A Story of Three Dragons

First published in Australia in 2001 by
perdiem PUBLISHING Pty Ltd
ACN: 095 883 355

Copyright © 2001 By Bob Jones

All rights reserved. No part of this
publication may be reproduced, stored
in a retrieval system, or transmitted in any form
or by any means, electronic, mechanical, photocopying,
recording or otherwise, without the prior written permission
of the copyright owner.

ISBN: 0-646-41725-8

The names of a minority of individuals in this book
have been changed.

Edited: Edward Caruso
Printed and bound: Griffin Press
Cover design: Bob Jones
Artwork: Michael Kenna
Final draft: Steve Nedelkos
Disrtibution: Kirby Books

The publisher wishes to thank copyright holders for granting permission to reproduce the following articles: Colin Talbot, 'Bob Jones', © The Weekend Australian, 10 July 1977. Bill Birnbauer 'Miss Ronstadt Sings to the Tune of $60m', © *The Herald & Weekly Times*, 24 February 1979.
The author and publisher also wishes to acknowledge the following sources: Monica Braw, 'ABBA's Dygnet-Runt-Vakter', © *KvP*, 3 March 1977. Mick Fleetwood and Stephen Davis, *Fleetwood: My Adventures With Fleetwood Mac*, Sidgwick & Jackson, London, 1990.

www.bobjones.com.au

BOB JONES
A Story of Three Dragons

*Dedicated to
the three women
in my life:
Faye Mary Thomas
Tracey Lee Smythe
Ishoa-Jade Cook*

Laissez Le Bon Temps Rouler

Let The Good Times Roll, a story of three dragons, is the first part of my autobiographical trilogy. This book represents the Yellow Dragon, which is a metaphor for the intellectual and psychological realm.

This first installation is an insight into the more than twenty years I spent touring as a personal bodyguard, where my clients included the most elite celebrities of the rock 'n' roll industry in the often-claustrophobic settings of hired cars, hotels and planes, which taught me much about human emotions and relationships, philosophy, and even a lot about business consolidation and empire-building.

The early years of my story are linked to the Red Dragon (which is a metaphor for the physical level) and will be depicted in the book of this series, *The Violent Years*.

Having been born in the year of the Dragon, and after taking the name Jones from my stepfather (my father had been one of many unsung heroes who'd never returned from World War II), I'd been blessed with my mother's Celtic red hair and ferocious Irish temper (plus my father's Scottish blood and, from his side of the family, my grandmother's Jewish blood). I'd never be out of the influence of mischief and constant fighting.

After dropping out of a grammar school education for what I'd believed to be the exciting life of a gang member, I'd graduate from rebelling against the education system and problems with teachers, to bucking the social system and problems with the police. I'd joined no ordinary gang. The Phantom Twins were by the far the largest gang of the era. It comprised 500 members and controlled the streets of inner-city Melbourne. The Phantom Twins were headed by a good-looking set of twins renowned for their ability to disappear off the city streets within seconds and reappear several blocks away, whenever necessary. It'd take a special squad of six tough cops, known as the Bodgie Squad, to make the Phantoms totally disappear before the Melbourne Olympics.

 A good flogging at the hands of these cops one night would see me disappearing back to the suburbs to join one of Melbourne's northside gangs, and more violence would follow in a climate of inter-racial gang wars, which saw me honing my youthfully acquired fighting skills.

 Next came a teenage marriage and parenthood that had no chance of survival because of our living on the fringes of all this violence.

Through the frustration of the breakdown of my marriage, I'd become involved in, and eventually took control of, the night-club realm of the bouncing industry.

For almost a decade I'd spiral, seemingly out of control, down the bowels of the nocturnal other/underworld.

In my role as a protector, I'd experienced vicious assaults, encountered pimps and prostitutes, strippers, very violent criminals and crooked cops.

This also, is the time in my life where I'd meet my lifelong enemy: The Black Dragon Society, which is what I call the ever-powerful narcotics kingdom. The white powders they use to peddle death...I call The Black Dragon.

Just when it seemed there was no way out, along came the miracle of my life: I was introduced to the philosophical principles of the martial arts. I became instantly addicted to what has since developed into a lifelong pursuit.

During my world travels as a bodyguard, I'd searched for and sought out various martial arts masters. By adapting this newfound knowledge to my own street sense, I'd developed the first, truly, Western martial art. My system was thus a learning/training process of freedom of thought, which eventually became known worldwide as Bob Jones' Martial Arts Freestyle.

By taking only the *truth* from the traditional styles and teaching a *purist* freestyle by precept and example, 1 further developed this form of self-defence in which youthful strength and spirit would be employed in the exercising of the mind.

In the long term, this practice would enable me and my students to continue to develop self-esteem, the true meaning of courtesy and, above all, the discipline of temper, thus nurturing personal improvement.

This part of my trilogy is represented by the Blue Dragon (spiritual level), and will be portrayed in the book *The Greatest Story Never Told*.

The summer of 1972–73 had been a time of serious contemplation about where I'd been, what I was doing and what I'd planned for the future, both for me and my organisation (the BJC – Bob Jones Corporation).

This was my thirteenth year of working in the rock 'n' roll and entertainment industry. A particular instance at a free outdoor rock concert promoted by radio station 3XY at the Frankston oval had provoked my summer of soul-searching. For me personally, this event climaxed a thirteen-year career of a turbulent and, at most times, violent lifestyle.

The security industry had always been good to me and I'd made a lot of friends. I was very respected in the industry and the security empire I'd built up was expanding each day. What had seemed my greatest strength had become my greatest weakness. The Australian media had always had good things to say about me until now, as a result of the injuries inflicted during this concert. This being the reason for my contemplation, I'd thought about my adolescence, of growing up in gangs.

The deeper I'd searched the more I'd realised that after almost twenty years of violence, something was going to have to change.

The years 1972–73 were also a time of change in Australia. After twenty-three years in the wilderness, the Australian Labor Party had won victory in the federal election. Within ten days the new Labor Prime Minister, Gough Whitlam, had ended conscription to Vietnam.

Adelaide (the city without a convict past) also had to do some serious soul-searching that year: a group of men had violently assaulted known homosexual Dr George Ian Ogilvy Duncan, who as a result, drowned in the River Torrens. This was the beginning of an eleven-year span of sexual serial killings involving homosexuals. A witness identified three vice-squad police members. He had also been beaten and thrown into the river with Dr Duncan and watched him drown. The police were eventually charged (fifteen years later), but found not guilty.

It was also in this city of churches that, on 21 October 1972, Joe Cocker would get busted with enough marijuana for a couple of joints. Within days, he would be found guilty and deported.

The headlines that involved Joe Cocker made the biggest splash of the year. The news flashed out of Australia and around the world, taking the media pressure off the cops and Adelaide's dead homosexuals. The drug culturalists, especially within the entertainment industry, could not believe this Joe Cocker situation.

Unknowingly to me at the time, it was to be this Joe Cocker bust that would open the door for a:
Bob Jones change of lifestyle!

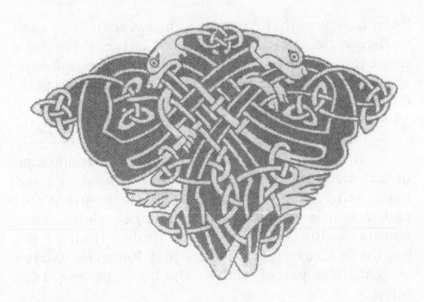

21 November. I'd looked up my diary early on that sunny Melbourne morning. There were several meetings regarding my dual role: my involvement as a martial artist and as a security consultant. There was a security luncheon booked for 12.30 at the Southern Cross Hotel: I had to meet a Paul Dainty of the PDC (Paul Dainty Corporation). This was to be a very important meeting: on the phone he'd mentioned 'making me an offer I could not refuse'. I knew from his eloquent English accent he was not in the Mafia. I was intrigued, and on asking how I'd know him he'd answered: 'Don't worry about that, I know you.'

We'd arranged to meet in the lobby of the Cross, one of my stomping grounds. I'd worked here during the 1960s as a supervisor (bouncer). As I waited, old names and faces came to mind: The Beatles, comedian Shelley Burman, Terry Riley, the Tavern Bar manager, Vinnie Scott and that funny man of the bouncer fraternity, Pat Housley.

Then here was that American chiropractor who used to fix our occasional occupational hazards. He did a great job on an injured shoulder of mine one time about four years earlier. What was his name? Oh yeah, Gus Mercurio.

'Hi Bob, we're both early.'
It was 12.25. I turned around to see a young man of sartorial elegance. Very British, groomed hair and nails, impeccable English-tailored three-piece suit and patent leather handcrafted Italian shoes. They were as shiny as the polished timber floor of the Southern Cross foyer, and I just knew he'd have bought those patent leathers the last time he was in Milan.

Over lunch we small-talked about the Australian rock 'n' roll scene, then he slowly led into, 'Bob, I've checked you out, I've heard about your promotional days with the suburban dances, your trouble-shooter days, the years in the discotheque arena, and the last couple of years you and your martial arts empire have secured all of the major outdoor rock festivals ...'

I didn't bother responding that I'd checked him out, that at only twenty-six he was a multi-millionaire, had a worldwide organisation with its head office in London, that he was now spending most of his time in Melbourne and was annoying many of our local entertainment entrepreneurs due to the quality of the acts he was beginning to bring out ...

'I've spoken to a lot of industry people, both here in Melbourne and Sydney, and also my Australian manager of the PDC. All highly recommend you and your organisation. At the end of the day, I was wondering if you could manage the security for a big-name band I am touring here later this summer season?'

'After a rap like that, I damned well better give it a try. Who's the band?'

'The Rolling Stones.'

Shit! Shit! Shit! Did he just say The Rolling Stones? Since The Beatles rolled over, The Stones were possibly the biggest act in the world. Okay, okay, look cool, don't muck up ...

'Look Bob, the problem I've got is that bloody Joe Cocker bust a month ago, those bloody headlines ricocheted around the planet. Now, The Stones are paranoid about coming here. After what Joe got done for, they're afraid they could get life down here.'

Keith Richards and Mick Jagger, I could see the reason for their paranoia.

'Their tour manager Peter Rudge is due in three days and he's said that unless I can guarantee them the best security in the country, they just won't come. That gives you three days to get your act together, do a proposal for the tour with your plans to give them the best security there is in this country. Oh, and by the way, I could use a good security manager for my tours; pull this off for me and there could be quite a bit of work for you in the future!'

Shit! Shit! Shit! The Rolling Stones, I thought as we shook hands and as I gave Paul Dainty one of my most confident smiles.

Three days later, at 10 a.m. on the button, I arrived at the PDC Melbourne head office. That was when I saw who Paul Dainty's Australian manager was, an old buddy of mine. We'd been rival dance promoters back in the early 1960s. That was why I'd got such a good rap from Paul at lunch.

'Ron "the Con" Blackmore, I don't believe it! Haven't seen you for a coupla years. Thanks for the character reference extraordinaire! I owe you one.'

'Yeah, well in about an hour when we pick up his royal highness, you impress him and we're square.'

It was off to Essendon Airport to pick up The Rolling Stones tour manager Peter Rudge from his Qantas New York flight in what must have been Australia's longest stretch limousine. A limo, wow, I could get used to this!

'Bob Jones, eh! You must be this martial artist security guy I've been hearing so much about. What bands have you toured with recently?'

'Argh ...' This was my first communication with The Rolling Stones tour manager.

'Okay, I was only joking, I know this is your first tour gig. I also know you've done just about everything else, so this should be a piece of piss. You got your prop for me?'

We shook hands and all I said was 'Argh!'

On the way back, Paul, Ron 'the Con', and Rudge were busy at it, talkin' tourin. For the next two hours, and back at the PDC office with raves about per diems, backstage trailers and riders, I was exposed to a whole new language 'I knew I just had to learn'.

'Bob,' Peter Rudge finally switched his attention to me, 'we got a 10.30 a.m. to Brisbane and in nine days we've got to check out every state, as well as New Zealand's venues, hotels, travel arrangements, anything you think that might go wrong, and while we're at it we'll double-check that bloody "City of Churches," Adelaide. We gotta do it in nine days coz I'm due back in New York and Mick Jagger's expectin' good news, so 10.30 a.m., eh!'

Paul Dainty had given me the tour itinerary. Wow, I'd never seen anything like this. More than sixty people on the road, flight times, baggage pick-ups, drop-offs, one-day-on, one-day-off concert dates, hotels, check-ins, check-outs, buses, limos, more limos, sound checks, and so on ...

'They arrive on 14 February and it's around six weeks with New Zealand. How's that fit your schedule, Bob?'

How does that fit in with my schedule? I'm still spinning from sixty people with two or three bags each, and what did it say? Five semi-trailer loads of equipment to follow us around, but set up ahead of us, plus their own cargo plane carrying their personal equipment ... shit!

'Ah, no problem Paul. I've got a one-day concert for 3XY coming up in a month, on Boxing Day at Frankston, Australia Day weekend. I've got the second Sunbury Festival that's on 28, 29 and 30 of January. I've put a quote in for the Aquarius Arts Festival in New South Wales at Nimbin, that's in April over the Anzac Day holiday weekend ... But The Stones finish end of March'

'Just like clockwork, eh! Bob Jones, you should come work in New York sometime.' This was a compliment, coming from The Rolling Stones tour manager!

Nine days with Peter Rudge around Australia and New Zealand, now that was an experience! That guy sure knew his gigs and I didn't miss a trick. I wanted to learn and this was just the guy to learn from.

'You know Bob, for a guy that's never done a

big gig like this before, you were right on the money with that prop. I've marked a couple of things you probably know by now you wouldn't do again, but, you know, a couple of your ideas were new. I'm lookin' forward to tryin' them. You and your boys will do just fine. The Stones are a great bunch o' guys. Charlie has been playing drums that long he's turned into a grumpy shit. I don't think he even likes touring but his bark is worse than his bite. Keith likes his space, don't crowd him and you'll be fine. Mick's a real breeze; easy to get along with unless ya fuck up. The other boys are bringin' their old ladies; you won't hear a beep out of them. Anyway, if you got any problems, that's what I'm there for, I'm the problem-fixer.'

After the nine days Peter Rudge was on his way back to New York and I figured I'd made a real good friend and he made me feel 'I was on the team'.

The boys looked tired when they'd arrived at Sydney International Airport after what would've been around twenty hours of airtime. We'd whisked them through the airport terminals after they'd cleared Customs, directly into their waiting limousines. At the Kings Cross Hyatt, even I was impressed: my security guys were everywhere. I had my Black Belts at the front doors of the reception foyer, at the elevators on the ground floor and more again to greet them on their floor. The twenty-second floor of the Hyatt had been totally booked out for the members of the band (plus guest musicians, 'Gentleman' Nicky

Hopkins on piano and 'Wild man' Bobby Keyes on saxophone), and us, their bodyguards. Mick Jagger was the first to comment, 'Good security men, I like 'em, because they don't look like some of those stuffed shirts we often get lumbered with. Yeah, they look cool; they don't look like regular security. Hey man, when we have some time, someone's gotta tell me how come everyone of you is wearing those square crosses around your necks.'

Even without time for intros they each filed into their rooms to rest and freshen up after their arduous international flight. About half an hour later a call came over the hotel intercom, 'Bob Jones to reception, please.'

An irate female had called the desk and wanted to talk to the head of security.

'Hello, Bob Jones here, can I help you?'

'Yes you can! Fuck you and fuck that promoter, Paul Dainty, he couldn't organise a fuck in a brothel!'

I had no idea who this was and was about to make some sort of comment about her language, that was when she cut me short...

'Fuck all of you, you stupid lot of shits! My husband's Keith Richards ... that's right, you heard me, Keith Richards of The Rolling Stones just arrived here from Los Angeles, and I just got in after fucking twenty-eight hours from London, stuck in Singapore for fucking four and a half hours, then I arrive here in Sydney! I have a fucking Paul Dainty itinerary here that reads, "someone would be at the airport" to pick me up. Now, if you don't fix my problem immediately, when I see Keith and Mick you won't even have a fucken' security job.'

She hung up in my ear. The tour hadn't started; I hadn't even met the band yet. I knew Mr Problem-solver would get me out of this. But wouldn't you know it, when you need a cab, a cop, or problem-solver there's never anyone in sight.

Peter Rudge, Ron Blackmore and Paul Dainty were off at a meeting or something. The band was resting, could've even been asleep (sometime later I learned Keith Richards never slept). Oh shit, what could I do? Show some head-of-security initiative; fix this slight problem on my own.

I told two of my bodyguards, Richard Norton and Dave 'Bungles' Berry to keep an eye on the fort.

'Hey, "Lifesaver" Stuey, come with me, we'll grab one of our standby limos and hightail it out to the airport. Keith Richard's wife is stranded out at International; she's just got in from London and she's a little upset.'

(Stuey 'Lifesaver' Lomax had been a good back-up in times of need, particularly at that outdoor rock concert in Frankston.)

I told the limo driver not to get us all killed, but I needed to get to the airport in half the time it had ever taken him before. When we got there, there it was: British Airways Flight 207, flashing *landed*. I looked around for what I figured could become my nightmare. She saw us before we saw her. A tall, slender model of a woman, long brown hair and complete with designer clothes.

'Rolling Stones security,' she'd stated in a sultry voice with a touch of shy sexiness, added to the tone. 'I'm so sorry for my reaction on the phone, it's just that I've been in flight time, and it was such a drag of a flight, held up on the stopover for dreary hours.'

Man, was I relaxed that she was relaxed. When we got back to the Hyatt, I was feeling a little more positive.

'Stuey, take Mrs Richards into the bar and get her a drink. I'll get Keith.'

As they left for the bar, I headed up to the twenty-second floor and knocked on Keith's door. When he opened it the volume blasted through me and filled the corridor. He had his super stereo cranked way above maximum.

'Hi Keith, I'm Bob Jones from Paul Dainty's security team and I've had a slight problem that's been fixed.'

'So, you gotta problem?'

'No, not anymore. It was a problem with your wife but it's okay now. We've been out and picked her up from her London flight. She's down in the bar with one of my guys.'

'Yeah, well we betta go see.'

On the way down Keith looked puzzled, 'Bob, is it Bob Jones?'

'Yep.'

'Well, listen Bob, my ol' lady, Anita Pallenberg, is in London but there's something wrong 'ere. There's no way, short of a death in the family she'd come 'ere without telling me.'

'Without telling me,' ran through my mind as the elevator came to a stop on the ground floor. My brain started working overtime and I asked myself, how come, if that was Mrs Richards, didn't I just take her straight up to Keith's room? Seemed logical so how come I didn't? How come I didn't register that she had no baggage when we saw her at the airport? Oh no!

'Hey Bob, is that one of your guys in the bar, and is that my ol' lady with 'im?'

A funny question deserved a funny answer.

'Yep.'

'Fuck man, now I got a problem. That's this crazy chick I got myself tied up with last time we toured here. Now we've got a problem, and if you fix it for us we'll be square. Fuck man, she's a real nutter, you gotta fix this situation!' He turned and headed back to the elevator.

My god, I had to think of something – anything – quick!

'Mrs Richards, ah, Keith's not here. He's at a meeting. I just rang him, he's so excited you're here and said to take your time and Stuey and me will take you to him.'

She smiled and finished off her drink. We wandered out front and I told the limo driver to 'take Mrs Richards to the Sebel Townhouse.'

'Keith and Mick are in the club bar; you have a nice time now and we'll catch you later on.'

The first gig was the Western Springs outdoor stadium in Auckland, New Zealand, a huge natural amphitheater set in a circular valley that slopes up so that the 30 000 to 40 000 fans become a sea of heads with a perfect view down to the stage.

Around 38 000 Rolling Stones fans approved the support acts while warming up for the big moment. It was the late afternoon of what had been a pleasant sunny afternoon. Well, it had been pleasant except for the last half hour or so: we'd had three complaints from different people about a bad-arsed bunch of bikies up on the hill to the left-hand side of the stage.

How could you count them all? I figured there were about thirty Highway 61 gang members on the hill responsible for the complaints.

At the time Richard Norton was my right hand. (In years to come he'd become a famous movie star.)

'I'm gonna head on up the hill and have a talk to these Highway 61 boys', I said to him.

'Hey, uhm, sure you don't want some company?' my lifesaver remarked.

'No. I don't want to piss them off. But I tell you what, if the shit hits the fan, I'll be expecting you and the rest of the guys to join me. There's no way I want to die on my own. Definitely not on our first tour of duty.'

'If the five of us bodyguards go up the hill together it'd cause World War III.'

As I headed up the hill I thought, am I mad? I could feel a murmur in the crowd: hey look, it's that red-headed Australian martial arts guy the media have been talking about. A month ago a dozen or so of his guys put about a hundred sharpies in the hospital, but now he's headed up the hill on his own towards the Highway 61.

The gang members lay about. My walking into the centre of them had the desired effect: they must have all been thinking: this white boy ain't got no M16, he's gotta have his pockets full of grenades or something.

'How ya doing, guys? Listen we've had a few complaints about someone throwing cans or junk over there, and hitting some punters, and rather than spoil a good show Paul Dainty, the promoter, and The Stones themselves suggested I come up here.'

That was when I pulled out my *grenades* from my security jacket and handed them out by pecking order, starting with the biggest, ugliest and meanest looking of them all. My grenades were twelve Rolling Stones World Tour 1972–73 T-shirts, complete with Mick Jagger's loveable lips ...

'Hey bro', ya wanna beer?'
'Ya wanna?'
'Ya?'

They all wanted to share a drink with me; I could've had at least a dozen beers with this crew, I'd just made a bunch of new mates.

'Hey yo all black shit for brains!' The leader turned to his gang. 'Don't let me see any of you guys chuckin' cans around. Someone could get hurt. Hey, let's have a drink for the promoter and The Rolling Stones.'

'Hey, what's your name, bro'?'
'Bob, Bob Jones. I'll catch you guys later.'

I walked back down the hill humming Billy Thorpe's hit single 'Most People I Know Think That I'm Crazy'. The best thing about these situations, as they happened and as I'd live to tell the tales, was that I'd won a few more points of respect from my guys. To me that's the name of the game.

With bands of the caliber of The Stones travelling around the planet on their tours, there's a sort of friendly rivalry that creates, on occasion, very spectacular stunts. On every tour the Paul Dainty Corporation likes to carry out several of these stunts.

In LA, at a major gig, prior to The Stones coming to Australia, one of the US's leading promoters, Billy Graham, had filled the stage's overhead tarpaulin with thousands of ping-pong balls. Dozens of black flouro tubes had been strategically placed around the stage. During The Stones' final encore Graham had released enough ping-pong balls to cover the stage and bury the entire band and its equipment. On cue, the lighting guys had killed the access stage lights and the black flouros made all the white balls luminous. From the audiences' perspective, the stage was flooded with glowing purple balls. The band's movements as they continued to play, and Jagger's gyrating, caused the balls to slowly dissipate off all sides of the stage.

It took an encore for The Stones to come back to view. (This was filmed as part of the tour and looked amazing on film.)

Due the size of the Western Springs crowd, Ron Blackmore had decided to use an idea none of us had seen since the grand opening ceremony of the Melbourne 1956 Olympics. It was an idea to rival the ping-pong story. Unbeknown to The Stones, he had sneaked in a covered semi-trailer full of homing pigeons, and there were nearly as many pigeons as ping-pong balls in LA.

As most people know, homing pigeons on release fly high into the sky, circulate several times to   orientate themselves with the direction to fly home.

Just on dusk, as The Rolling Stones were introduced and they'd run on stage and hit that first electrifying cord, the Western Springs audience would see the sky disappear momentarily, followed by a   massive circle of fluttering wings before the pigeons would fly home. Great idea, but wrong! There must have been a north-west wind blowing because when the birds were released, they flew off on a 45-degree angle for three blocks directly away from the backstage area, then they circled three times and flew off into the night. The only problem was the driver of the truck, Ron Blackmore, and us bodyguards were the only ones who witnessed this great idea.

A few days later at our hotel in Melbourne, and after a hundred ribbings like 'Ron, where's your pigeons?', Peter Rudge left a note on the door of Ron Blackmore's suite. 'Ron, we found your pigeons.' When we all got back from the sound check, Ron Blackmore had entered his room trying to figure this note, but not for long.

Apparently, Peter, Mick and Keith Richards had, before we'd left for the sound check, about three hours earlier, put around fifty pigeons in his room and the whole suite – the bed, the dresser, the carpet, and the bathroom – was covered in pigeon shit.

Mick Jagger had been commissioned to play the lead role of Ned Kelly. During this time, and during his travelling around the North Island and South Island of New Zealand, he'd developed an empathy with the plight of indigenous people.

Mick had surprised me with his awareness of the racial problems he'd seen in this region and this empathy had surfaced again when we'd arrived in Brisbane. We had a couple of days off before the band's performance at the Milton tennis courts. On the second day someone had invited a group of thirty Aborigines from the same tribe, including elders and young warriors, who'd been painted with ceremonial markings, and an abundance of indigenous musicians complete with didgeridoos and other traditional instruments. This *someone* had booked one of the Park Royal's function rooms with an interesting mix of Western and Outback cuisine. This same someone had organised an invitation for Mr Michael Jagger to attend this ceremony.

Despite the function room surroundings, the evening had the earmark of a modern-day corroboree. But, alas, like many a good story this one had a sad ending. At around 3.30 a.m. it turned out that the someone who'd been responsible for this cultural exchange, dressed in traditional
Aboriginal attire (including dark, total body makeup), was, you guessed it, Sydney's, now becoming quite famous, Mrs Richards.

Thus Keith's comments from Sydney came back: 'Bob, she's a fucking nutter – get rid of her!'

Mick Jagger yelled the same thing, but it was easier said than done. After trying to take hold of the nutter, covered in little more than black oily makeup, Richard Norton and I both wrestled with her down the hallway into the reception area where she broke loose and made her way back to the hall, with a tirade of abuse that made her phone conversation from the airport with me seem like a Sunday School sermon.

The elders and most of the musicians slithered by as if all us white folk had just got off the First Fleet. The warriors stood in total bemusement, fascinated by the tribal markings Richard and my handgrips had created all over Mrs Richards' body in the attempt of eviction. I did the only sensible thing I could think of, demanding that the manager or hotel security took over from there.

By the time the police arrived, Mrs Richards had seen herself out, threatening to get even with:

'*You*, Bob Jones, you fucking piece of dog shit. You'll rue the day you ever fucked with me. You haven't heard the end of me, I'll give you shit you'll never forget!'

Oh well! Some you win and some you lose.

Threats of bad weather (Brisbane's tropical climate at this time of year, thanks to the rainy season) had almost threatened cancellation. It had held off until after the capacity crowd was seated, after the support band and after The Stones' grand entrance. But then boom! Down it came, a torrential downpour so heavy The Stones could hardly see the audience. Although the stage was covered by a huge tarpaulin, with all the electronics on stage, it was dangerous for the band. However, there was no way Mick Jagger and The Rolling Stones were not going to give this rain-soaked audience its value for money.

'Sure is wet here tonight ... We love you,' screamed Mick over the amplification.

The Milton tennis courts' audience (all 8000 of them) waved, with arms outstretched, their brollies and plastic sheet coverings. They were sitting ankle deep in water on this steamy hot summer night, doing a fair impersonation of Dame Edna Everidge when she waved her gladioli.

In unison the multitudes sang,
'Weeee love yoo, Rolling Stones.'
Some you win ...

Back at the Park Royal, Mick Jagger phoned me and said that he, Keith Richards, Nicky Hopkins and Bobby Keyes were going for a trip to the Gold Coast (about an hour away), and that he'd need 'a couple of limos and four bodyguards until the sun comes up'.

Our search for the next morning's sunrise saw the two limos stopping in Southport. That tropical storm had just blown over and we'd picked up a guy I knew to be a well-known dealer. I wasn't happy with this but I figured, after all, I am a bodyguard, not a cop. (Through the *dojo* (training academies) that I'd opened in Brisbane about a year earlier and my trips there since, I'd got to know many of the local haunts, bikers and bouncers, especially in Brisbane's downtown, Fortitude Valley and the sleazier clubs of the Gold Coast. This always served as an occupational requirement in this, the security industry.)

The limos cruised the main Gold Coast strip and turned right into Cavill Avenue. We parked and entered a seedy club known then as the Mousetrap. This was the first time I'd ever gone into a club with a band the caliber of The Rolling Stones. I gotta tell you, it's different ... Ron Blackmore had rung earlier and organised a private section of tables to be set aside. Ron 'the Con' must have also organised half a dozen really beautiful ladies, along the style of the meter maids who pumped coins into your car meter during the day.

The Mousetrap was a small club with about, I figured, a capacity of 120, but probably licensed (if in fact it was) for about eighty. Within an hour of The Stones and us arriving, around 200 patrons had squeezed in, with about as many outside; the local bouncers trying to organise them into an orderly line that could not fit in. Within the next hour Mick, Keith, Nicky and Bobby were on the stage jamming with some local Surfers Paradise band, that would surely tell their grandkids about the experience of being on stage with Mick Jagger and Keith Richards of The Rolling Stones.

The boys played with as much zest as any of the large commercial gigs on the tour. As for the bodyguards, well, someone had to keep the meter maids happy! We hoped for the sunrise to take it's time!

The next day was a quick stopover in Sydney between the Brisbane, Melbourne and Adelaide gigs. The band suffered from a lack of sleep (except for Keith, of course) as the security and bodyguards mistakenly tried to outdo Keith Richards! However, we'd covered all our points. An entire floor of the Hyatt had been booked out to the band and us. One of my ideas that Peter Rudge had liked was that on this floor I had the hotel change the locks to one way. Hence, you could go out to the stairwell, but no-one could access our floor from the other side. We had our own local security man at the elevators on this floor when we went out. He had the right to ask for the identification of and record everyone that entered any of our rooms.

When we came in our local boys would go down to the foyer and reception and we would secure our elevators. Our other two bodyguards, Paul Flemming and Tum Joe, were out to dinner, bodyguarding guitarists Mick Taylor and Bill Wyman, who had their ladies with them and were having early nights. Stuey the lifesaver was virtually a spare, as his job was to look after drummer Charlie Watts – practically the only time we saw Charlie was on stage at the gigs.

Meanwhile, all I could hear was the rock 'n' roll blasting through the doorway of Keith Richard's suite. Richard Norton leaned against our doorway watching an Aussie Rules match on TV and Lifesaver Stuey was near me, eyes closed, nodding his head to Keith's stereo-blaster.

I took the moment to peruse the pre-tour regime Paul Dainty had sent me on the background of The Rolling Stones.

This was the tenth year of The Stones being together, they'd formed in London in January 1962.

Mick Jagger and Keith Richards had been born in Dartford, Kent, in 1943, and first met at primary school. Their friendship really came together via a mutual friend, Dick Taylor. The three of them played together in fledgling bands around the London R&B scene. Around this time they'd secured drummer Tony Chapman and pianist Ian Stewart, and then with Brian Jones, who actually came up with the name for the band, they finally had the first Rolling Stones lineup.

In mid-1962 they got their first break when Blues Inc. recorded a BBC radio session gig. Shortly after they replaced Dick Taylor with Bill Wyman, then Blues Inc. drummer Charlie Watts replaced Tony Chapman. This new lineup's first single, released in June 1963, was Chuck Berry's, 'Come On'.

Their then manager Andrew Oldham fostered and promoted the band's bad boy image, which established a huge cult following among the nation's youth. They recorded an EP, *Five By Five* (mostly covers) that topped the charts in the UK in 1964, and they toured with The Ronettes. The EP had been recorded in Chicago to a background of rioting crowds who had assembled outside. On 10 July 1965 'I Can't Get No Satisfaction' became their first US number one single; it didn't reach the number one spot in the UK until September.

A change to American manager Allen Klein, however, was not the recipe for instant success. Their third album *Out Of Our Heads* (1965) was less impressive than its predecessors.

Aftermath (1966) was their first wholly original album, followed in 1967 by *Between The Buttons*, which reflected the problems of the band: that year Jagger, Richards and Brian Jones were all busted for drugs. They were found guilty and sentenced to prison. However, on appeal they had their sentences quashed; this drew them more international press.

Meanwhile, The Beatles were promoting Aleister Crowley, England's most notorious occultist by putting his photo on the cover of their psychedelic album *Sgt. Peppers Lonely Hearts Club Band*. The Stones showed their 'own sympathy for the devil' with their *Satanic Majesties Request* album, which fell far short of the standard of Sgt. Peppers.

The Stones then returned to a more straightforward rock sound for their album *Beggars Banquet*, with the smash hit single 'Jumpin' Jack Flash'. It was followed by *Let It Bleed*. Both are classic rock albums regarded as the band's finest. However, in the middle of a wave of Satanism and occult adventurism, Brian Jones was found dead in his swimming pool (on 3 July 1969).

Rock festivals Woodstock and Altamont finished off 1969, with members of the Hell's Angels stabbing a black man to death in their role of stage security. Mick Jagger, dressed as Satan on stage, had been singing The Stones' hit single 'Sympathy For The Devil'.

Brian Jones' death allowed new guitarist, ex-

John Mayall's Bluesbreaker, Mick Taylor, to make his debut in London at the free concert in Hyde Park.

A live album from the tour *Get Yer Ya-Yas Out* was followed in 1971 by *Sticky Fingers*, with the single 'Brown Sugar' topping the world's charts. In 1972 *Exile on Main Street* was released, with another world hit 'Tumbling Dice' accompanying it.

And here we were in 1973 at the Sydney Hyatt. The doors of the elevators opened. There was a national florist convention with hundreds of the industry's representatives from every state in the country. There were at least a dozen flower delegates lined up behind their spokesman, all with large bunches of flowers.

'I'm sorry people, this floor is closed to the general public.' Lifesaver Stuey had sprung to his feet.

'Who says a whole fucking floor can be closed off?'

'Ah, I do sir. Coz that's the way it is. There are people who want the privacy of this floor.'

'Yeah, well I'm the president of the Australian Florist Convention, and these are all state representatives and we've heard there's a fucking rock band or someone up here, and I've promised these people they can have a look at whoever the fuck it is on this floor.' He was a big frame of a man, an executive-looking gentleman – except for the alcohol. He started to lead his party off the elevator as Lifesaver Stuey placed his open hand on his chest and stopped him in his tracks.

'I say, who the fuck do you think you are?'

'I'm sorry, I believe I've already explained ...' Lifesaver Stuey replied.

A short-arm push had the gentleman stumbling backwards, knocking down two or three of his state representatives flat on their executive arses. The gentleman's wife saw the error of the situation and tried to console her husband that perhaps they could go and make better use of their time than mess with us. However, he wasn't having any of that; in fact, he wanted a piece of Lifesaver Stuey, and he was going to have it now. In front of all his friends.

He came out of that elevator like a charging bull. Lifesaver Stuey gave me a quick glance as if asking for permission. Whack! He let a reverse punch fly (a power punch coming from the rear of the body as opposed to a jab off the front side). Lifesaver Stuey's calloused knuckles hit Mr Flower, our gentleman executive's chest, sending him crashing again against the back wall of the elevator, rocking the crap out of it.

He wanted to come back for more, except that the doors were closing. We could hear him cussing and punching the buttons to open the doors. The women in the elevator screamed as he started kicking the control buttons. The doors would not move; in fact, the elevator was not moving. They were not going anywhere for he had totally jammed the whole works.

We rang hotel management and its in-house security. Within minutes security, managers, Peter Rudge, Ron Blackmore, Paul Dainty, road crew, and just about everyone, had come up for a look. Even Charlie Watts had come out of his room. It was 12.15 a.m. and Mr Flower swore and threatened the hotel management with the cries of, 'I'll find out who the promoter is and I'll sue him and the fucking band and those fucking security guys.

I'll fucking sue the elevator company, I'll sue the fucking lot of you!'

The management apologised and phoned the repair company. By 12.30 everyone had wandered off, except of course for us, the bodyguards.

Unfortunately, the elevator repairmen didn't show until 3.30. This meant our friends were in the elevator for almost three hours. At 1.30 Nicky Hopkins was amazed at the amount of abuse our gentleman executive kept giving out. Nicky had asked all to be very quiet for a moment, and suggested he'd make a 'cuppa tea', and almost had everyone giving him the milk and sugar listing.

At around 2.00 a.m. Keith came staggering out of his rock-a-rooma and told them that he was the elevator technician.

'Now listen in there, can you hear me?'

'We can hear you, but we want to get out,' said a woman's voice.

There must have been plenty of alcohol inside as no-one else sounded as if they were sober.

'Well the problem is, it's out of balance,' Keith said, winking and shushing us, his index finger over his lips. 'Now listen, I'm the elevator technician and I want to see if we can centralise you all as a group.'

'Well, what do you want us to do?' replied that woman's voice.

'Well, stand around the walls in a circle with an even distance between you all.'

We could hear them shuffling around the elevator.

'What will we do now?'

'Well now, you all hold hands in the circle.' Once Keith had achieved this he had them holding their breath, bouncing on their heels, stepping, jumping and even kicking out in front. They may have woken to the fact they were being had when Keith suggested they all perform a forward roll into the centre of the elevator.

'Oh look, I'm sorry,' said Keith 'I'll have to be off to bed now.'

We all knew that also was a lie.

The next morning we flew to Melbourne. Paul Dainty suggested we switch Lifesaver Stuey for another bodyguard. The flower power executive guy had been down the reception threatening to sue, and wanted the security guy who'd 'bashed him' to be charged with assault. Lifesaver Stuey was pissed off but knew it was the best thing to do. Nicky Pappas replaced Stuey on the tour and met up with us in Melbourne. That day in Melbourne the local press were having a field day with this flower power situation. Since the Frankston riot the press had been hunting me. The droogs (a new form of skinhead, according to the press) were going to get the Bob Jones boys at Sunbury. When we pulled that off with barely a problem, then of course these gangs would get their vengeance at any of The Stones concerts. This gave the press pretty good odds on a national scale and the flower incident was right down their alley.

Meanwhile, I'd gone into Mick Jagger's suite to co-ordinate the times for the pick-up of the sound check. He had several newspapers, all carrying various headlines: of Bob Jones, bouncers, droogs, sharpies and now a respectable florist convention executive after our blood.

'Ah, Mick, I'm sorry about all this drama.'

'What's that Bob, what have you got to be sorry about?'

'All these newspapers from all over the country carrying headlines about the heavies, on tour as security for you guys.'

'There ain't no such thing as bad publicity, 'ere look at all of this: BOB JONES bodyguard to THE ROLLING STONES. There, they've spelt everything right, and if it's spelt right, it can't be bad publicity, can it?. An' another thing you need to know about this entertainment industry, it's far better to be on the front page tellin' them a lie,than on the back page tellin' them the truth.'

Well, seeing Mick wasn't upset, then I wasn't even going to give it the time of day. That's it, any press is good press, long as they spell it right.

After the floods at Brisbane's Milton tennis courts we now had a pleasant sunny afternoon on Kooyong centre courts in Melbourne. I covered my spot on the side of the stage in front of Nicky Hopkins on piano and next to Bobby Keyes on saxophone.

Mick Jagger by now had several 4 a.m. martial arts lessons with Richard Norton and myself. Mick would look at me, wink, smile and throw some punches and a kick, then launch into his regular gyrations following along the shape of a huge Chinese/Celtic dragon that was painted over the entire floor of the stage. He'd glance back as if to check my approval of his new stage techniques.

The Melbourne reaction to songs like, 'I Can't Get No Satisfaction' and 'Brown Sugar' was awesome. After the show it was out to dinner and back to the hotel, out to a few Melbourne clubs, and back to the hotel at around 2.30 a.m. For Mick it was an early night and Keith said he had some tapes to listen to – as usual he played them loud.

We'd sent our local Black Belts down to the lobby and foyer.

'Bad luck about Stuey getting involved with that prick in Sydney, but all the press would need is for one of us to get done on an assault charge,' Richard Norton remarked.

'Yeah, but it's great to have Nicky Pappas on the road with us,' I countered.

'Hey, it's great to be here!' Nicky couldn't contain his excitement. 'Fuck man! Nicky Pappas on tour with The Rolling Stones! Fuck, what a spinout! Did anybody see that babe, front row on the right of stage with that long blonde hair, and did anyone besides me notice the size of her fucking ...?'

'Yeah!', 'Uh, huh!', 'Did I?', 'Wow!' It seemed everybody had worked overtime at today's gig.

'Security!' Mick Jagger screamed from his room. 'Where the fuck's my security?'

'Nicky, get on our radio. Tell our guys to get house security up here. Tell 'em it's urgent. Richard, let's check it out!'

Mick's door burst open and out he came into the corridor dripping wet with nothing but a towel around his waist.

'Man that fuckin' nutter's in my room! You guys have got to get her out of there; she's fucking totally out there.'

Richard and I ran into the room, and there was my psychopathic nightmare standing in front of me, her hands spread like cat's claws with fingernails that could rip the skin off our bodies to the bone. Mrs Richards, as I had come to know her, was dressed as one of the hotel maids.

How could she have got a key, and how could she have known which room Mick would be staying in? Considering that one of my bright ideas was to have the band registered under false names, but then again this was Mrs Richards.

She stood in a fancy-fighting stance, as if she'd trained in one of the arts. I shaped up defensively. Christ, am I about to do battle with Mrs Richards? I thought as Richard Norton saved the day, grabbing the bedspread from Mick's bed and throwing it over her body and wrestling her to the floor. By now, Nicky Pappas was in the room and the three of us picked her up and carried her to the corridor, laying her down gently and sitting on her as she contorted and foul-mouthed us.

'Thank God for the Jones boys, that's all I can say,' Mick said as he slammed his door behind him. The hotel security, plus a night manager and my Black Belts from the lobby, showed up. (Thank God, we needed plenty of witnesses!)

There we were, three bodyguards sitting on one woman with a half dozen guys all wondering what our next move might be.

'Okay guys, maybe she's settled down enough to let her up,' was my intellectual observation.

As we stood up Mrs Richards unravelled herself out of Mick's bedspread.

'You bunch of fucking heroes! Three of you on

to one female! You all want to lay on me so bad, I'll give you something to fuckin' well lay on.' This was almost two decades before the movie *Fatal Attraction*, but at the time I couldn't help thinking about Clint Eastwood's *Play Misty For Me*.

'You all want to lay on my body so bad, and being against my wishes, I'd call that rape, wouldn't you?'

Right then I thought *rape*, is she for real, and was Mick Jagger right when he said as long as they spell it right, there's no such thing as …?

That's when she started screaming: '*Rape, rrrape! Help me somebody, Bob Jones and all the security guards and Mick Jagger have raped me!*'

It didn't matter how anybody would spell this, I was headed for trouble!

'Fuck you, fuck you all! You can't get away with this!' she screamed, tearing off her housemaid's uniform and beating herself up – punching herself in the face and scratching her arms and shoulders with her fingernails.

Managers, security and bodyguards were all flabbergasted, no-one with a clue about what to do as she was now down to her bra and nickers, with her uniform torn to shreds. Next she ripped off her bra with one hand and used her other hand to step out of her nickers.

Enough of this strip fiasco, I thought.

Richard Norton read my mind; he went for the fire escape door and opened it. I went for her. Nicky went for her torn bra and uniform, and between the three of us she landed on her naked arse in the fire escape stairwell.

'Fuck you Bob Jones, and all you other fucking heroes! You won't get away with pack rape! I'll get even with you over this, you pack of cunts.'

We slammed the door on her, knowing she couldn't get back on the floor with us; that is, without the cops.

'House security and *you*, the night manager,' I began, 'this could get ugly, get down to your office and write this up as you just saw it. Do it now while it's still fresh in your minds. I'm sure your bosses need this lot about as much as us or the band needs it.'

They must have sensed the urgency in my voice as they bolted to the elevators. For the next hour we sat around in a state of paranoia. However, as it turned out, there was no need: luckily we never heard a dammed thing from Mrs Richards; well, not until the final show in Sydney.

Next on the itinerary was Adelaide, the city that didn't share in the nation's penal settlement history. It was the city where it wasn't just a crime to be homosexual, it was a death wish. This was also the city of the Joe Cocker bust, which had drawn international attention. I'd told all of my guys that this was also the city where we could not drop our guard.

The first show was hot, The Stones played a really tight set that left their fans frantic. As the limos dropped us back at the hotel there were hundreds of fans around the grounds and our local boys had been working double-time to keep the lobby and foyer clear of Stones' fans. It was a real battle getting the guys from the limos into reception. I had Mick by the arm and could feel the adrenaline still pumping through his veins. As we were walking to the elevators my guys had the doors held open for us, but one female fan had wrangled her way past security.

'Mick Jagger, I love you!' She threw him a neatly gift-wrapped package, complete with ribbon and a double-bow.

Up to our floor and the boys went off to their rooms to unwind. We did our usual position changes with the locals and all six of us bodyguards sat around thinking well this is Adelaide, there's one down and one to go.

'*Bob, Bob Jones, I need you in my room, now!*' Mick yelled from his doorway.

A cold chill ran up my spine; no, it couldn't be, she couldn't possibly have got past my guys, not after the drilling I'd given them about our Mrs Richards, the tour nutter.

Mick read the expression on my face. 'No, it's not her, she's not here. But fuck man, it could be worse. Have a look at what that chick in the lobby threw at me, and fuck, this is Cocker city.'

That neat little gift-wrap was a box of dynamite to us: a box of dope!

'Fuck there's enough in that score to keep even Keith and me going for a fucking full moon.'

Strange girl in a lobby, dope in a gift box and as Mick said, 'this is Cocker city'. Shit! Shit! Shit! My brain patterns were running every which way.

'Come on, Bob Jones, you're in charge of security, think of something!' Mick requested.

All I could think of was these Adelaide coppers bursting in at any second with a bunch of German shepherd sniffer dogs, like on TV. Another electric shock ran up my spine: *assualt* in Sydney, *rape* in Melbourne, *drugs* in Adelaide. Christ, I didn't care how the spelling worked, this publicity we didn't need. I grabbed the box off the bed, ran to the toilet and flushed the contents down the toilet, tore the box into pieces and flushed that too. I walked back to Mick's suite, feeling like a real clever fart ...

'Was that the toilet flushing?'

'Yep!'

'Don't tell me, did ya flush the shit?'

'Yep!'

Well, Mick had told me to think of something!

'You got any idea what that shit would've cost?'

'Nope!' Maybe I should've taken more time and thought of a better idea.

'Well, you can believe me, that's the most expensive shit that has ever been flushed down that fucking toilet.' Mick laughed so hard he collapsed on his bed.

We never did see any sniffer dogs in Adelaide, but I copped the brunt of a bunch of dopey shit jokes for the next few days.

The second show resulted in our most controversial headlines of the tour. Not through any of our doing, but this second show just wasn't big enough for the amount of people that wanted to see The Rolling Stones. The scalpers got higher prices for their tickets than any of the other shows. The venue was packed, a total sell-out; there must have been at least another 5000 fans out the front without tickets, and they wanted in.

The second show was even better than the first, The Rolling Stones rocked and the fans competed with the band's volume. However, large numbers of fans had jumped the fences and, with all seats sold out, this extra group made conditions not only uncomfortable, but also extremely dangerous as the front of the stage and the aisles were filling up.

'Bob Jones, Jesus, you've got to sort this out!' Paul Dainty was quick to the scene.

'Paul, there must be a fucking thousand of them coming over the fences. What do you expect me to do now they're in?'

'Bob, it's not the front of the stage that's the priority problem, there's about another five thousand about to break the fences down. If the fences go, they'll stampede into the concert, and there's nowhere for them to go except the stage.'

The spotlights on two stands floodlit the problem area where the police and fence security were having their major problem.

All of us checked out Paul Dainty's dilemma, it was reminiscent of the Frankston riot. A crowd of thousands, with hundreds of fans pushing, pulling, kicking and bodily throwing themselves into the two-metre-plus wire cyclone fence with barbed wire on the top.

During our training prior to this tour there had been seven of us, which I'd humorously referred to as the magnificent seven. Tonight, I had only five, but on this occasion they were truly the magnificent five.

We stood defiantly in a line in varying bouncer/bodyguard poses. Under these spotlights we were in full view of the crowd. Like in some sort of miracle, the fans damaging the fences stopped their attack, and murmurs drifted across the Adelaide concert night.

'Ah shhhitt, it's those karate guys! It's those martial arts bodyguards! A coupla months ago in Melbourne, a few of them had put a coupla hundred sharpies in the hospital!'

It was as if the six of us were suddenly a super-force. However, the moment of truce was broken by a loud 'Crack ... crash.' About twenty fans had climbed a huge tree, crawled out along one of it's larger branches for a view of the stage. Fan twenty-one was too much and all fans and the branch tumbled down over whomever was underneath, with multiple injuries to a multitude of fans.

It was time to head backstage and prepare for an emergency evacuation.

As we turned to move away from this troubled ares the crowd attacked the fences again, with a handful of very tired-looking police and fence security guys trying to support the swaying fence from their side. Backstage, our five limos were parked in all directions. I got the limo boss to turn them around, facing the gates ready for an emergency, just in case.

'I want the drivers standing by all cars and I want all the doors front and back open, and I want them running. Keep those engines turned running, and if we come off that stage with the guys in the band, I want us out of here within seconds. No! I want us out of here instantly.'

'Hey, are you Bob Jones?' The question came from behind as I'd said *instantly*.

It was Ron 'the Con' Blackmore, accompanied by a police superintendent and a police officer of, I guessed, at least senior sergeant rank.

'These fellas need a big favor, Bob!' Ron said with trepidation.

The superintendent continued: 'When you and your guys appeared under these spotlights it was the only time that mob eased up on their onslaught of the fences for the last twenty minutes.'

'Yeah, that was a freak out for us too.'

'Look, those fences haven't got much left in them, they're about to fall and my guys are exhausted.'

'Excuse me, I'm missing a point here somewhere!'

'Well it's like this, we need your assistance. I've been in communication with headquarters and our entire dog squad is on it's way, but we're asking you guys to do a repeat of that trick you pulled off before. Help us just till the dogs get here. If the fence goes first, we'll have a riot on our hands.'

I simply nodded; I guess Ron took that as a yes. The superintendent and his police officer shadow went back to check on his boys.

'Ron, my concern's the band. That's my job, isn't it? To protect the band?'
Ron must have felt the need to share with me, who actually was the boss.

'Sure Bob, but there's the PDC to consider as well. In the next coupla weeks this fucking band'll be gone, and we'll have to work this gig all over again with a new band.'

'Okay, okay, we'll try that magnificent five stunt again, but if that fence breaks and the dogs ain't here, well, my guys and The Stones won't be here, either.'

'Cool, I'm with you. I'll tell Dainty and Rudge, and guess what, if that fence goes, we're with you.'

I filled in the magnificent five and grabbed the guy who was in charge of the pit crew (the pit crew worked the front of the stage, there were at least a dozen of them, behind the barriers). They were all working their arses off with those extra fans, who'd already jumped the fences.

I began filling the head guy in. 'Look man, if for any reason you see me and these other bodyguards whisk The Stones off the stage you make damned sure no punters come on, or back of the stage.'

'Gotcha!'

The local guys were always keen to impress. The head guy didn't know (and neither did The Stones) that if the fences blew, there'd be approximately another 5000 for him to keep off the stage area.

There we were, back under the spotlights, me and my magnificent five and guess what? It worked like a dream, with that same murmur as before and the crowd growing still! No more branches breaking.

Just then the Adelaide police *marines* arrived, and with at least a dozen beautiful black 'n' tan German shepherds with cop trainers that made me wonder which of them would have the worst bite. The crowd roared it's anti-police abuse as it does when there's a two-meter fence between them and a dozen police dogs.

The dogs settled the crowd just like we had, but I knew they'd hold the mob's respect longer than we could. But hey, we did it, the superintendent thanked us, and we wandered off backstage. The Rolling Stones finished off a great set and were none the wiser of what had gone down as they'd blared out 'Street Fighting Man'.

I loved that song.

On a long flight from one city to another, with nothing better to do, Richard Norton and I answered Mick Jagger's questions about the origins and philosophical background of the martial arts. We had a mutual interest in comparing what we knew to music.

Keith Richards, on the other hand, sat next to Mick, with his tape blaring out a recent Stones performance (this was Keith the critic doing his own sound check). With his eyes closed, he looked as interested in our conversation as he was in the flight.

Richard had just explained to Mick how, with martial arts beginnings, there was one, only one form of fighting, and that was the *source*. Mick's interest was heightened as Richard explained the original musical connection.

'In warfare, the concept of the source was to choreograph every defensive and offensive manoeuvre to musical notes. This was set to a rhythmic drum beat, so it looked more like dancing.'

'So what you're telling me Richard is there's this martial arts source? While we're touring the world we've noticed varieties of martial arts in almost every country. Now we come to the South Pacific, we get you two guys as our bodyguards and we're told about a martial art and it's called Bob Jones Freestyle'

That got my blood pumping ... 'Mick, humans have roamed the earth for millions of years and archaeological findings prove we've fought one another since the beginning: the source. Now in 1973 we imitate what we see, what our masters show us and we meditate to try to comprehend the source, or the beginning. Now, around the world we see this music and dance-type fighting of the Ram-Muay with the Thai boxers in Bangkok, the Flamenco style of Spain, with two men, their heels tapping, constantly fighting over a woman. Here in Australia, our Aborigines with their corroboree have danced for tens of thousands of years.

'And, yes, Bob Jones is guilty of imitation, but we do it well, we know we have contacted the source.

That's why our freestyle has spread to every city in Australia and New Zealand!'

'You're right, Bob. Yep, you're right.' Keith Richards interrupted with his usual energy. 'Imitation's the key word! Fucking imitation, the whole world is full of fucking imitators, that's what makes the world go around.

'Like you guys say about martial arts, music has only one source. There's really only one song in the whole world, and probably Adam and Eve hummed it to each other, and everything else is a variation on it in one form or another, you know? We need masters we can imitate, whether you're a fuckin' White Belt or like when I got my first guitar. When we fail to produce an accurate copy, we invent ourselves, our own style.

'The Johnny know-alls talk about imitation; virtually everybody starts out by copying somebody else. It's logical. Isn't imitation the greatest form of flattery?

Music, martial arts, anything, its all the fucking same: imitation!' Keith sank back in his seat, closed his eyes; his face had a satisfied look.

Suddenly, on that flight from one city to another the plane prepared to land.

'Could you all be seated please and fasten your seatbelts.'

Jesuz! And I hadn't even thought that Keith was interested ...

It was summer. The entire city of Perth closed down on weeknights after 8.30 p.m. Our flight from Adelaide was on a Tuesday night and we were due to touch down at 9.30. Keith Richards, as usual on all flights, as well as all night in his hotels, had his stereo-blaster set up in his first-class seat with it's speaker boxes split on either side of the plane at the front row. The Stones had created their usual party mode to pass the time on this three-hour flight.

Keith had his blaster blasting and those flight attendants on flight TAA 109 didn't stop laughing for three hours. By the time we'd landed, Ron 'the Con' Blackmore assured us he knew the owner of the best Indian restaurant (one of The Stones' favorites was Indian cuisine) in Perth and he'd be open and have the place jumpin' in a jack flash by 11 p.m. Between Mick Jagger and the band, and Richard Norton competing with Paul Dainty (both were natural chick-magnets), they had every hostess and many female passengers looking forward to meeting and eating with the band. I'd become used to the limo-lifestyle by now, but it was still hard grasping how easy it was for The Stones to light up a town, even if it was Perth in 1973.

Neither I nor any of the bodyguards could drink alcohol while on tour, but that didn't stop us from having a good time. The band, its bodyguards, the management crew, and several of the stage crew, arrived at the restaurant at around 11.20 in the limos and a local tour bus. As we were welcomed in by the owner, there were already about thirty women who had gathered, all eager to meet the band. Paul Dainty had organised a few female celebrities and Ron 'the Con' had made sure there were at least a couple of strippers and off-duty hookers, and Peter Rudge had requested a selection of Perth's better groupies.

It was midnight at the only restaurant open in town. Around sixty of us were about to party to sunrise, knowing that Mick loved to see the sun come up and Keith, well as you know by now ...

Sixty were about as many as the place could fit. The Stones were eating Indian food so they were happy, and all those beautiful girls that had come to share the band were all smiling. And why were the bodyguards grinning from ear to ear? We'd worked out how many band members there were (two of them had their ladies with them) and how many of these glamour's there were, which meant that at some time during the night there'd be more than twenty spares floating around. It was no good competing with Richard Norton, we all knew one day he'd be a movie star. Paul Dainty was the boss, and a very smooth-talking entrepreneur millionaire to boot. Mick and Keith; well, they were Mick and Keith! So, I made a point of hanging out with Bobby Keyes, the sax player. He was one of those smooth-talking Yanks who'd cottoned on to a couple of honeys. Nicki was a petite blonde made to order for Mr Keyes.

Her girlfriend had introduced herself to me during dinner as Renee. Renee apparently didn't have a surname; she was as tall as me with very long hair, which coincidentally was the same colour as mine. She had a slight Irish accent and wore a black full-length dress, backless and pretty much frontless with a split up the front to her pelvis line that tastefully didn't show much of her long white legs until she sat down to dinner.

Over the meal and a couple of bottles of wine, she made interesting conversation about her job as a secretary to a budding Liberal politician and what type of weight training she did four or five times a week.

For the rest of the time she asked me about what it was like to be a bodyguard to such high-profile rock 'n' roll stars. This was my fourth week at the new job and I had Bobby Keyes and Nicky Hopkins (who'd joined us with a friend, Lisa, who looked about seventeen and who made a living stripping at a local joint) pissing themselves about Mrs Richards and the probable thousand bucks worth of shit I'd flushed down the toilet.

By about 3 a.m. I sat back and looked at all my guys. No-one had had a drink. Yep, everyone was working as well as having a good time. Paul Dainty and Richard Norton, as usual, were competing for the best looking babe in the place. Sorry, second best, I figured; after all, Renee by this time had cottoned on to yours truly.

By 4 a.m. the grog ran out. Mick and Keith both looked as if they were ready for room service. The leaders of the pack, Paul, Ron and Rudge signalled to me that we were about to make a move. As we walked out the restaurant there were a few cabs, our four limos and the tour bus idling away. Paul Dainty, the forever-English gentleman announced,

'Ladies, thank you all for a wonderful evening. The cabs are covered for anywhere you want to go. Just in case you might want to continue on with our party, the cabs will drop you at our hotel and we've organised the bar to be open for us, and anything you want is on the tour tab.'

'Bob, I'm sure you're busy doing that guarding thing, we'll jump in the cab and see you back at the bar,' Renee purred.

She and Nicki floated off towards the cabs, and I couldn't help thinking this bodyguard stuff sure took first prize over bouncing.

Back at the bar it took no time at all for Mick and Keith, and the leaders of the pack, to disappear to our floor with their suitable partners. The tour tab was of no use to me, just as I was practising all my favorite lines, Renee cut my thoughts in their tracks.

'Wow, would you look at that, it's 4.30! Oh, I'm so tired and I've got to work in the morning. Looks like you don't have any bodyguarding to do. I don't suppose you and I could call it quits and go upstairs to bed?'

In the shower I couldn't help but notice that Renee's workout routines had been kind to all parts of her body. Now, that was a routine I'd have to ask her about sometime. The rest of that night was the best part: Johnny Ray, that crying crooner, had once sung: *'Oh, oh what a night it was ...'*

After Paul Dainty organised a day on a multi-million-dollar fishing launch and a night on Rottnest Island, The Stones performed before yet another sellout crowd at the WACA.

The four-and-a-half-hour flight from Perth to Sydney for the last leg of the Australasian tour saw The Stones and everyone connected with them in party mode. Keith Richards had set up his stereo-blaster, cranking the sound *up loud*. Our group filled up first, business and around one-third of economy class with hardly anyone seated. Sensing that there was only one week to go, people talked and laughed about everything that had gone down during the previous five weeks. After ten years of touring the world, The Stones really enjoyed doing their thing.

About two hours into the flight, I'd told Richard Norton to check out the back of the plane. Almost every flight attendant call sign light flashed – all the attendants were at the front of the plane partying!

That evening, Paul Dainty had organised a get-together celebration tour dinner at the Bourbon and Beef, a popular American-style restaurant at the top of Kings Cross. The Bourbon and Beef in the 1960s and 1970s with its open-style front windows had a raging bar alongside the restaurant area. Downstairs was a popular discotheque nightspot. The place got that packed out it was hard to move. Patrons were as diverse as you would find anywhere in Sydney's Kings Cross: transvestites, Bohemians, tourists, punters, pimps, prostitutes, strippers and an array of local gangsters and drug dealers.

My knowledge of the 'Cross' meant that I knew who was who in the zoo. Local bad boy Grant Anderson was a stick relation of mine (a double-o-seventh cousin by marriage). His old man was Jim Anderson, who literally ran half the 'Cross' in those days with his partner, Abe Saffron. This guaranteed me safe passage throughout the 'Cross', including the Maori bouncing fraternity and the *striptease* strip of bouncers. It also gave me reasonable clout with the crooked local cops.

Even though I had a gist of how the Sydney scene worked, it still was not easy to appear in public with a band of the calibre of The Rolling Stones. Us bodyguards had to rely on our previous bouncer skills to keep the peace, thanks to our years of door work dealing with the public, which enabled us to identify potential problems.

After dinner and back at the Hyatt, Mick Jagger wanted his usual late-night martial arts training session to brush up on his punches and kicks, which were now a regular part of his on-stage antics. After the workout us bodyguards hung around by the elevators and shot out the odd kick and punch and laughed at one another, it was, after all, about 11.30.

At 12.45 a.m. Mick and Keith Richards came down to give us another lesson in The Rolling Stones party power philosophy.

'Bob, Richard; you guys come with Keith and me for a bit. We're gonna have an end-of-tour party,' Mick boasted.

'Yeah, and your other guys had better be on the ball when we get back!' Keith warned.

Mick, Keith, Richard and I caught the elevator down. There was no warning: the bottom floor of the Hyatt was the hotel's own inhouse night club. As we entered Mick said, 'Bob and Richard, you guys hold back and keep an eye on me and Keith. Just in case, you know!'

No, I didn't know.

As we stepped off to one side and scanned the patrons of the club, Mick and Keith had walked on to the middle of the floor to be illuminated by one of the club's downlights.

The DJ was playing some funky background music, and long before he'd a chance to say, 'Hey, there's ...' every girl in the place (and they were all here praying that something, anything like this might happen) screamed and flocked to the dance floor.

They tried to get as close to Mick and Keith as they could. All I could do was look at Richard and he looked at me. (Was this a *just in case*?)

'Hey ah, all you girls, it's great to see you here tonight. Keith and me, and our bodyguards over there, we ah, we were thinking of having a party up on the twenty-second floor. That's our floor and we just thought all you guys might want to come and join in the party.'

Mick looked our way and then towards the elevators. Next thing, four elevators packed with us guys and every girl that was on the dance floor made their way up to the twenty-second floor.

As the elevator doors opened, Mick said to Nicky and Bungles, another of my boys,

"I'm sorry'

'All the girls are cool but no guys, this is a private party.'

Some of the girls were attached to guys and I remember the sight of one couple in particular as Bungles responded to Mick's request by putting his hand on the chest of the guy. His girl, mesmerised by the thought of partying with The Rolling Stones, just kept walking.

'But, but ...' the boyfriend said, as his hand grip slipped to a finger grip, and one by one the fingers of he and his girlfriend's hands slipped apart. ' ... *but* we're engaged!'

'Sorry man', Bungles consoled. 'You heard the boss, it's a private party, girls only.'

He and Nicky bundled him and several guys back on to the elevators and pressed 'down'.

The next couple of hours saw a steady flow of room service calls – the tour tab for this party would surely rival our entire tour security bill!

The party rocked till dawn. If you've never been on tour with a band like The Stones, you wouldn't believe what they can get girls to do, and that engaged guy should definitely not have married that girl!

The funniest thing that night was when Bobby

Keyes called me to his suite. There were girls everywhere, getting drunk and getting into the various stages of undress. He was on the phone having a very drunken conversation and actually seemed to be arguing.

'Bob, I need a hand, man. I'm on this call to the Gold Coast and I've got reception trying to hook that other phone up with a call to the States to my wife, and I don't want any of these chicks answering that call. That would not be cool at all.'

'Bobby, what are friends for?' I replied, waiting by his bar next to the phone. Just as I was admiring the scenery, wondering if Sydney had a Renee equivalent, the phone rang and reception advised me the US call had been connected.

'Hello, ah hello. Yes, this is Sydney, Australia. My name is Bob Jones with security, hello!' The noise in Bobby's suite had picked up as several more corks popped from champagne bottles and the girls kept laughing, drinking and spilling lots of the bubbly wine.

Bobby was still arguing with his lady friend on the line to the Gold Coast.

'Hello, security here, can I help you?'

'Well, I hope you can. I'm trying to get through to my husband, Bobby Keyes. Is he there, please?'

'Yes, he is. He's been waiting for your call. He's on the other phone, I'll just get him for you.'

'Oh, thank you very much! It sure is noisy there; it's hard to hear what you're saying.'

I put my hand over the receiver. 'Bobby, hey Bobby!'

Oh no, his arguing with that lady friend had turned into a swearing match.

'Bobby, it's your bloody wife.'

'Oh, thanks man, I've been waiting for that call,' he said, as if he'd forgotten what I was doing there. It turned out the Gold Coast call was a girl he'd met when on the Brisbane show. The argument was about him wanting to fly her down for the last show in Sydney, and for some reason that appeared to be a problem. He'd rung his wife to let her know he missed her and there was only one show left.

Now Bobby was too drunk to hang up either of the calls, so he carried on the two-way conversation between the Gold Coast and the US, a phone by each hand and pouring himself another drink at the same time. He screamed and swore into one phone and talked lovingly into the other. He'd mix up the phones when he'd pour himself a drink, swearing at his wife and making love to the girl that couldn't make the last concert of his Australasian tour. It lasted an hour.

The final night of The Rolling Stones tour was a sellout. That Randwick Racetrak audience were treated to the most spectacular stage entrance of possibly, this entire world tour. At least a dozen spotlights floodlit bright as day, six glorious white horses drawing a London carriage suitable for the Royal Family. All members of the band looked absolutely elegant. On the night the Stones played their best set, as if to say: 'Thank you Australia, you've been great.'

Mick Jagger gyrated with new-found aggression: punching, kicking and reverse-elbowing. He'd wink at me in approval of my martial arts instructions.

In the audience a large bodybuilder ushered his girlfriend through the massive crowd that was up and dancing by the front of the stage. Both he and his girl had painted their bodies silver. He was dressed as a gladiator and she was dressed and made up as Cleopatra. Suddenly, he'd hoisted her high above his head and sat her on his shoulders, both her silver thighs hanging down the front of him. As she shared the spotlight with the band, the Paul Dainty tour signature exploded.

This huge fireworks display illuminated a sign as big as the Hollywood sign in the hills of California. It read: 'Paul Dainty Thanks the Rolling Stones in Australia'. The audience, The Stones and us bodyguards were blown away, Paul Dainty had done it again.

'Street Fighting Man' was the next number in the set. Charlie Watts counted it in and his drums set the beat for their song about the recent uncontrollable Paris peace riots between police and demonstrators.

Mick this time really got into his new martial arts repertoire, punching and kicking in all directions. The bodybuilder and his girl punched in rhythm to Mick's punches. When he strutted over to centre stage and touched her hand, she took him by the wrist and pulled him in and kissed him. The crowd went wild: Cleopatra had kissed Mick Jagger.

Without missing a beat, Mick strutted back over to where I was standing near the piano and he laughed.

He put the microphone behind his back and screamed at Keith Richards, Nicky Hopkins, Bobby Keyes and Bob Jones:

'*That fucking Cleopatra, she's Mrs Richards!*'

Having completed my first rock 'n' roll tour after keeping pace with Mick Jagger and Keith Richards for six weeks without the aid of the substances that had kept the both of them going, I found I needed several long periods of deep sleep ... It was also a time of looking back and taking stock.

In the early 1960s I'd been married to Pauline. Friends and neighbours believed she looked like Elizabeth Taylor! My own Pauline was not just a pretty face; she was also a natural book-keeper.

Since we'd married and experienced parenthood through the birth of our daughter Tracey Lee Jones, Pauline always had the knack of knowing exactly when I needed to earn extra money. Back in the early 1960s, Melbourne had a 6.00 p.m. curfew on alcoholic sales that stretched to 9.00 a.m.

The hours between these times provided the opportunity for young entrepreneurs like myself to indulge in an extra income-earner and sell illegal booze to drinking patrons.

So Bob Jones worked three normal jobs, and indulged in the proprietorship of a sly-grog bottle shop. And with the added opportunity of becoming a dance promoter, and with Pauline's ability at handling the books, how could I fail?

During the mid-1950s, on the north side of Melbourne, Heidelberg had been selected to be the site of the Olympic village to house all Olympic contestants.

In the middle of this residential development, a huge auditorium had been built for all local and international contestants to work out or just hang out.

With the Olympic Hall as the venue and the influence of Alan Freed's 'Big Beat' in the US Spring of 1958, when he'd planned to play sixty-eight shows in thirty-eight cities in forty-five days with stars such as Chuck Berry and Jerry Lee Lewis, I planned for the 'Big Rock', which was the biggest Friday night dance in the northern suburbs.

Stan 'the Man' Rofe was my own Alan Freed, working as the Big Rock compare. Along with my radio advertising budget, he'd occasionally give airplay to the bands playing at the Big Rock and he wasn't shy in mentioning this great new dance and the fact that he'd be at the Olympic Hall Big Rock on Friday nights.

From my gang days, I was well aware of the capabilities of the unscrupulous promoters hiring gangs to tarnish the image of well-run dances or even close down new dances. For this reason I hired a couple of guys I knew from around the traps: Bill Sabotka, who was a 183-centimetre tall, blue-eyed blond-haired Austrian, and Dave Milne, who stood at 194 centimetres. Both were extremely popular with the ladies, weighed well in excess of 100 kilograms, were of good fight shape and were a formidable sight. They were Big Rock security regulars and I backed them with the Red Coat Bouncers from West Melbourne's Festival Hall, which was of the Wren family fame.

My major opposition included the big five: Ron 'the Con' Blackmore, Ivan Dayman, Col Jones and his Capri-circuit in the north, Brian De Coursey and Bill Joseph, both in the south-east quarter around the bay. All of my opposition was well established. At the time the Capri-circuit had twenty-two suburban dances operating and the other big four had at least half a dozen or more in their circuits. This gave all of them a degree of control and they could make it hard for me (and of course they did) to acquire good-name bands).

Pauline and I persevered and eventually built up a good stock of bands and performers, including Normie Rowe, Bobby Bright and Laurie Allan, Johnny Saxon and the Saxons, Mike Brady of M.P.D. Limited, and The Hearsemen, to name just a few old friends.

Before long, dance number two in my planned Bob Jones Circuit started up in Eltham. In those days the Heidelberg Olympic Hall was considered to be the outer suburbs and Eltham was known as the bush. We humorously called the Sunday afternoon Eltham dance 'Lookout'. Both dances exploded in popularity and I figured that if I could look after two dances, then I could look after a hundred and two. This meant my other jobs had to go (one of these, interstate truck-driving, had become very time-consuming).

The Jones' family abode at the time was a small dwelling behind a single-fronted shop. This un-let shop, which stored our alcohol supplies, was in Station Street, Fairfield, alongside Crappers Ice

Works, and opposite the Crapper Family wood yard. It was the perfect address for a sly grog location.

With the government's six o'clock curfew on all licensed premises, it meant that all year round there was a huge demand for wood 'n' beer or ice 'n' beer, and there was never any concern about the traffic flow. Not even as Pauline and I had bands practising a couple of nights a week, one band in the garage and another in the lounge room. However, the cops, in unmarked cars, started *keeping book* on who was buying wood, ice and booze. There was a rumor that some local gangsters weren't happy with their new opposition. Thanks to my capital *A Attitude* from my gang days, I wasn't the least concerned.

Instead, I was concerned with the cops, but my *Attitude* would not let me negotiate a deal in that direction. After the three jobs, next to go was the sly grog. This had me thinking even more seriously about my future as a dance promoter.

Dance number three was on the drawing board. We were planning to launch 'Jailhouse Rock' on Thursday nights, coinciding with the recent Elvis Presley hit of the same name. This new venue was at the Coburg Town Hall, which was just around the corner from Pentridge Prison.

Things had never looked better: Friday night was the Big Rock, Sunday afternoons at Eltham was The Lookout. Now we were booking our acts at a third venue to launch Jailhouse Rock on Thursday nights.

Many years earlier I'd been a member of the gang, the Phantom Twins. This gang was forced to disband prior to the 1956 Olympics. Thanks to the police, so many gang members went *northside* to their suburban gangs in the northern suburbs.

Possibly the first, if not, definitely one of the very

first rock 'n' roll dances in Australia – the weekly meeting place of all of these gangs – was the Arcadia Ballroom (more commonly referred to as the 'ARC'), a first-floor premises in High Street, Thornbury. Inside the dance hall each suburb had its area, including areas for such guest gangs as those from Collingwood and Richmond, who were associates of the northside, particularly in times of strife.

It was here that I met Vin Scott. (This was an alias that Vinnie used for his boxing career.) Vin ran the security for the ARC and was the most feared name on the northside (with constant challengers). He was reputed at the time for being the hardest hitter in the Australian boxing scene, thanks to the lethal punching power he had in both fists.

I never found out if it was my own bad karma or if one of the big five had sent them to 'tarnish the image' of Big Rock. I should have spotted it from the beginning. So many times I'd left the ARC with Vinnie and the guys to visit opposing dances in the south, east and western suburbs for the odd night of tarnishing. The tell-tale sign of the gangs was their ranks swelling the Olympic Hall. Irrespective of what this venue had originally been designed for, the gangs were hell bent on creating their own blood sport.

Since my time with Pauline, marriage had become a healthy change from my previous violent lifestyle. Also, fatherhood and marriage had softened many of my street instincts.

Perhaps that's why I hadn't noticed all the familiar signs. The Preston boys would congregate around the front of the stage, perhaps the Northcote boys would hit the cloakroom, or maybe the Thornbury boys were assigned to the ticket box take of the night. Lalor would cut the phone lines and

Heidelberg would service the car park.

The faces milling around in the centre of the hall would be from Reservoir. Among these Reservoir Boys would be the new recruits, including a younger member about to prove his worth. He'd be the one to wipe his sweaty hands, form a fist and throw his king hit at the target. A punch that he'd remember for the rest of his life.

This king hit was the signal for everything to happen at once. I was on the stage at the time checking some minor problem. I didn't see a thing, not even the *target* hitting the floor.

Everything would be over within five minutes.

Outside, their getaway cars would be lined up ready for the five-minute exodus. Meanwhile, the Preston boys came up to the stage in waves. Their job was to smash the equipment.

My years with Vinnie Scott had taught me well. I could punch damned hard, but some of those guys were getting up again. That's when I grabbed the microphone stand (this was a couple of years before I'd begin martial arts training) and swung hard. They went down like bowling pins. This time they stayed down and a couple of them had trouble breathing. Pretty soon other mike stands and a couple of drum stands were swinging and whistling through the air all around me on the stage.

Jesuz, what's going here? I thought. All the musos had thought fuck him, why should he have all the fun, as well as this it's our equipment these pricks mean to do a number on.

I left the Bobby Brights and the Mike Bradys to capably fend for themselves and protect their gear. My Red Coats were outnumbered, but breaking even thanks to two of their big-hitters, Billy 'Kid' Lewis (an Australian boxing champion) who's eulogy was that he never had to hit anybody twice in a street fight. His main back up was Snowy, a veteran pro-bouncer with then around twenty years of working doors. His stint in the big war made this war zone a game. They had bodies falling everywhere, and all they needed to turn the tide was my attack from the flanks.

Just then I could hear Pauline screaming, loud enough to be heard above all this. Jesuz Christ, I hadn't had time to think about her welfare. She was standing on a chair against the wall yelling my name repeatedly. I surged my way through a lot of now tired scuffling and wrestling opponents. When I reached Pauline, she yelled: 'These bastards, they've wrecked absolutely everything. Our boys on the front door, they're in big trouble. There are just too many of these mongrels out there.'

She then shrieked even louder, 'Bob! Dave and Bill need you!'

I grabbed Pauline's hand and she ran with me. As we entered the foyer of The Olympic Village Auditorium I said, 'Pauline, get back into the ticket box room and lock yourself in.' That's when I noticed the door had been wrenched totally off its hinges. Also, Pauline's ticket reception window had been smashed. The reception foyer was covered in broken glass from the floor-to-ceiling glass doors. There was blood along the floor, and splattered and smeared over the walls. People were unconscious everywhere.

Meanwhile, Dave and Bill were both hopelessly outnumbered.

A decade of gang warfare had taught me a lot about street survival skills. It was as if time had stood still as I'd tried to gain full momentum over approximately ten metres from reception to the front steps where Dave and Bill where getting into what was a life-or-death situation.

A lot of innocent bystanders had been hurt. Each gang's intention was to hurt my friends and to specifically get me. Hurting my wife Pauline would definitely have been bonus points.

My fears turned to anger. The release of this anger was like a stick of dynamite and exploding adrenaline to all points of my body. With hands full of hair I clashed heads together, thrusting them towards the concrete steps, taking them two at a time out of action. I deliberately smashed teeth, compressed cheekbones and split eyes.

Dave and Bill picked up on my passion and the three of us set about doing what we'd do together for the next ten years, whenever the situation warranted: causing maximum damage.

Meanwhile, Pauline was behind the three of us.

'Now you're exactly getting what you came looking for you fucking mongrels ... Real brave bastards when you were smashing my door down to take our money, you weak bastards ... Don't run away, come and get some more of what you were looking for.'

But run they did! The plotters were retreating to their waiting vehicles as per plan, so as to regroup, lick their wounds and prepare to fight another day.

And the aftermath of this horrific five minutes of carnage: the cars of my patrons, mostly broken into; property stolen and damage en masse; the Olympic Village Auditorium wrecked; our food stall tipped over and the takings stolen; and people everywhere, bloodied and injured, some seriously. The cloakroom had been raided and bags, jackets and valuables stolen. The band and backstage crew had helped me save the stage and Billy 'Kid' Lewis and Snowy and the Festival Hall guys would've survived without my help, although the *thank you* was nice.

The evening's crowd had been the biggest we'd had due to the bands I'd booked (as it turned out they didn't have to play), and this northern gang had all bought tickets to get into the venue, assuming they'd get it all back.

Pauline could read my mind (she was good at that): 'You didn't think I'd let those arseholes get all the night's takings, did you?

'Well, it took them three goes at breaking the reception glass, and as they were kicking the door in I put the money bags between my thighs, pulled my dress over the top and stood there screaming like there'd be no tomorrow.

'They kicked the door in, grabbed the cash tin; they thought I was about to have a heart attack ... Oh, and here's the entire night's takings, less, of course, the few pounds and shillings in the cash tin.'

I tried to kiss her for saving the night's takings, but Dave, Bill and me were too busy exploding into uncontrollable laughter.

Did I already mention that Pauline was good at balancing the books?

Not long after this rambunctious evening at the Big Rock Olympic Hall, Heidelberg, I suffered a rare moment of extreme depression. In less than six months I'd gone from having a well-paid interstate trucker's job and two part-time labouring jobs to promotional activities. The cops had applied some pressure at a time when I didn't need it, and caused the closure of the sly grog enterprise that was building itself into a thriving business. After the big brawl at the Big Rock, and the press it received along with the damaging word-of-mouth, the three local councils connected to my promotions cancelled my permits. My all-too-short career as a dance promoter was over.

These events were not the only cause of my despair: Pauline and I had also gone our separate ways. My daughter Tracey Lee would no longer be a part of my life, without the agreement of her mother.

Pauline and I had been doomed since our wedding day. We'd been two teenagers drawn together in times of uncertainty, typical of the youths of these changing times, demanding to be heard, but with nothing, as yet, really to say. We were two teenagers about to become responsible parents who were not even old enough to vote.

There'd been a marriage war between her Catholic mother and my Protestant father over which of their churches would sanction this unwanted pregnancy. At least both Pauline and I knew that we wanted to have Tracey Lee.

To end all family arguments, we snuck off to the registry office to recite a bunch of vows we didn't understand. Being pronounced man and wife' was the fun part. All we had to do was move in together, set up living quarters with some cheap furniture and play out this Mr and Mrs Jones scenario.

When, six months later, the doctor said something that meant: 'I now pronounce you *mother and father*,' Pauline and I realised we began a journey of something we knew nothing about.

Just over three years later Pauline decided it wasn't going anywhere. In this situation the father/husband has no say in the matter.

To add to this my financial status was zero.

I'd lost everything.

All I could think was, *the world could go fuck itself!*

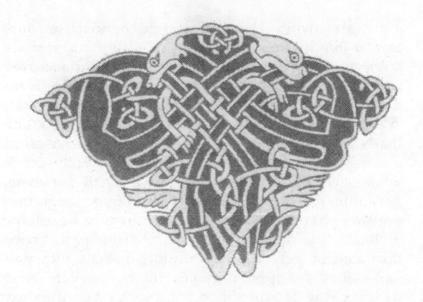

Ron Stefani's Spaghetti Bar, 12:30 p.m., Friday, 22 November 1963. Dave and Bill had an offer they hoped I'd be interested in.

The bar was, and still is today, in a complex called Leo's, which is located in Fitzroy Street, St. Kilda. Leo's was a landmark in those days frequented by pimps, prostitutes, trannies, would-be gangsters, crooked coppers, TV personalities, St. Kilda beach trendies, every tourist in town, and the who's who of the corporate profilers from anywhere south of the inner-city of Melbourne.

It was the perfect place for Bob Jones to discuss the launch of his new lifestyle. Ron Stefani had sat us at my regular table in a quiet corner, surrounded by photos of Ron with Frank Sinatra, Ron with Sammy Davis Jnr, Ron with Cole Porter; in fact, there were photos of Ron with just about everyone who was anyone. Within a decade, even yours truly would appear on the wall with Mr Stefani.

Meanwhile, Dave cut straight to the chase. 'Bob, the reason Bill and me called this meeting today; we got to thinking after that all-in-riot at your dance, the way you came out and backed us when the chips were down. Well, first up we both gotta thank you for that. We noticed you've got a flair for expansion, you know that's why the big boys set that gang on our arses.

'We want ... what we want is for you to sort of manage us. Bill, me and you – we'll call ourselves "Trouble-Shooters" and we'll only bounce gigs that are out of control. Gigs that are having excessive violence. The catch is we work for triple pay. As we take control, get rid of the trouble-makers, they pay new bouncers supplied by you the normal rate. And us three, the Trouble-Shooters, move on to the next gig prepared to pay triple time.'

Jesuz, I thought, Dave and Bill were offering me this gig to get into something I'd been doing all my life. On top of that they were saying it was worth triple the pay.

Hmmm, there was no conflict of interest due to the fact that all my recent opposition had dances with more violence than they wanted. If any gigs did not want to pay the extra money then we'd send them the trouble-makers we were having problems with. That should work, I reasoned, and in time it did! Plus bringing in normal bouncers for normal rates backing us up could be expanded to possibly every gig in town. On top of this it'd give me somewhere to release all this anger I'd been bottling up as a result of my current circumstances.

'Dave and Bill, what can I say? I'm in!'

We all shook hands, but with only one point I needed to clarify: 'Dave, when you said, as we take control new bouncers move in supplied by me, what exactly do you see as *me* and what is the role of us in this new venture, Trouble-Shooters?'

'Mate, Bill and me don't want to know about any corporate bullshit, that all sounds like the too hard basket. All we want and what we want for the three of us is the cream of the crop. Any television or radio lunchtime promotions, strip shows and the private party's – you know, all the best gigs – at the top pay rate. At the end of the day it's pounds, shillings and pence, that's what counts. We want you to run the expansion coz that's what you do, that way it's a win–win situation. We need the expansion so the Trouble-Shooters get the reputation and can continue to move on and chase the bigger pay cheques.'

The following morning, no sooner had I flicked on the radio than the announcer had stated:

'Yesterday, at 12:30P.M., on this Friday, 22 November 1963, the President of the United States of America John F. Kennedy was shot as his cavalcade was moving slowly through the city of Dallas. JFK was pronounced dead 30 minutes later ...'

All that day I was numb. JFK shot dead? I kept thinking. The whole world had just fucked itself – at exactly the same time I'd been given a brand new lease of life.

Trouble-Shooters was an overnight success and as the numbers grew the organisation became known as the Bob Jones Security. In the industry we were referred to as The Bob Jones Boys, and within a decade a bouncer would have difficulty finding employment if he didn't work with us.

The Trouble-Shooters worked seven days and seven nights and it wasn't long before extra teams of Trouble-Shooters had to be formed to cope with the demand.

The team after Dave, Bill and me included Gary 'Maneater' Spiers, he'd go on to work for years as a bounty hunter for insurance companies in downtown London. He'd develop his own bouncer syndicate and his own martial arts organization (unfortunately Gary would pass away in 2001). Then came Dennis 'Animal' Williamson, who would possibly find his fate while encountering the wrath of some wife's jealous husband. Sandy Fricker, always one of my favourites, would stay in the business for years before fading out of the scene.

Brian 'Chops' Suey (still working in the Melbourne scene today), would become the right-hand man to Dave Hedgcock, who, on my retirement from bouncing, would take over from where I'd left off – he still controls the Melbourne nightclub scene and has been shot four times and lived to tell the tale. (That's another reason why I got out when I did.) Frank Romani was one of my best back-ups ever; however, his involvement with The Black Dragon Society, would have us eventually parting ways.

The third team of Trouble-Shooters comprised Ivan Check, who feared no man; Little 'Crusher' Joe (thank Christ he was on our team!); and Tony Hill, who, when he stopped working for me, restarted The Lookout and ran that Eltham Dance successfully for years.

In May 1964 I received a call from a Mr Terry Rielly, a manager at the Southern Cross Hotel in Exhibition Street. I remember thinking, Christ, the bloody Southern Cross, Melbourne's biggest and most prestigious hotel complex, what could they want with me?

'Bob, I've heard good things about your security organisation. Next month we've got The Beatles coming to Australia. While they're in Melbourne, they'll be staying here at the Southern Cross. I'm sure you'd be aware of the difficulties surrounding them and security? We're working with the police as far as the crowds we're expecting out front and around the hotel. We'd like to talk to you about extra security to help out our regular hotel staff internally. You know, foyers, lobbies and elevators around the hotel grounds and things like that. Could you come in and maybe we could share some ideas and see what you can do to help out?'

A couple of days later I went in, and we all pretended to know, very professionally, how it would all go down on the day. But none of us were prepared for the actual turn of events as they would unfold.

The Beatles had arrived in Sydney on Wednesday, 10 June, and were expected in Melbourne on Saturday, 13 June.

The reaction to The Beatles was something unheard of in this country. The crowds were bigger than those of the recent Royal visit – whether at Sydney Airport, in transit or at the hotels, there were thousands of teenagers everywhere.

The Commonwealth and local cops had trouble coping with the unexpected response and one Sydney journo had described the musicians as the 'four hairmen of the apocalypse'.

On the Thursday, Terry had rung me and said with a touch of panic in his voice, 'Bob, have you seen what's happening? We've talked to the police and they've upped their numbers from 150 police on duty to 300, plus we have 100 military servicemen coming. That *dozen* we thought would be enough from you, can we make that 25, especially on the Saturday when The Beatles arrive?'

'Of course', I told Terry, 'no problem.'

As it turned out, it was everything else that was the problem. Estimates of between 10 000 to 15 000 screaming, mostly female, teenagers, had packed into Exhibition Street.

The Beatles appeared briefly on the verandah of the Southern Cross Hotel. The crowd lost control (the fact that Ringo Starr, laid up from tonsillitis, had been temporarily replaced by English drummer Jimmy Nichol had no effect on the hysteria of the crowds) and the authorities were forced to set up emergency casualty facilities in the hotel foyer to cater for the more than 150 people who were injured or had collapsed in the frenzied crush.

A Sydney doctor staying at the hotel, Dr Ivan Markovic, while helping out commented, 'I've never seen anything like this.' However, something deep inside of me said, Bob Jones, you'll see a lot more of this as time goes by! This I certainly did.

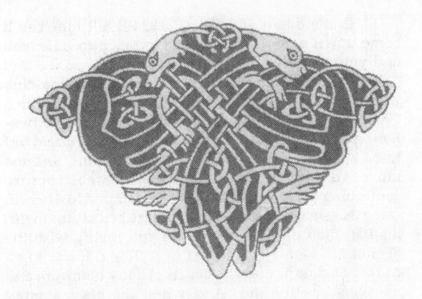

1965 was definitely another stand-out year for me and my career. I'd had an intense desire to get involved in martial arts for a couple of years; however, there was very little instruction around in the early 1960s. Luckily, in the new year I'd been doing weights at the California Gym in Collins Street. There was this guy down one end in a white uniform, wearing a black belt and taking a martial arts class.

After the lesson I made a point of asking, 'How does a guy get to take lessons?'

He looked flustered, answering, 'Aren't you Bob Jones, that bouncer guy?'

'Yeah, but what's that...'

'Listen Bob, my name's Jim, Jimmy Wilson, and I'm not really a Black Belt. The gym here pays me a couple of quid an hour to teach, but really I'm only a White Belt and I train in St. Kilda several nights a week in Tae Kwon Do, a Korean style. My instructor is a Brown Belt; his name is Jack Rozinsky. That's where you gotta go if you want instruction.

Come down and meet Jack; I'll tell him you'll come down next week. He'll be pleased to train you and your guys.

I went down to Jack Rozinsky's St. Kilda club with a bunch of my hard-nosed bouncers on 3 March 1965. Jack introduced me to my crossroads, a two-hour gruelling physical torture session that turned out to be a beginners' class. As we knocked off, and the more advanced students took a break before continuing on, Jack had five bricks clamped to a bench.

He smashed every one of these bricks, first with his fist, then palm, elbow, knee and finally with the heel of his foot. He smashed everything, including a couple of clamps and the bench. All my bouncers and me were spellbound. And when the class started again, Jack went into advanced mode. This was not even the same guy who'd taught us beginners. Mr Rozinsky was now working out with his boys; his kicks cracked the air with explosive power, and I wanted into this advanced class with a passion – for all my years of fighting, if I could've broken bones like bricks and kicked arse with Jack's devastating power ...

I trained every day in my new-found art and still in the new millennium I train every day! Jack Rozinsky, on that Monday night, put me on my path, and I'm eternally grateful to Jack, the first of many instructors.

The Trouble-Shooters got bigger every day with new venues coming on board. One market I'd not been able to get near was the new discotheque scene that was spreading all over the inner suburbs and especially within Melbourne's CBD.

A year after The Beatles and The Southern Cross incident, I received what I'd come to call that *magic* phone call.

Graham Geddes described himself as a rural schoolteacher, and he was going to open the most controversial nightclub, or discotheque, in the world. He asked if I could visit the following Saturday. He was still renovating The Catcher, but he wanted to talk to me about running the entire security for his new adventure. Remember, it was almost Christmas 1965 and the liquor laws still had licensed premises in Victoria closing at 6 p.m., which was the reason for the six o'clock swill: the workforce attempting to get drunk in an hour after work (making us Victorians famous internationally as fast drinkers).

Without a license (The Catcher would in time become famous as an unlicensed BYO venue), Geddes' newest and biggest discotheque (all of three storeys) was going to open at 8 p.m. and rock till 5 a.m. with all the biggest bands. True to his word (although totally unwanted and unwarranted), Graham Geddes made his Catcher and Bob Jones' bouncers household names.

From The Catcher, now my state headquarters at the bottom end of Flinders Lane, I began a systematic takeover of all the city's nightclubs and discotheques, All, that is, but one, 'The Thumpin Tum', where one of my best mates (outside of my immediate organisation) Max Ouzis was head bouncer.

The story of this place and the colourful characters such as David Flint, who ran the original

Thumpin Tum, the Knight family (Anthony and Phillip), who ran 'Birties and Sebastians', and Graham Geddes, who'd created The Catcher, which had six weeks of front-page headlines in the smut-rag *The Truth*, is a whole book in itself.

February 1966. Sixteen years of Menzies' rule had come to an end. During the leadership of new PM Harold Holt, the Victorian Premier Henry Bolte initiated the long-awaited decision to extend drinking hours to 10 p.m. And, as we drank for the extra four hours a day, we'd also pay bucks for our beers (thanks to the new currency), just like our Yankee mates who stopped over on R&R (rest and recreation, or 'rooting and randiness' as Barry Humphries quipped at the time) on their way to and from Vietnam.

The security industry had exploded, and the Bob Jones boys now had plenty of competition as the pubs experienced trouble getting patrons to go home at 10 p.m.

Two years after The Beatles' visit, the Southern Cross had become the place to stay, but with this new 10 p.m. closing time, they too were having trouble, especially in their famous 'Jockey Club Bar' in the saloon bar arcade. the Southern Cross rang me, but this time it was like a ten-year blast back in time to the violent 1950s.

'Hi Bob, this is Vin ... Vinnie Scott. I'm in charge of all the Southern Cross Security. I'm in here with a good mate; his name's Pat Housley. Hey, and he's the funniest fucker in the bouncer business. He's just one of those guys who without even trying breaks you up every time he opens his mouth. Makes you piss yourself laughing. You'll like him. Anyway, call in and see me. We need to talk; we need a good third guy and I want it to be you.'

When I called in Vinnie made me an offer to good to refuse. It was good money (he was working the same concept as the Trouble-Shooters, which by now had become quite famous, proving the business adage: when you become successful you create your own competition), and the hours were outside my current commitments. Plus, I had all the discos now and the Southern Cross could have been the wedge to move into the hotels of the city.

By mid-1966, after six months of being at the Southern Cross, I'd learned to watch my 'Ps' and 'Qs', due to the clientele in the 'Business Bar' and the five-star restaurant 'The Mayfair Room'. And down in The Jockey Club Bar on public holiday's things could get real tough. This Bar served as a meeting place for punters before and after all sporting events. The upstairs bowling alley was a popular hang-out for the skinhead gangs and sharpies of the city.

I worked there six days a week before starting at regular club gigs that went all night like Birties, Sebastians and The Catcher. The regular drinkers who called in at least a couple of times a week included members of the special police squad, 'The Silent Six'. Their job was to keep an eye on the city's gangs' movements. A new breed of kids bucking the system had recently appeared that the media referred to as skinheads or sharpies, due to their extremely short hairstyles and their sharp code of dressing. The Silent Six, who operated under Sergeant Bruce Huxtable, were almost the same coppers who'd given me a clip in the mid-1950s.

Vinnie turned out to be right, Pat Housley was one of the funniest guys in the bouncer industry. Every shift he'd make us laugh with his antics. On top of this he'd score cocktail waitresses at the rate of two a shift. He'd take them out of the bar to an unrented penthouse, which would have been serviced and waiting have a freemeal with a bottle of wine delivered and then do his thing. By the time they showered and Pat returned to Vinnie and me at The Jockey Club Bar, the penthouse would be serviced and readied for the next client.

I often found myself in the role of supervisor, as the Southern Cross preferred us to be known. More often than not, I'd daydream of a future in the close protection personal security industry. One day it would happen ... somehow ...

Then Vinnie made me an offer ...

'There's this guy, he's a comedian from the US and he's staying here at the Southern Cross. His name is Shelley Berman; he's appearing in Melbourne for five nights. The deal is he needs three bodyguards. Are we in for this?'

'Yeah Vinnie; hey, any work I can get as a bodyguard, I'm in. What do you reckon, Pat?' I asked.

'If you fuckers think you can get in on this without your old number three, then you're mistaken. Show me the money!'

The next day Terry Rielly took the three of us up to the suite of Mr Shelley Berman and introduced us, saying that we were just the guys he was looking for.

Shelley was a medium-build, medium-sized man. He had a thick lock of dark hair, impeccable dress sense and sparkling eyes. It wasn't hard to tell that he could easily survive as a comedian, his face beamed constantly with a huge New York smile.

'Okay, so you're the guys interested in looking after me. I might not look it, but sometimes I can be a handful.'

'The three of us can handle a handful of anything,' Vinnie replied, 'but why as a comedian do you need three bodyguards during your show?'

'Well guys, it's like this. My act is super popular. Look at these shows here in Melbourne: sold out five nights in a row before I move on to Sydney. Now the format of my show is I do an hour of my regular stand-up working on the stage, then for the second hour I move down into the audience and I feed off them.

'I look for exceptionally fat people; I look for exceptionally ugly people. Super straights from the suburbs are my favourite, while my specialty is good hecklers.

'Now all of the above are to be crucified; they have to be sent up to the max. That's what my audience pays for: a good meal, some good booze and a good old send-up at the expense of my victims. Now at these tables every now and then someone in the party will take offense. You know the type: no sense of humour. They should know what I do, or shouldn't be there in the first place.'

'But how do you expect us to work during your routine?' Vinnie asked; I was also thinking the same myself.

'Okay guys, that's the easy part. I have a system of five basic body language postures that will show you how to respond. And make sure your response is diplomatic! There are five basic decorum rules that you need to follow to handle and defuse problems. It doesn't matter whether you're reading one of my hand signs or if you're using decorum, just follow the one-to-five system and don't jump the gun; that is, don't get to number five by mistake or we could all be in a lot of trouble.

'Okay, this is simple. I've left the stage and I'm down working the audience. I'm on to a table of ten. Let's say hypothetically that there's six guys and four women. The four women have all got the most outrageous bouffant bird's nest hairstyles. I mean, these bitches were born to be sent up by Shelley Berman! Meanwhile, the six guys are all interstate truck drivers from the same trucking company. You can bet they're all covered in tattoos from their wrists down to ankles under their Saturday night go-out-to-dinner attire.

'Imagine one of the bird's nests is yellow with a tinge of green. It's the highest bouffant and the one most like a bird's nest, with the customary distasteful length of black root hair regrowth showing through. Just enough to make the whole affair quite disgusting. And her makeup looks like it was applied by her three-year-old daughter using her favourite crayons ...

'To top it off, she's got these obscenely exposed Jane Mansfield-type tits, except they bounce like offset jelly every time she giggles. She's come to my show hoping for five minutes of fame and I'm giving it to her ... The whole place is bustin' arse laughing at her, and she's that stupid she's even giggling at herself and her jelly soft tits are bouncing every which way.

'Now there's a problem: hubby Harry and his brother Hewey are getting pissed. Not just by alcohol, but getting really pissed at me and starting to let me know about it. Now with the three of you in what I call a delta position; that is, I've come off the stage and I need one of you facing me and the others on either side. Now as these truckers are buying into my act of defacing the queen of their kitchen, I need to have you guys in tune with how I'm handling the situation at hand. Thus, the one-to-five hand signals.

'*Number one* is me tugging on each ear lobe with thumb and index finger centre nuckle. This means you should tune in and listen to what is unfolding.

'*Number two* is me wiping my chin with the bottom of my index finger, signifying that this bullshit is or could soon be out of hand.

'*Number three* is if I run my hand back through my hair, this situation may become a hair-raiser at any time. You should start moving in closer, just in case.

'*Number four* is the back of my hand wiped across my forehead, which means everything's fine, I've got control of the situation. These variations occur due to the audience only hearing what comes over the microphone and I'm always in control of the mike.

'My lighting guy knows my hand signals and knows when to open the spot or close in tight on me, depending on what we want the audience to see. It's the private dialogue cross-firing around the table between me and these hostile truckies that dictates my hand-signs to you guys.

'Now, *number five* is the big one! That's when I pinch the tip of my nose. I'm letting you guys know I could possibly be punched on the nose within three seconds. At this point I'll take the spot off to another table. On number five you guys will move in; one will do the talking and remember diplomacy ...'

It turned out that this hypothetical case became reality several times during the week, thanks to America's Mr Shelley Berman. Though I wanted more than anything to work as a bodyguard, facing altercations with irate husbands responding to family valor didn't spark any passion. Vinnie, Pat and I were a real team, and Shelley Berman responded by offering any or all of us the chance to continue on the road with him. Of course, we all declined and went back to our passion: protecting The Southern Cross Hotel. However, Shelley Berman, for all his routines, is on record as my first-ever paid job as a bodyguard. Berman's five signs body language would later come in handy in all the bigger venues I'd be securing. The Catcher, for example, was a huge floor space in an old three-story warehouse. On any Saturday night we had a crowd of over 3500 between 8 p.m. and 6 a.m. We would refuse admission to up to 500 punters on these busier nights. Our communication via hand signs gave us an advantage in violent confrontations. We kept them basically the same, except for number five, which was changed to, 'if I ever pinch the end of my nose – anytime within three seconds – I am going to punch everybody'. This was a commitment that had to be followed through, which usually meant everyone would cut loose and punch everybody. This gave us the advantage in violent confrontations. Berman's one-to-five system of different situation escalations and the use of common sense diplomacy became the ground rules for future development within my security industry. My guys' tolerance in coping with all the variations of dealing with the public created even more of a demand for our style of security work.

By the mid-1960s rock 'n' roll was in its tenth year. It had successfully brought jazz via rhythm and blues to a worldwide audience. There was, however, one remaining domain for the fans of folk and jazz: the weekend outdoor festival. Until then it seemed that only folk and jazz fans were rugged enough to venture into the wilderness for a weekend of back-to-nature celebrations of open-air live music.

In 1967 I'd heard, through the rock 'n' roll mainstream media, that during the early summer in California we'd be introduced to a new phenomenon, The Monterey International Pop Festival, which would become yet another pivotal event in the history of rock. It would only be a matter of time before this concept would also reach Australia.

Monterey was the talk of the town with musos, promoters and even my bouncers asking, 'What d'ya reckon?'

I started to cut, paste and file any media exposure I could find on these rock festivals!

Monterey was the brainchild of a quartet of California's heavyweights: promoter Alan Praiser, agent Benny Shapiro, publicist Derek Taylor and John Phillips from The Mamas and Papas. Well aware of the tide of countercultural idealism, this group had decided to take what was originally designed to be a modest commercial venture into the realm of a massive fundraising exercise.

A list of up-and-coming names from San Francisco's psychedelic citadel, such as The Grateful Dead, and mainstream acts, such as The Mamas and The Papas and Simon & Garfunkel, were booked to headline the festival.

Tensions had developed between the laid-back 'Frisco bands and these LA-based entrepreneurs. Such bands had been used to free festivals in Golden Gate Park and were deeply suspicious of this new commercial enterprise.

Eventually, the differences were resolved and the rest is rock history: approximately 250 000 people turned out to see thirty-two major acts from around the world during the weekend of 16–18 June 1967.

Within two years both Woodstock and Altamont would each attract double that crowd, but only Monterey captured the essence of the moment of the flowering hippie culture.

Peter Stripes, I'm not even sure if that was his real name, around the traps in the early 1960s. He was the man about town, best known as a fashion designer on the Melbourne scene, an out-there kinda guy, way ahead of his time. In the mid-1960s he'd shocked Australia as the first man to go on national television and admit to regularly smoking marijuana among other things.

'Stripes' was a uni-sex fashion shop where Peter retailed his designer wear. It was a large shop on the corner of Bourke and Elizabeth streets with an awning painted with black and white stripes.

I knew Peter from around the usual traps: Birties, Sebastions, The Catcher and The Thumpin Tum.

One Saturday night at Birties he'd asked, 'Hey, ah Bob, any chance you could call by the shop during the week? I have a business proposition I'm pretty sure you'd be interested in.'

'How's Tuesday?'

'If you can make it around one o'clock, then lunch is on me.'

Not being one to miss out on a free lunch, I'd arrived at the Stripes store at one o'clock sharp. We walked the three blocks up Bourke Street to Pellegrini's, where Peter had booked a table. This was the place in the city to be *seen*; you could already hear the murmurs: Peter Stripes and Bob Jones having lunch together. *'Something must be going down!'*

'Have you heard about these pop festivals recently in the US?'

'Yeah, especially that Woodstock! Five hundred thousand punters!'

'I heard that too man! But that Altamont, fuck man, that got spaced out. Like The Rolling Stones were halfway through their fucking set and the Hell's Angels cut loose ... I mean literally man, and cut this black dude to death.'

'Yeah Peter, bad for business, but good for security. It's a pisser how something bad like that makes me busy in my business.'

'Well, that's what this lunch is about, man. I'm actually doing the ground work for the first-ever outdoor festival of this type in Melbourne later this year. I plan to promote it as the Miracle. The way you got this town wired with security, man I figure I'd be mad to even be thinking about doing this without you and your boys looking after the gig.'

'Peter, deal me in.'

After all, that was why I'd done so much research.

Over the rest of lunch we tossed the idea around and the excitement grew. I hit Peter with an hourly rate by ex amount of guys working the gig for one day before, through the concert and one day after at twenty-four hours a day, plus my security management fee. He didn't even blink. Peter wanted to be the best and didn't mind paying for it.

The site was up in the Dandenongs, outside a town called Launching Place. It was just the place to launch the Miracle of the first-ever outdoor rock concert in Melbourne.

Peter and I arranged to meet a couple of weeks later at the site.

'Tell me, Bob, what do you think? You've been a promoter yourself; for ten years you've worked all the leading gigs in town – who should play the Miracle?'

'Jesuz Peter, I work seven days a week, day and night with the best: The Wild Cherries, Vibrants, Town Criers, Python Lee Jackson, Grown Up Wrong, Healing Force and Axiom, just to name a few ... Last year Somebody's Image had a great hit with 'Hush' and The Executives are doing well with 'Windy Day'. My favourite's Max Merritt (reminded me of Joe Cocker) and his Meteors with songs like 'Western Union Man'.

'There's Billy Thorpe and The Aztecs. They pack out anything or anywhere they play. Plus, there's the guy that's killed them at The Catcher for more than two years, 'The Big Time Operator', Jeff St. John (born with Spina Bifida) who does amazing things in and out of his wheelchair. He's sharing centre stage with a voice that's just got to be the answer for an Australian Janis Joplin ... Wendy Saddington.'

'Hey, thanks man. I'll keep your suggestions in mind,' Peter replied.

I figured I hadn't told him anything he didn't already know. It was time for me to cover what I knew best.

'Seeing as you want me for the security, that's where I'm coming from. That natural valley for an amphitheater to throw the sound up here at the punters is great ... St Johns and a tent hospital and you're caterers over there, that's all great. But, from my point of view, there's no where on this property that caters for parking when a huge turnout arrives.'

'That's your department, how do you plan for us to get around that?'

'That farm over the other side of the road. Its got a nice slope and it could be a natural car park.' Peter and the farmer bartered a compatible price and I had my car park.

One month prior to the concert my martial arts organisation was the talk of the town. The media had lapped it up: 'Karate experts to police pop concert.' Of course, they already knew that the promoter smoked marijuana ...

The weather was beautiful the week before the concert. On the Friday morning, twenty-four hours before concert time, I had this bright idea for the car park. I brought a large hessian bag full of flour, a reel of string and a few buckets and funnels to match. By about lunchtime that Friday my guys and I had that farmer's hill turned into a grand car park to rival Disneyland. We'd walked out fifty meters at a time with the string line for all the parallel lines and had walked out all of our access drive ways. Another team used car-length string lines and a bucket and funnel to pour the flour. (The farmer, as a part of his deal, had cut the grass right back for us.) We had that acreage of beautiful short green grass all white lined out with cooking flour. I also purchased yellow waterproof (just in case of rain) jackets and high-powered torches to show off our ingenious white lines in the concert car park after dark.

By mid-afternoon they started coming. They came all night, the next morning ...

They set up their tents and out of the bright blue sky it came – a few drops of summer rain. Then a light shower developed.

All day Saturday more fans kept arriving. And so did the showers, later into the afternoon and on the Saturday evening. The traffic got heavier, but so did the rain.

The car park idea had worked like a dream. My guys worked those white isles as if they were ushers filling seats at the theatre. I was so proud, all those cars in straight lines. My other idea, the yellow raincoats with 'Bob Jones Security' printed on the back could be seen from anywhere. And the torches showed every car exactly where to go, even during the now, torrential downpour.

The weather was sultry; nobody seemed to mind the heavy rain.

By now, everyone was into the booze and Peter Stripes was not the only person smoking marijuana. The fans were also getting their arses into gear with the best speed in Melbourne at the time.

The bands had played spasmodically on Saturday and during the night. On Sunday it was near impossible for them to play, thanks to the continual downpour.

Funnily, no-one complained. The crowd just drank, smoked dope, swallowed and snorted more speed, and partied.

Two of my main guys, Tum Joe and Dave 'Bungles' Berry, and I spent most of Saturday night fishing for guys 'n' gals who'd collapsed face down in the mud. Some were close to drowning. One teenager had nearly suffocated before Bungles and I dragged his head up out of the mud. His heart rate was so slow, Joe, Bungles and I hoisted him up and we alternated carrying him to the hospital tent in the pouring rain.

Thirty years later that teenager now owns one of Melbourne's biggest night clubs and every time I go there, the drink card, everything, is on the house. Occasionally, he embarrasses me and tells people, 'If it wasn't for Bob Jones years ago ...'

As it turned out, our first-ever Miracle was a washout, but everyone made the most of it. However, as the concert that hadn't really started finished, the fun and games really began ...

Remember that car park idea of mine? Well, all that rain had flooded it out and all those long straight lines of hundreds and hundreds of vehicles had all slid down the hillsides to a valley of solid steel all jammed together at the bottom. Tow trucks and' dozers were there for a week untangling the mess!

One thing Monterey (mid-1967) and the Dandenongs Miracle (1970) had in common was that they were both firsts. Woodstock (1969) and Sunbury (1972) also share many things of common interest. Both were staged on properties that bore an uncanny resemblance.

Farmer Max Yasgar's 600 acres, actually at Bethel just outside Woodstock, and farmer George Duncan's 300-acre Glencoe Property, actually in Diggers Rest just outside Sunbury, a small township north-west of Melbourne, were both properties with sweeping valleys that served as natural amphitheaters. Both drew the largest crowds, although Sunbury's 35 000 was a long way short of Woodstock's 500 000 (though crowd estimates varied, with some as low as 300 000). However, the Sunbury crowd is still comparable on a population per-capita basis (at this time Australia numbered only 13.5 million). Each festival was filmed and turned into feature-length movie with box office success. Sunbury was released and shown Australia-wide, while Woodstock went to audiences worldwide.

The Woodstock Music and Art Fair was the brainchild of Artie Kornfield and Michael Lang. And what had been proven many times during the 1960s was that if it happened in the US it would also happen in Australia.

The world had now seen Woodstock and its

fans had made the statement of wanting to share a communion of peace through this new music for the young. Woodstock was also a statement against Vietnam and, as a counterculture, a political statement against the then system.

However, on 9 December 1969, four months after Woodstock, the major event to finish off the decade of the 1960s would also serve as the Yin and the Yang to the music at Bethel. Almost the same amount of music-lovers would be drawn to San Francisco, the peace city of the planet and The Rolling Stones' promotion at Altamont, a festival of nothing but violence.

The Hell's Angels had been asked to do the security, but that was probably the most thought put into organising this macabre event. These Angels came from neighboring chapters in San Jose, San Francisco, San Bernandino and Oakland, and they came on their Harley's fully armed with weapons: knives, lead pipes, tyre-irons, chains and an array of sawed-off billiard cues with lead-weighted ends. They came with their own Hell's Angels schoolbus that was stocked with beer, rotgut wine and questionable LSD tabs. They'd ridden menacingly through the middle of the crowd, up to the front of the stage, which was only half a metre off the ground instead of the usual two to three metres. As a result, there was no buffer zone between the audience and the performers.

No pit area, a low stage and the Hell's Angels for security were the contributing factors to the debacle that this festival was to become.

The drama started from the beginning. Santana opened and as soon as anyone started dancing or ventured anywhere near the front of the stage they'd feel the wrath of the Hell's Angels' billiard cues.

Second up was Jefferson Airplane. With Grace Slick, their lead singer, they'd performed several fundraising benefits in the past with the Hell's Angels and figured they'd be in the gang's good books. This was not to be. As soon as Grace began singing 'We Can Be Togther', the Hell's Angels started playing pool with everyone in sight.

Grace stopped the music and appealed to the Hell's Angels: 'Hey you guys, why are we hurting each other?' This was to no avail. One of the members of her band, Marty Balin, dived off the stage into a group of Angels who were flogging a black guy. They immediately beat Marty unconscious along side the black kid. When Jorma Kaukonen, the lead guitarist, announced to the crowd what the Angels were doing in front of the stage, a huge hulk of a Hell's Angel who was standing on the stage grabbed the mike and yelled: 'Fuck you ! Fuck all of you!'

Several bands later, and for some unknown reason, as Crosby, Stills and Nash began their set, the Angels went berserk and belted everyone within range. People lay everywhere, bleeding and unconscious. Crosby, Stills and Nash grabbed their instruments and bolted to their waiting helicopter. Stretcher-bearers entered the war zone in an attempt to clear the injured off to the already overcrowded medical tents.

Medical staff had been working frantically since the festival began, overrun with patrons who'd used the bad drugs peddled by syndicate pushers. The weather had been grey and chilly; hence, the festival site had a morbid atmosphere, As night drew near, the fans' bonfires made flickering shadows of the remains of a thousand nearby demolition crashes, there were rusty auto parts belonging to the skeletons of deceased and decaying abandoned ex-racing stock cars. The festival had a food shortage, water was almost non-existent, and there were not enough toilets for one-tenth of the crowd. Also, plenty of drugs – Mexican grass, cheap Californian wine and amphetamines – circulated.

The Hell's Angels had escorted Mick Jagger on to centre stage. He was wrapped in a satin cloak that glowed red under the special lighting effects. Not only were The Stones perceived as rough anti-establishment renegades, that night the crowd saw Mick as Lucifer. All day they'd been awaiting this messenger from Hell with these barbarian Hell's Angels as his nether world entourage.

The satanic ritual began. Satan threw open his red cloak and pranced, singing his theme song, 'Sympathy for the Devil'.

Their fans stripped off and crawled on to the stage as if it were the high alter to Hell. The more the Angels beat them with cues and kicked at them with their studded boots, the more the fans just keep crawling up, as if offering themselves through some supernatural force as human sacrifices to these agents of Satan.

Right in front of the stage, an obese girl, loaded with acid and her breasts exposed, had tried to reach Mick, only to be belted to the ground by several Angels and stripped naked to then be kicked about the body and face, and to be hit again with pool sticks.

'Stop that one!' Keith yelled, as if the other half a dozen Angels weren't even there.

'Hey! Hey! Hey! Hey! Hey! Hey!' Mick yelled; each 'hey' for each of the Hell's Angels present. 'One cat can control that chick, you know what I mean? Hey fellows, one of you can control her, man.'

Having given it his best shot, Jagger launched the band into a succession of their more popular singles: 'Under My Thumb', 'Brown Sugar' (where the lyrics have him singing about whipping women) and 'Midnight Rambler', a macabre song about a night-killer who stalks the corridors with a knife ready to stab a victim.

Whether these words inspired or if Meredith Hunter, an eighteen-year-old African-American kid, was just in the wrong place at the wrong time is not known. Some say his only mistake was in bringing a white girl to the concert. Whatever the reason, the Hell's Angels set on him, punching and kicking and clubbing with those familiar pool cues. Young Meredith Hunter drew a gun, several Hell's Angels drew large knives and he was brutally stabbed repeatedly, until he was dead.

'John Fowler here, Bob. We need to talk.'

It had been three years and four months since Woodstock.

'Bob, I'm going to promote the biggest outdoor rock concert ever; on Australian standards it'll be as big as Woodstock. I want you there to make sure it's not another Altamont.'

During the two years since the Miracle, I'd flown to Sydney for several festivals, but it was in February 1970 that the New South Wales first Pilgrimage For Pop was held at Ourimbar. It drew 10 000 people to hear bands such as Tully, Nutwood Rug, Heart 'n' lSoul, as well as the better known Aztecs, Chain and Jeff St. John's Copperwine.

In January 1971 we did the security for two festivals in the same month: the Fairlight Festival in Mittagong, Victoria, and the Odyssey Festival in Wallacia, New South Wales.

This was the brainchild of an old mate from Sydney, Lee Dillow, who would go over to the US in years to come with Paul Hogan's *Crocodile Dundee* in a management capacity.

I'd just signed contracts for Rock Isle on the shores of the Murray River at Mulwala, which was to have been an Easter festival in April 1972. The organisers had booked two international acts: Canned Heat and Stephen Stills and his new band Manassas.

'Bob,' John Fowler continued, 'I represent Odessa Promotions who are putting the finances together. We're looking at a site near Sunbury for the Australia Day weekend of 29, 30 and 31 January.'

That was three months prior to Mulwala with two international acts, but I knew by his attitude and tone of voice that John Fowler, managing director of Odessa Promotions, was about to put on the biggest festival we had or would see.

His pre-publicity machine was bigger than any before it. It promised our best would be there. The return from overseas of Max Merritt and The Meteors, plus Daddy Cool (who didn't show), Spectrum, La De Das, Billy Thorpe and The Aztecs, Indelible Murtceps, Chain, Carson County, Healing Force, Opus Big Band, Wild Cherries, Pyramid, Langford Lever and Leaping McSpeddons was only the beginning.

'Is there anyone else you can imagine?'

To really widen his crowd appeal he had Adrian Rawlings and the outrageous 'Wizard' to act as MCs. He also boasted acres of car parking.

I remembered thinking, whatever you do, don't

mention the catastrophic Miracle car parks!

At the Sunbury site during our first inspection, John explained where everything was going to go: from the proposed flea market, open-air art show, carnival, barbeques, stage and backstage, medical area, and our security caravan and tent for sleeping quarters for the 150 guys who would be working the three eight-hour shifts, every twenty-four hours.

The music area was almost identical to Woodstock. It was a huge valley that would serve as a natural amphitheatre, *and* it had a bonus over its US counterpart: the moderately flowing Jacksons Creek that snakes its way around the camping and backstage areas, making it perfect for cooling down for anybody at the festival.

'Bob, this is what we know – entertainment, production, marketing – we'll get them here. They'll have a good time; they'll be looked after. What we don't know and the main reason we're hiring your organisation, is that we have 300 acres in between two major highways surrounded by nothing but open farmland properties. How do we get a possible 50 000 people to pay to get in, to return the investment and hopefully have some profit left over for the exercise? You just tell me what you want. You're expenses are not a problem, whatever it takes to protect Odessa's investment.'

Through the variety of guys at my martial arts academies, we had access to our standard twelve horses, twelve security trained dogs and twelve trail bikes. Along with our own horse-floats we had an old Bedford one-tonner tray truck used to deliver meals in the middle of our security shifts. Besides being our meals on wheels this old Beddie also doubled as a trouble-shooter vehicle in case I needed to get a dozen of my A-team Black Belts to any danger spots in a hurry. With the horses, trail bikes and our one-tonner, we handled all potential situations with the minimum of fuss.

After six hours of walking around the site I'd worked out my major hook for doing any festival security contract.

The placement of my security towers was devised through the use of the area map I'd picked up from the Sunbury Council Chambers. It showed the major elevations around the festival site and had me estimating that we'd need four towers: two towers at a height of five meters, one at ten meters and one on the festival hill at twenty meters.

With binoculars by day and high-powered torches by night, my guys could watch and communicate any grave circumstances on walkie-talkies (on our own security frequency) to all our team leaders. As we secured the festival area perimeters using horses and trail bikes during the day and our dogs overnight, we guided everyone to the ticket boxes – and that's what the promoters paid us for. Plus, we doubled up as just about everyone's problem-solvers.

John Fowler was happy with the towers. He said they'd double up as good vantage spots for the television and the Cambridge Film Crews that would be shooting the entire event as a feature movie. John would set up all facilities, including our security tent, public toilets, showers and where the patrons would be allowed to pitch tents and park their cars.

John was going to open the fences of George Duncan's property for the cars coming in off the highways and along the double-lane road. He would drop enough gravel to form four, maybe six lanes of traffic to the ticket boxes, to keep the peak time traffic moving. This strategy proved perfect for an idea of mine to build a three-metre hessian-covered wire-strand fence, 200 meters along the eye line of the lay of the land, and parallel to the entry road. We created corners and ran the fence off on 45-degree angles at both ends, around thirty to forty meters until the fence disappeared due to the natural slope. This would give everyone the impression that the festival site was totally secured, plus fence off John's idea of where his car park was going to be. (Killing two birds with the one stone!)

Six hours on site saw the completion of my major festival MBO (management by objective) sheet, which detailed everything I'd be responsible for during the seven days: three days prior, three days during and one day after the festival. John Fowler was happy with my lot as I'd informed him that I'd document the hire fees for everything: my guys' working hours and my admin. fees. I'd get the contracts to him asap.

'Bob, I'm really happy with everything you and I have arranged. I'm really happy with the cost and I'm sure the quality of your work will have you continuing to get all of these major events that are worth doing. Plus, I've got a bit of a surprise for you: I'm renting something for you that'll be a great little publicity banner for you as the head of Sunbury Security. This is a vehicle that is quite capable in any terrain, plus it will drive straight on to and across Jackson's Creek. It's called a *Goannamobile* and it will drive across on top of water!'

John was right: I'd milk the media with that Goannamobile for all it was worth.

Early December 1971. Two months prior to Australia's biggest festival, John Fowler, festival controller John Dixon, Odessa publicity director Jim McKay and yours truly, who wore the title 'security co-ordinator', were at a major meeting at the former Russell Street Police Headquarters with all the big brass of the day.

The Assistant Police Commissioner R.I. Miller, Superintendent G. Hickey and Superintendent R.H. Warne and another dozen or so cops represented traffic control, drugs and major crime squads. The concept of this meeting was to have us all aware of who was doing what and where there might be any crossovers and, if so, how these situations might be handled.

During our talk the police ran through their problems and solutions concerning the local council, the negatives of the surrounding farmers, the Victorian Fire Authority and their fears of grass fires due to the dryness of the area at this time of the year, and their plans for the medical care of possibly 50 000 music fans who'd turn up to this event. So here was Bob Jones in Russell Street Police Headquarters actually working and liaising with what was once the enemy. (I'd always seen the cops as the Gestapo!)

It bought back to mind something my stepfather had told me as a young kid. He'd been brought up on a farm in Silvan (40 kilometres from Melbourne) and his father would flog him and his five brothers with a stock whip to get a hard day's work out of them and to keep them on the straight and narrow. I don't know the quality of truth in this statement, but the mere thought of it in my adolescent years had me tow the line most times. These floggings apparently made my stepfather, at eighteen years of age, run away from farm life to the city to join the police force to fight for the cause of justice and to make the world a better place (this was his first lesson on life).

'To catch a thief, you have to think like a thief. If you're going to mix all day with the garbage – you eventually turn into garbage,' he'd maintain. When World War II was declared my stepfather gave me his second lesson on life: 'War, I didn't want to know about any bloody war in Europe. At twenty years of age I wanted something better. Christ, world depression, farm life, floggings and now a world war ... Anyway, I enlisted simply to get myself out of the bloody police force.'

I remembered this advice many times over the years, especially one month prior to the Melbourne Olympics. Several of the hierarchy of a notorious Melbourne street gang known as the Phantom Twins and me had been jammed into a holding cell in the city down a lane off Degraves Street. Six seasoned, hand-picked coppers beat the crap out of us, one at a time. (The beating was not as bad as we'd been giving one another in our own wars with rival suburban gangs, in an effort to keep control of our turf: the square kilometer of Melbourne's CBD). The boundaries of this territory had been Spencer, Flinders, Spring and Latrobe streets.

For a long time after this beating I remember thinking; well, stuff the system ...

As the senior police continued to detail the mechanics of the upcoming Sunbury Festival, I recalled the many altercations I'd had with the law during my violent years.

The most recent of these had only been a few months earlier, when six drunken men had taken on Brian 'Chops' Suey and me. We beat them up bad and the coppers charged the *two of us*. Then I recalled the Melbourne Magistrate who'd looked over the top of those spectacles hanging off the end of his nose. He'd gazed down at me and Chops and said: 'Bouncers, can't stand them; in fact, I detest them.'

Could he say that? Chops and I were not only bouncers, we were the bloody defendants, and this establishment prick was sitting in judgement over who was right and who was wrong in a situation of extreme violence.

The two cops responsible for charging Chops and me faltered under the interrogation of our defence council. The six drunks must have been six of the worst witnesses ever to enter a courtroom. (They wanted to be there as much as Chops and me.) They'd faltered at every point of pressure our Barrister had put them under.

When we were found guilty, everyone was in a state of disbelief. Two of us had defended ourselves against six drunken men and been found guilty. There was an appeal to the High Court, but that's another long story ...

'Bob, argh, Bob Jones!' Superintendent Warne called. 'Bob, so you and your martial arts organisation will be handling security. That's not a job I'd envy anybody for.'

I sat forward in my chair and almost pinched myself. Here's this high-ranking cop talking to me as if I'm human ...

'Our Sydney counterparts told us how you

did such a good job at Wallacia early this year, especially considering the problems you had with those New South Wales bikie gangs. You've been working the club scene since it all began and you've done all the major festivals that have worked. We'll be leaving the security of the festival in your capable hands. We'll handle the traffic flow in and out. We'll be on hand in case of any emergencies and Bob, if you do need a hand, don't be afraid to yell out.'

That was when I did give myself a pinch. There really were cops who genuinely cared about possibly 50 000 young people who'd be camping out for three days and nights. They understood and showed concern that many of them could overdose on drugs and would need attention, that some could cut themselves on broken glass, fall and break bones, suffer from heat exhaustion, or drink enough alcohol to kill a brown cow.

Now wait a minute, did he say that was my job and that he didn't envy me? But he did say, 'if you need a hand, don't be afraid to yell out'.

1 June 1970. I'd opened my first martial arts school at 48 Elizabeth Street in Melbourne (there are now over 1000 franchised schools around Australia and New Zealand, with plans to further expand). This proved popular so by Christmas I promoted my first-ever annual training camp at Mt Evelyn.

In 1972 we had our second seven-day *summer camp*, which ran from 8 to 14 January (ending just two weeks prior to the Sunbury Festival). For the seven days I had almost the entire security team training for the event, until everyone knew their jobs backwards.

I went in with my pre-concert team on the Tuesday. Though three days early we set up our security signage on our caravan, our sleeping tent and placed black plastic sheeting over the wire fence, creating a security compound large enough to house much of our equipment, such as our trail bikes and Goannamobile. The horses and our dogs were catered for around the back and out of sight of the main festival area.

Backstage we found Billy Thorpe and his wife, and a bunch of other musos and friends who'd been here for a week already.

By Thursday we'd tested our walkie-talkies from security towers one, two, three and four. The number one tower was the twenty-metre see-almost-everything site, and what it couldn't see was picked up by towers two, three and four. The guys came in and went out with their commands via their two-way radios, proving they could communicate anything that was going on anywhere. Our horses, dogs and trail bikes arrived on Friday; the horses and dogs looked happier than us for being back on the job at another festival.

Although show time was for 10 a.m. Saturday, the crowds started pouring in Thursday and all day Friday. Like at Woodstock on the Friday evening, this gave a bunch of the early-bird musos the opportunity to jam on the Friday night, and it had to be one of the best times of the festival: just an impromptu get-together of some good buddies for the purpose of making good music together.

Saturday was hot, *damned hot* and they came en

masse all day. There were thousands and thousands of young people, and a few not so young, from all over the country. Some had flown from Perth and some had hitch-hiked down from Cairns.

On stage, filling in between the fabulous voice of Carsons' front-man Broderick Smith, followed by Taman Shud, then the La De Das, was the festival's odd couple. First came Adrian Rawlings, an eccentric poet from around the traps with his 'Laugh In' floor show. He'd be at a club and between band sets at, say Sebastians (Exhibition Street) Adrian would lie on the cloakroom floor, or anywhere else that could be deemed eccentric, with a microphone and start laughing for what would turn out to be thirty minutes.

Sooner or later everyone in the place would fall ill with this contagion. Thirty years later a tribute statue to Adrian, on the corner of Brunswick and Argyle Streets, Fitzroy, was erected to remind the world to keep laughing.

Adrian's partner in the MC fun department was the most eccentric guy on the scene: 'The Wizard'. It was thought his name was Ian Channell, a semi-professional university 'Merlin' of the late 1960s.

A deregistered sociology student, he claimed to be researching tension resolution through absurd behaviour, leading to 'revelation of mutual interests' by 'behaving absurdly in small groups'. This, apparently, was sufficient reason for the University of New South Wales to appoint him its first, and only, 'official wizard'.

Like many of the celebrities of this period there was a touch of the despot, as well as the lunatic, about these two. Someone said they'd both thought their role as MCs at the festival meant 'much craziness,' and probably accounted for Adrian's laughing fits and what he and The Wizard would attempt to do by six o'clock in the afternoon: to behave absurdly in front of a 'very large group'.

All day Saturday, during the breaks between acts, both Adrian and The Wizard bantered about the stage, telling bardic tales and reciting obscure poetry, and every hour on the hour, and sometimes in between, Adrian would tell the Sunbury audience about the power of universal thought through transcendental meditation.

'You know, if we all believe in something together during one cosmic fibre of time, anything we would imagine together would be possible,' he'd preached.

'Why, I believe I could even fly across the sky!' The Wizard retaliated.

They'd kept this up for the following six hours (from 12 p.m. to 6 p.m.!).

All we kept hearing was, 'If you believe ... I'll fly across the sky ...' bellowed across the festival site as some of the patrons sipped red wine, and the hippies drew on yet another joint, and the 'juice freaks' sculled just one more beer, before the next ... Then it would be everyone's turn to chant: 'Yes we do believe!'

'Fly across the sky' was the regular chant as the crowd numbers and the temperature rose higher and higher. By 6 p.m. it was time for us all to believe as The Wizard, as promised, would climb to the top of a big-arsed old gum tree at the side of the stage. He was dressed for the miracle moment of transcendental movement for his flight across the sky as a bat, and, no, he didn't look like a poorly dressed version of the infamous Batman; he looked just like a bat!

At several stages of his journey up this ol' twenty-metre-high gum tree (it was the same height as my number one tower), The Wizard would stop for a breather and Adrian would have us all chant, 'YES, WE, DO, BELIEVE!'

How are they gonna pull this off? I thought. Maybe they've got John Fowler to fly over in the helicopter and The Wizard somehow is hooked up. Yeah, that's it! They'll all fly across the sky and we'll all piss ourselves laughing.

Finally, there stood The Wizard, in all his bat glory, at the pinnacle of the biggest backstage gum tree. Adrian got us all to chant our final affirmation as The Wizard flapped his wings and he took off. We all believed and gasped in dismay: The Wizard flapped his bat wings all the way down, belly-whacking the surface of Jacksons Creek. He must have dislocated both shoulders.

The thirty-five-thousand-strong crowd were definitely in shock; you could hear them thinking, what the fuck happened? How come he didn't fly?

As they stared at that big ol' gum tree the sun was setting over the back of the stage and the moon was already well up in the sky. Adrian Rawlings mumbled something that the cosmic fibre of time had been affected by the hole in the ozone layer that wouldn't happen for another twenty years at least, or something like that. Then he broke the silence with his outrageous laughing, and it wasn't long before he had that entire audience laughing right out of his hand as he screamed into the microphone, 'How about a huge round of applause for The Wizard and his flight into space ... And how about an even bigger hand for ... all the way home from England, just for Sunbury and you here tonight: Max Merritt and The Meteors'.

Just then, Max, Stewie, Dave and Bob ran on to the stage. Well, Max, Dave and Bob ran on to the stage and Stewie Spiers hobbled over to his drum kit, and by the time he'd placed his crutches on the floor and shuffled sideways on to his drum stool and led the band into songs like 'Try a Little Tenderness' and 'Western Union Man' we all knew why we'd come to Sunbury, even if it wasn't to make The Wizard fly across the sky.

On Sunday morning we had a pleasant spiritual change from the amplified music with acoustic guitar and the clanging of symbols by members of the Hare Krishna sect, who'd pitched camp as close as they could to our security compound. By lunchtime the record crowd had grown, thanks to the birth of two baby girls. One had arrived on Saturday afternoon and the other on Sunday morning.

Just after lunch a crew from the promoters' office called to see me at our security compound.

'Bob, we've got this guy disrupting the entire concert. He's on security tower number one and threatening to commit suicide. He's threatening to jump off the twenty-metre tower!'

It had been funny the day before with The Wizard, but I knew this guy would do more than dislocate his shoulders if he jumped and landed on the heads of people sitting below.

'Someone said he's popped a tab of bad acid or had an argument with his girlfriend, or both. Anyway, we need to get him down. In fact, the crowd are starting to chant that he should just go ahead and fucking jump!'

'But hasn't it been tried three times? I mean you guys tried first. A couple of St John's Ambulance guys climbed the ladder and tried. And wasn't that cheering and hooting from the crowd their response to the two coppers who couldn't get him to come down, not three minutes ago?'

'Yep, but we figured you …'

Sandy Fricker and Tommy 'the Bear' Makris were two of my bigger boys, both had huge chests and shoulders. It was not the bodybuilding look, they were just big, hard-looking guys. Off we tramped to the festival site and over to the base of security tower number one. I climbed the ladder and Sandy and Tommy went hand-over-hand, up the outside of the scaffolding. The crowd was breathlessly quiet in anticipation of what might happen next, except for the odd call of:

'Fuck, he's in trouble now!'

'He should jump now before it's too late!'

'Maybe if together, we all believe …'

As we reached the top of the tower and I stuck my head through the hole in the floor, the nutcase threatened, 'Don't you try and come any closer; I'm deadly serious!'

Sandy and Tommy appeared, heads, chests and shoulders first (on either side of me), and holding on to the safety railings, poised and ready to spring at him on my command.

'Keep them away; both of them – and you too! Stay away or I swear, I'll jump off and kill myself.'

I could see then and there: he was totally distraught. But then so was I, three times this had already been tried and three times it had failed, thanks to the jeering of the crowd.

I'd never been one who could cope with a crowd's jeering, especially if it were at me. However, I'd stare into this nutter's eyes with a gaze that would make him realise that I was also deadly serious. After three to five seconds, which, I swear, seemed like an eternity, I said, 'Listen to me you fucking idiot, I didn't climb all the way up this tower to be fucked over by you. If you don't come here within three seconds and climb down these stairs with us ...'

I paused and gave him his three seconds.

' ... these two rock apes will come over and throw you off this fucking tower.'

I knew full well the boys would excuse my description of them, given the circumstances.

I felt good about myself as the four of us climbed down from the top of that tower to a deafening roar of approval from the thirty-five, some say now almost forty-thousand crowd.

By about 4 p.m. that afternoon I was having my third *tour de festival* for the day in the chopper. The view was something else – Sandy, Tommy and I from the tower were up with the birds with a full view of the surrounding areas. We could see our horses and trail bikes working the perimeters. It was thumbs up from the guys working the towers, and there were our meals on wheels, that faithful old Bedford, delivering either a late lunch or an early dinner. The binoculars afforded a much better inspection of all the youths in varying forms of undress, mostly nude, as they swam along the banks of Jacksons Creek.

The friendly waving at the chopper meant there was no offence taken at the fact that we were observing the activities of the festival site; after all, we were security, weren't we? Plus, it'd only been an hour since Sandy'd had to carry one of the *damsels in distress* off – totally naked – after she'd cut her foot on a shard of glass (it took around ten stitches to fix it up). Because of the amount of blood loss she was experiencing, Sandy'd got her to St. John's as quickly as he could. His carrying her through the crowd might not have received the reaction of the suicide prospect, but it got a round of applause from the crowd.

Having the chopper overnight would've made life much easier in terms of catching night prowlers. Such punters would've tried anything to get into a festival during the moonlight hours to save themselves the entry fee. It was a near-impossible task for a concert fan to pull off, as our dogs took the incursions very personally – to them it was a big game and they just had to win.

Once the pilot hovered over the heli-pad, down we went gently.

Sandy, Tommy and I figured this was a good time for a coffee break in the security tent. The meal section had a long trestle with about twenty chairs for the guys to *chew the fat*. There was about a dozen of my main guys sitting around and goofing off. The main subject was my dialogue with the suicide candidate, plus the other fun-stuff they'd all been up to.

'How about Sandy Sir Lancelot carrying that naked chick off into the wilderness?' Dave 'Bungles' Berry winked and elbowed Nicky 'Schnappas' Pappas.

'Yeah, it's a cunt of a job, but, hey, someone's gotta do it.' Nicky had such a way with words.

'What about that character we sussed yesterdee? We watched him and his mates coming for a hundred yards carrying this big ol' acoustic guitar case in his right hand. In his left hand was a legal six-pack [half a dozen tinnies was the limit per person]. By the time he got to us he was draggin' the fucking guitar case along the ground.

'We pressed the flip on the clasp, keeping the guitar case closed. Talk about comin' out of the closet. Enough booze fell out of that fucken' case to completely stock any home bar!' This was definitely a Tum Joe yarn.

'Hey Chief!' Paul Flemming tried to get my attention. 'Yesterday, when the gate was about the busiest and the temperature was about the hottest, we had the traffic comin' in four lanes wide with four ticket boxes open. Still, it took about an hour and a half for the traffic to get from the highway, down to the site, up the 200-metre stretch to the ticket boxes. Anyway, I saw this character in a car by himself. No big deal, except he'd had gear and junk stacked every which way. I figured, either he's here for a month on his own or, "Hey buddy, mind if I take a peak in the boot?" Jesuz man, he had a mate and two skinny-arsed chicks packed in there with not enough oxygen to make it to the car park. Lucky I opened the lid when I did. They were cooked on all sides. It was around 94 [about 35 degrees Celsius] at four o'clock yesterday. Bloody hot! Anyway, I saw the humour of it all and let them buy three more tickets, and off they went sitting on the boot and singing that new single "Hayride", a bit out of harmony.'

('Hayride' was the top-selling single off the new album *Prepared In Peace* by The Flying Circus, one of Australia's most popular bands of the time. They spent much of their time in Canada where they developed a rabid regional following.)

'What about this? What about that?' went on for some time; my gang was in such good spirits. However, it would've been a matter of time before the calls of, 'What about that fucker you … I … we … and what about those chicks you … I … we …'.

I didn't feel the need to buy into my guys' violence or sexual encounters, so I quietly slipped away from the storytelling and wandered off to the edge of the festival site to soak up the atmosphere.

It was just on dusk, the Indelible Murtceps, a classic concert band, were playing and I nodded to the thump of the bass. The sun and moon were sharing the sky again. As I was looking at that ol' big-arsed gum tree and thinking about the Wizard's shoulder pain, someone called out: 'Hey Bob, is that you Bob Jones?'

The voice came from behind, as did the finger dig on the shoulder.

Friend or foe? I thought, taking the mandatory step forward (just in case) before turning.

The smile was hidden by a beard and a headband across the man's long hair.

I had no idea who he could be as he smiled and held his hand out in friendship.

Okay, enough on the paranoia. Shake the man's hand. As I did I could see that he looked around eight, maybe ten years older than me.

Strong face, piercing eyes, solid body and firm handshake that transferred warmth ... Yes, he was a friend.

'No idea, eh! Bob, maybe it's the long hair and beard and this fucking dippy headband. Five of my mates and me bashed you in 1956. Ten years later, in the days of The Southern Cross and Vinnie Scott, I think it must have been 1966, almost the same five mates and me saved your arse outside of The Catcher, down the bottom of Flinders Lane. That night you were caught out against an angry gang of louts.'

'Holy shit, I haven't seen you for six years! How's your boss? How is Bruce Huxtable?' I couldn't believe the coincidence.

'Big bad Bruce, he's made superintendent recently. That old bodgie squad from the 1950s, then the silent six ... that sharpie squad of the 1960s ... there's only a couple of the old team still together. By the way, you haven't seen me – we're here undercover, with the drug squad these days. But hey, we go way back! Thought I'd take the chance and say hello to an old mate. I've seen you at a couple of these festivals'. A moment later he disappeared into the beards and headbands.

Now this was an unusual relationship: the phantom cop and me. However, I never saw him again. I often wondered if he'd ever made superintendent.

It was time to pay another visit backstage. The Murtceps had just finished a damned good set. They were doing the usual roll call for Billy Thorpe and The Aztecs. This was Billy's favourite time slot: it was the best of both worlds; first, with the sun going down over the horizon, which gave off the sky's natural light; and second, on dusk the stage lighting kicking in with all its special effects.

Naturally, my 'access-all-areas' pass hung around my neck. Frank Chick and I shook hands, and I headed to the backstage tent.

Frank, one of my robust Brown Belts, and heading for Black, was a budding rock 'n' roll star in his own right. Because he spoke the musos' language he worked backstage.

Nearby, Billy Thorpe and The Aztecs were making more noise above everybody else as they prepared to go on stage. The scene reminded me of the Wallacia rock concert incident in New South Wales a year earlier. I'd found Thorpie, lost among the punters in a drunken, drugged-out state. After carrying him across the festival area, and finally helping him on to the stage to do his set, he'd fallen off the stage, face first. (Twenty-five years later (in 1998) Billy Thorpe would tell the story in graphic detail in his book *Most People I Know Think That I'm Crazy*.)

Suddenly, there was Norman-e Sweeney, The Aztecs' road manager. 'Hey Bob-e, did ya think we'd do another Wallacia on ya?' he stirred.

The Aztecs burst into laughter. Thorpie screamed out, 'Bob-e Jones, come and dig this set, buddy. Its that time of the *daight*, you know–'

'Yeah, I know, day–night, best of both worlds … aye,' I added.

The Aztecs ran up the stairs and on to the stage (and no, Billy didn't fall off this time). Meanwhile, I headed to the front of the stage to catch the show and to watch my pit crew. Twenty of my guys had been trained to work the pits, the area between the front of the stage and the barrier fence was generally about two metres wide at a one-night concert. At these festivals we had around five meters between the stage and the barriers. On each side of the stage the barrier fence cut back usually on a 45-degree angle to the speakers.

On the Saturday night Max Merritt had almost stolen the show, although he'd started off very slowly. The audience had taken a while to warm to the new numbers – Max had spent the previous twelve months in England. However, they really got going as The Meteors played their golden oldies.

In contrast, Billy Thorpe and The Aztecs, who'd been playing the Melbourne pub scene, from the first number got the crowd up and dancing. By the end they'd stolen the whole show.

Halfway through the set the crowd was clawing at the barricades. The Aztecs went into their latest hit, 'Most People I Know Think That I'm Crazy', at more than 120 decibels, which is the same volume generated by a jumbo jet taking off.

The mass of humans surged at the barricades from the front. The pit crew were stuck in the middle. It took all their strength to stop any breakages in the protective wall, which would've created an instant overflow and seen the human tidal wave surging under, round and over the stage and down into Jacksons Creek.

Some of the younger females suffered from fatigue, dehydration and shock. Many were crushed and trampled. My pit crew guys had to dive in and save them. The following day it was all over and everybody had thankfully survived.

Assistant Commissioner R.I. Miller had said to *The Age*: 'Festival fans were a credit to youth.' Superintendent R.H. Warne had stated in public, 'You couldn't have wished for a better behaved group.'

Not to be left out Superintendent G. Hickey also added that the crowd was one of the most well-behaved he'd seen.

After compiling these three statements into a press kit that told the story of my involvement with the festival, I booked a venue in Sunbury, organised and opened yet another successful Bob Jones martial arts school.

John Fowler perhaps unknowingly had also, with his concept of Sunbury, broken down some serious barriers in the music business. During the 1960s it was very difficult for Australian-made music to get any sort of airplay. The if-it's-from-overseas-it's-good syndrome prevailed. John proved that local artists had a following that were there and waiting, and that they just had to be shown the way. Sunbury did just that. Nationwide radio stations picked up on the credo: if you play locals, you play ratings points, so let's play.

We'd already been booked for the second Sunbury festival in 1973. The crowd, the bands, the show and the festivities would be 'similar'.

There'd be more skinny-dipping, much more pot-smoking, much more acid-dropping and much, much more booze. The very fast junk food lines and the unsanitary toilets and showers were no longer seen as adventurous.

It was time for us to move on; hence, the Bob Jones boys wouldn't be doing anymore Sunbury festivals. However, the best thing to have come out of this event was a young (eighteen years old at the time) Michael Gudinski, who'd come of age. He and Ray Evans had formed Mushroom Records and they'd recorded Sunbury with the title of *The Great Australian Rock Festival Sunbury 1973*. With a name like that guess what? Yep, tons more airplay again for our local Australian Acts.

The following two Sunbury festivals were staged without my security organisation and both times Odessa Promotions had, for their own reasons, a change of policy. In 1974 Odessa brought out the English band Queen, with costs slightly offset by allowing the 0/10 Television Network to screen edited highlights. This festival was less successful than its predecessors, as the crowd was very hostile towards the high camp performances of Queen and the local band, Skyhooks. (This wasn't to be their time and they were both booed off the stage.)

The non-presence of the Bob Jones boys was an open invitation for all of Melbourne's skinheads to partake in and suffer the effects of alcoholic over-indulgence. Naturally, such behaviour soured the atmosphere of both festivals.

The final Sunbury festival in 1975 had a dismal turnout. The perennial Billy Thorpe and The Aztecs produced even more volume than the imported Deep Purple, who were paid $100 000 for their well-received performance, which was more to the taste of the crowd than the previous year's featured band. Despite this, it was the innovative Ariel (led by Mike Rudd) and an invigorated Sherbert who offered the best music on what was a very wet weekend. Ironically, Skyhooks were also now very popular, as their first LP, released only months before, had broken down former hostility.

With the smaller crowds and increased overheads (associated with performance fees), Odessa Promotions sustained a financial loss for the 1975 festival that was estimated to be in the vicinity of $200 000 to $300 000 – only 15 000 people had turned up. The combination of these factors saw Sunbury ending as an event that was no longer viable.

During the Easter weekend of 1972 we were still riding high from the success of our security efforts at that first Sunbury. Eager to cash in on this notoriety, I had 500 T-shirts printed with *Rock Isle – Bob Jones Security* on them, so that my 150 guys could wear a clean ad-shirt every shift. This Mulwala – Easter '72 festival on the shores of the Murray drew a capacity crowd almost comparable with that of Sunbury;

however, the media's enthusiasm had already been exhausted. Irrespective, we made damned sure everyone there had a good time while we had only a few problems with the local bad-arsed stand-up, knock-'em-down farm boys who objected to us city lads declaring certain rules for the weekend on one of their farms.

The period after the Mulwala – Easter '72 Festival was a very exciting time for me. Many hours had been spent in trying to co-ordinate a training/competing tour of the US. My security and growing martial arts organisation thrived, thanks to the many concerts and festivals we looked after. Also, I'd been in constant communication with the current world middleweight full contact karate champion, Chuck Norris. We'd organised a particular date for me to meet and train with all the then martial arts celebrities, including world heavyweight champion, Joe Lewis, the *unbeatable* Mike Stone and the latest lightweight champion on the scene, Bruce Lee.

    There was also another reason why I was looking forward to this American tour. A couple of years earlier, after a seven-year separation, Pauline and I had decided to get back together and to make a go of it. The best part of the deal was that I got to train my daughter Tracy-Lee, and at this point in time she was preparing for her Black Belt, first-degree grading.

Unfortunately, the second time around for Pauline and me was worse than the first. We'd developed a real love–hate affair: we loved and hated ourselves with a passion, both at the same time.

The US had been the chance to spend six months away by ourselves, a chance to solve all our problems, but I was wrong. A year after the tour we'd separate, a year after that we'd divorce, this time for good.

We'd arrived on the date Chuck and I'd organised. However, at his main headquarters, Chuck's right-hand man Pat Johnson met me instead.

'Man, Chuck said to give you his sincerest apologies. This thing came up in Hong Kong. Bruce Lee said he had to have Chuck in this new movie he's doin' called *Way of The Dragon*. There's gonna be a showdown ... I mean, a real spectacular fight scene, real Coliseum an' all. Chuck just couldn't afford to knock it back, you know ... Ya never know where something like this might lead to. Chuck just hoped you'd understand. In the meantime he's asked me to help ya out where ever.'

As I thanked Pat for his hospitality, I had to do a good job in hiding my disappointment: after that twenty-hour flight I'd been looking forward to seeing Chuck and Bruce Lee.

Meanwhile, during the first couple of days Pauline and I were in California, all you could read about or see in the news was the big bust-up between the king of rock 'n' roll and his wife Priscilla.

Ed Parker (the promoter of the biggest martial arts tournament in the US) had been involved in teaching self-defence to Elvis and all his bodyguards (known affectionately as the 'Memphis Mafia').

Elvis had also wanted to involve Priscilla in the

training routines with him and his guys.

'Harney, wha' done yo' all give this self-defence trainin' a shot? If yo' all don' wanna train with me 'n' the boys, then Ed Parker said he's got a buddy tha' can teach yo' all private lessons.'

This was the story that Ed gave to Chuck when he was trying to convince him to take time out of his busy teaching schedule and get down to Graceland.

'If yo' all gets some lessons while I'rm on the road, then when I'rm home, we'll have this martial arts trainin' as a common in'erest.' Ed Parker's quoting of Elvis had convinced Chuck and he started giving Priscilla private lessons.

Then along came this movie and Chuck unexpectedly had to hightail it off to Hong Kong and play movie star. He'd asked the martial arts champion Mike Stone if he could do him a big favour and fill in with Priscilla. Mike agreed and everything went fine until there was a major catastrophe.

Pat Johnson and I were having a workout. 'Hey Barb, you got what it takes man, but I just need to polish up some little timing tricks for yo' all to take home fo' those Aussie students of yours. Yo' all gotta get yo'self off that back leg Japanese style an' get yo'self fightin' off the front leg like we all doin. Makes yo' all take-off much fastar.

'Hay now, I'rm real busy for the next coupla days, but I've organised for yo' all to train with the best tournament fighter on the US circuit. Here's tha address to Mike Stone's gym an' he's expectin' yo' all at trainin' there tonight.'

Now this would be a workout: between Pat Johnson and Mike Stone, I was learning more per day than I'd learn back home in a month.

By now I'd had something like twenty years of experience on the street and I'd practised martial arts for seven years. But what if this guy cut loose in self-defence, how much damage would he be capable of?

I guess that's why he shocked me so much after the workout ... 'You got what it takes, man. I can see you got that eye of the tiger; that street thing. Lotta guys in the martial arts, they don't got that. Say man, if you gonna be workin' out regular with me, how 'bout we go out Saturday for dinner with our women folk. But arh, I betta warn ya – my lady is Priscilla Presley.

'I was sorta helpin' Chuck Norris out, and me and Priscilla; well, we sorta got this thing goin' an I'm a bit concerned about Elvis and that Memphis Mafia shit. You know?'

Mike was testing me to see how I'd stand up, but I figured I needed this guy to teach me his stuff. Should anyone mess with that, then all Hell was likely to break loose – and some!

I continued to train at Chuck Norris' studios during the day and met and trained with seasoned tournament fighters, John Nativitad and Super Dan Anderson (both lightweights) and we all competed together at the Four Seasons – Summer Series – Tournament Circuit.

I managed to win the middleweight section and at the end of the day the three champions (heavy, middle and lightweight) had to fight one another in a sudden-death point system for the honor of grand champion.

Unfortunately, I'd won a twenty-man middleweight division only to be beaten by the lightweight champion on the day, Super Dan Anderson.

Super Dan also beat the heavyweight division winner, and on this day the little guy won through to become the Four Seasons – Grand Champion.

Every night I'd train with Mike Stone and we both continued to look out for those Memphis Mafia boys. On the weekends, I'd fly all over for competition tournaments: to New York for venues like Madison Square Garden for the famous Aaron Banks Bashes, if you got knocked out at those karate tournaments you definitely lost the battles. There were no trophies for the unconscious. Of course, every time I went to New York, I'd venture downtown and train at the infamous Peter Urban's *dojo*. I was lucky one night there, training with East Coast legend Ron Vanne Clief.

I went on to compete in Chicago (but only once!) at the Jimmy Jones Tournament, which was sanctioned by the BKF organisation.

Because the promoter had the same name as me, when I'd phoned I'd said, 'Hi Jimmy, I see you've got this big tournament on the weekend. I'm from Australia. My name is Bob, sorry, my name is "Barb Johnes". Maybe we're family or something.'

That's when we both laughed.

Pauline and I had flown in from Los Angeles to Chicago in plenty of time to catch the opening ceremony. That's when it hit us: BKF stood for Black Karate Federation. And this was a time when the Black Power Movement was happening.

There were 4000 competitors, 1200 of which were in the Black Belt divisions.

There was at least 8000 in that auditorium audience. Add this number to the competitors, all African-Americans, and that meant Pauline and I were the only two white dudes in the entire venue – and not related to Mr Jones, the promoter!

Also, back then everyone wore a white karate uniform. However, in Australia we'd been wearing coloured and black uniforms for quite a while. Think of it: 4000 African-Americans in white uniforms and me wearing black.

After I'd won my first four bouts, Pauline said, 'Are you sure you know what you are doing?'

In the semi-final I had the pleasure of fighting Joel 'Jiu-Jitsu' Ward, possibly the biggest man in the place. He'd been told to beat, maim and kill me. There was no time limit and no rules; however, no-one had told me a damned thing, and we went for it until eventually someone did ring the bell.

On points 'Jiu-Jitsu Joe' was several ahead; that's when Pauline said something she would not have said at any other time,

'I'm so glad you lost, now are we out of here?'

San Francisco, the city where ten years earlier the Haight–Ashbury era had been in full bloom, was next on my competition list. In a city whose sweeping hillsides and Golden Gate Bridge resembled the rolling hills of Sydney and its Harbor Bridge, I'd trained downtown with another co-star of *Enter the Dragon* at the Jim Kelly *dojo*. By now, after having trained all over the US, it seemed that many African-Americans had a natural rhythm for developing martial arts skills. Jim Kelly was a classical example of of the fighting arts being poetry in motion.

I next headed further north to Seattle, in search of a tenth degree (the top of the ladder) in the Ishin-Ryu system. Grand Master Steve Armstrong had introduced the Okinawa-based system to the US after World War II. From my first meeting with Steve I was inspired. His knowledge of the history of the oriental arts (I wouldn't experience this again until in Australia when I met and trained with the Irish-Canadian Patrick McCarthy twenty-five years later) had me spellbound. His esoteric understanding of the spiritual realms intrigued; he could fascinate for hours with meanings from within my *ennead* forms (the nine sets of esoteric movements that contain the understanding of martial arts).

Steve's main *dojo* had a serene atmosphere that comprised a shrine of remembrance to his own deceased Chief Grand Master. It contained a photo set among memorabilia, probably relevant to Steve and his Master's time together in Okinawa. Incense and thick candles burned day and night. The floorboards of the *dojo* were polished and kept impeccably clean. An extended play tape at moderate volume played Carlos Santana's albums back to back. The *Abraxas* album with the singles 'Black Magic Woman' and 'Oye Como Va' was followed by *Santana III*, his current number one hit album. Plus, at this time Carlos was becoming a devotee of the Indian guru, Sri Chimnoy.

This music was relevant to the mood; the *dojo* was the perfect setting for me to experience a little TMT (Transcendental Meditation Technique), something I'd learned years earlier through another fellow martial artist, Bernie Frazier).

The next morning I woke up ready for Los Angeles. Chuck Norris was back from Hong Kong and it was celebration time. He'd invited me to do some demonstrations with him as a special guest. One was to a medical research convention of several hundred doctors from all over California.

I trained for a week with Mike Stone, whom I'd missed during my competition jaunt around the US. Mike introduced me to Joe Lewis of the 'Tracy System'. Joe was the first Western martial artist to don boxing gloves. Two years earlier he'd established the first kick-boxing US title. Joe was a definite cog in the wheel of the LA action. On a good day he could give even Mike Stone some stick and in the late 1960s he'd reigned supreme as the king of the heavyweights. This was around the time of his first movie *Jaguar Lives*. Back then I'd figured that out of all of us, Joe had the looks, the physique and the attitude to really make it in the movies. I was wrong.

With only a week before I'd head back home, Chuck introduced me to Ed Parker, who ran a chain of *dojo*s along the west coast.

'Barb Johnes, eh! I've heard a lot about you lately from Chuck and some of the guys around the traps. They tell me you're a good martial artist, you're here to learn with a good attitude ... Well, you'd better not go back to Australia without having a look at one of the strongest styles in California: Ed Parker's style of US kempo.

This was no understatement by Ed Parker: his annual tournament promoted under the banner of 'The Internationals' was by far the largest and most popular martial arts tournament in the US at this time. It needed dozens of fighting rings, all operating at the same time, to put through the thousands of competitors that this competition attracted from all corners of North America and overseas, giving it it's international status.

This annual tournament became best known for it's musical free-forms competition. This was separate from the fighting divisions: it allowed for complete self-expression of the individual. Free-forms are a set of self-defence movements created by the contestants; these movements are choreographed to music and presented to the judges and audience. Personal musical preference has a variety of classical, rock 'n' roll, R&B and any other style that complements the mood of the competitor and his or her free-form.

Ed Parker was an advocate of mirror training. He'd often give me a set of combinations and leave me in front of a mirror practising on my own. This style of training had me contemplating the oneness of my reflection in the *dojo* mirrors; of the sense of individuality and the emptiness that comes with it; and of my beautiful wife Pauline, who'd gone back home to Australia two months earlier. This US trip had done nothing for our relationship: Pauline and I were only a matter of time.

Aggression had been building inside of me; that feeling of emptiness absorbed the heavy beat blasting from the sound system in Ed Parker's studio. For a while, I'd vented the anger of my personal problems through my martial arts movements to the bass and drums combination of Pink Floyd's double set *Ummagumma* and their recent number one album *Atom Heart Mother*. David Gilmour's howling lead guitar solos had electric currents shooting through my veins and nervous system, extending into my punches and kicking techniques with devastating lethal power.

During my final week in the US I spent every night working out in different Ed Parker *dojo*s, depending on where he was teaching. On my final night Parker had me in front of the mirror again, practising what I'd been learning from him.

'Good, that's good Barb. You got that ready now to take back home to Australia.'

We were just finishing off when a new exciting energy swept through the place: a group of about a dozen men had started training at the far end of the studio. Parker excused himself, explaining, 'That's one of my groups that ah teach private like. Barb, ah'll catch you tomorrow.'

Parker moved into the centre of the group, training just one of them. This particular student wore a very flamboyant martial arts uniform and dark, large-framed sunglasses. He seemed to be looking down at me and asking Parker questions. This had me thinking, could that really be Elvis Presley?

Priscilla came to mind. What if Elvis recognised me as the mate of the guy who'd stolen his wife? After all, it'd been the number one topic in all the major media since I'd arrived in the US.

There he was, with a full crew of his Memphis Mafia that wouldn't have thought twice about blowing this Aussie away!

At the airport the following day I'd phoned around saying thanks and goodbye to everyone. Parker confirmed who this private group was, that Elvis had asked, 'who was that guy down thar with Orstralya and Barb Johnes, embroidered across thar shoulders of a *black uniform?*'

Either way I didn't care what Parker had replied: I had to psyche myself up for the twenty-hour flight back home.

Once home there was a quick three-states tour – Victoria, New South Wales and Queensland – of my martial arts clubs. When I was back in Melbourne the papers headlined Joe Cocker's drug bust.

The second Sunbury had been all the rage around the traps due to the success of the first Sunbury (although it would only be a shadow of the original).

A booking was on the board for a planned 3XY radio station outdoor festival (that would turn into a massive riot and give my organisation and me national media exposure).

Christmas and the new year had come and gone. Before I'd had time to settle into any sort of routine, there I was: on tour with The Rolling Stones and having that phone conversation with the infamous Mrs Richards.

In 1975 I'd had the choice of either working as bodyguard to Paul and Linda McCartney on their world Wings In Concert tour, or doing my second *tour of duty* with my favourite, Joe Cocker. For years Richard Norton had been an interviewer with the Immigration Department concerning passports, visas and residencies. He could not get the time off needed to look after the tour. I assumed this was due to the Department having decided it was time for him to fulfil his governmental responsibilities.

There were now twenty-eight Bob Jones martial arts schools across three states. Queensland had added nine new schools with the opening of the Sunshine Coast, and there were nineteen clubs in the Melbourne suburbs. New South Wales was just starting up.
      Billy Manne had helped me build my organisation. At the time he was looking after the south-eastern side of Melbourne, from Frankston to Rosebud. This kept him busy.

However, we'd also planned for Billy to open up a full-time, seven-day a week, self-defence academy, complete with a weight-training gym.

I'd called him to talk about an additional project, Richard's unavailability for it and my desire to tour with Joe Cocker.

'Billy, this will be great for you. A month looking after the McCartneys ... and the publicity you'll be able to generate after the tour ... it'll help with the launch of your new training premises.'

'But I haven't toured before. Doing a gig like that, I don't want to blow it with a band like Wings.'

'Don't worry, I'll help out. We'll have as many sessions as it takes. The more you know about the band pre-tour, the better. It doesn't matter if they know nothing about you – you're an unknown quantity, a surprise ... Let's make it a pleasant surprise.'

We got together that weekend, and Billy saw the advantage of getting to know his protégés. By the time we'd finished, Billy and I both knew the three daughters coming on tour from the eldest Heather, the twelve-year-old; to Mary, named after her grandmother and just turned six; to the youngest Stella, who was four years of age. (Their brother James wouldn't be born for another two years). At the time Paul was right on $33\,^1/_3$ years of age and of course as pro-bodyguards we knew better than to divulge Linda's age.

Billy Manne and family had come to Australia from war-torn history of France and The Netherlands. Billy's dad had suffered horrific injuries during his time in the Dutch Underground during World War II; however, a failed business venture in Adelaide, South Australia, had dad, Billy and his German/Irish Celtic mother set off to Africa chasing yet another rainbow. Eventually, Billy's dad would save enough money to return to his country of choice: Australia.

Now what does Billy the bodyguard remember most about these days of 'Billy the kid'?

'Within three hours of being in Africa, dad, mum and I were walking downtown. Suddenly, this huge African set on us, brandishing a bloody machete. Mum was frozen with fear, dad was worried, not for himself but for mum and me. My father handed over his watch and what little African money he had on him. I was scared, but remember thinking that one day I was going to learn how to protect myself, my mum and my dad.'

Such hardships were the real tools I'd been given to produce, within a decade this absolute martial arts machine that had Billy in my top three students. This was why I'd selected him to be bodyguard on the McCartney Wings tour.

Billy Manne, a third-degree Black Belt, was a martial artist of very high morals: a non-smoker, non-drinker and definitely an anti-drugs campaigner who'd put the welfare of his clients above everything.

Billy was the *complete-comitatus* (protector).

I'd already been on the road with Joe and it was great to be working again with my favourite artist. Joe Cocker and Bob Jones had developed into a couple of good mates, and it was not only because of his music. I never did tell Paul Dainty, but I'd have done these tours without pay. In fact, I'd have paid to do them.

However, this was a bad time for Joe. Out of all of our tours together this was his worst in terms of binge-drinking. He'd cut back on the drugs but, he was drinking on his days off and his days on, plus heavily prior to gigs and even on stage.

During the last days of October, Billy Manne, Paul Dainty, Patty Mostyn and the crew had flown to Perth for the arrival of Wings; the Australasian leg of the world tour had been plugged under the banner of 'sold right out – and letting go'.

At Perth airport, Billy met the cast one by one as they cleared Customs. The first through the terminal were Joe English and Jimmy McCulloch, followed close behind by Denny Laine. Then came the whole gang: Paul, Linda, Heather, Mary and, still waking up from the long flight, Stella, who was being looked after by Rose, the children's tour nanny (who was honored on the *Red Rose Speedway* album).

Paul Dainty had Sydney publicist (the best in the business) Patty Mostyn on the tour, to keep up a momentum of PR as the travelling circus made its way around Australia. The group headed from Perth to Adelaide to Melbourne to Sydney to Brisbane, then back to Melbourne and Sydney for second sold-out shows before heading to the US for an extensive American tour.

At the Sheraton, Billy secured them into their fourteenth-floor Presidential Suite, an exclusive penthouse with fabulous views of the Swan River.

Patty Mostyn had organised a boat cruise for the following morning, allowing them to rest on what was left of their arrival day. After the river cruise, Patty had put together an invitation-only buffet luncheon for WA's 'who's who in the zoo' to come and meet Paul, Linda and the band and crew at the Cottesloe Centre at 11:30 a.m. They'd be back to the Sheraton by mid-afternoon for the 2:30 p.m. press conference, in the Sheraton's Convention Centre. Of course, that night the PDC (Paul Dainty Corporation) staged one of those extravagant functions and launched the tour's first pre-gig party, which would last most of the night.

The next day it was down to the Perth Entertainment Centre for the sound check that night - the show was sold out.

Billy called after the performance. 'You were right about not getting much sleep, there's always something going on.' From the excitement in Billy's voice this was not a complaint, it was an affirmation. 'The show was great. The Perth crowd went berserk!'

Meanwhile, Joe Cocker was working his arse off, doing small gigs and drinking even heavier as the tour progressed. We were staying in three-star accommodation, and limos were a rare occurrence. It was mostly hire-cars and the occasional cab. This was fine since the smaller venues should have made Joe's performance more intimate and accessible, but something was wrong. On a couple of occasions I tried to steer our conversation in a direction that might get whatever it was into the open, but each time he'd put those regular barriers right up.

Joe had not released any new material for some time, and it'd only been about eighteen months since his last tour. Ticket sales were down and mostly diehard fans had attended the gigs. Most of them didn't care about his recent hits, or even if Joe was a bit off key on a few notes ('What would we do if he sang out of tune/Would we stand up and walk out on him?') – if you're a Joe Cocker fan, it's enough just to be there. However, like me, there were many fans concerned about his welfare. People could see he was drinking far too much.

The tour had us travelling south for gigs to Wollongong and as far north of Sydney as Newcastle. However, I wasn't seeing that much of my best mate. All that alcohol had him in his Mad Dog state and that sometimes produced another side of Joe Cocker that tended to make me real sad.

Norman-e Sweeney, my Sydney buddy, hung out with Joe and me. He drove the hired cars for the north and south of Sydney trips. As we stayed at the Chateau Commodore, just near Benny's Bar, our regular late nightspot, Norm-e kept an eye on things while Joe was sleeping it off. This allowed me to catch up with Billy at the Wings' press conference at the Hyatt Kingsgate.

Billy was excited to see me after two weeks on the road with one of the biggest bands in the world at this time. He was confident the job was going according to plan. It reminded me of my first two weeks with The Rolling Stones.

People waited for their cue to enter *the coliseum* – that's what most bands think of press conferences: it's like this huge battle that they either win, lose or on a good day they draw.

My boss, Paul Dainty, was there. I could see how he also was psyched up for the battle: promoters, of course, see the media as the front line. Sometimes, good or bad, the press can make or break a big tour. That's why Paul Dainty had hired the best in the business. And there she was, my good mate Patty.

'Bloody Hell, between the Wings' bodyguard and now you, this is one war we can't lose!' Patty tilted up on her toes to give me that customary kiss on the cheek.

Just then the band, including Paul and Linda, must have been thinking who is this character?

'Ah, everyone ... this is my martial arts mentor, whom I have told most of you about. Ah, this is Bob Jones.' Billy's introduction seemed to conjure some serious conversation.

'*Lets do it*' sounded every bit like a commanding officer about to lead her army into the front lines, and that is exactly what Patty was doing. This was Sydney Town, and in the world of public relations, Sydney Town belonged to Patty Mostyn.

After her *warm-ups* and introductions on behalf of the Paul Dainty Corporation, Patty suggested that if they (the media) wanted a good response from the band in general, they should refrain from mentioning his former group, as this does tend to 'make him rather cross'.

Then entered Paul McCartney and his new band, Wings. They took up their positions, seated behind their trestles, facing the national firing squad. In typical form, a journalist from the *Sydney Telegraph* fired the first shot, 'How does it feel, at your age, to be still doing rock 'n' roll?'

This was certainly designed to inflict injury ...

Unperturbed and relaxed, Paul turned on the charm. Thanks to almost twenty years of professionalism he responded, 'Age does not make any difference as far as our fans are concerned – even in The Beatle days (Paul took the offensive by using that word himself) we had older fans. Our aim is that everybody, of any age, should like us. After all, I am currently $33\ ^1/_3$ years of age, and I look forward to speeding up to 45 and eventually 78.

'It's now five years since we [The Beatles] broke up. At that time, there was a certain amount of acrimony between the four of us – me, John Lennon, Ringo Starr and George Harrison – with several writs flying. Today all our differences are sorted out; they are all great blokes. George is now living in an Oxfordshire Mansion with a new girlfriend. John is in America, carrying on a long fight against a deportation order. Ringo is finding a new career for himself in films.

'... the Myer Music Bowl in Melbourne was our best show so far. The audiences are getting better as we are warming up. The audiences were also very good in Adelaide and Perth ... tomorrow night, here in Sydney at the Showgrounds, promises to be our best show yet!' Paul was doing his damnedest to bring the line of interviewing into focus of this tour and this his new band Wings.

However, that *Sydney Telegraph* journo wanted to prove he had staying power in the obnoxious department: 'Why, as one of the most famous men in the world, a super-rich ex-Beatle, do you bother to keep on touring? Just what motivates you and keeps you going?'

'Drugs,' replied Paul earnestly. 'I must have them. No seriously, I just like music.'

'Have you seen The Beatles recently?' A journo identifying himself as being from *The Truth*, a national (smut) newspaper, asked.

'We run into each other and stuff – we're just good friends.'

'Would you ever want to re-form The Beatles?'

'It's not within my power to bring back The Beatles. It was a four-way split and we all wanted to do different things.'

Linda, deciding it was time for a little crossfire, devised up some Machiavellian divide and conquer tactics. 'You could go on talking about The Beatles forever; all four of them really get so bored with it.'

The battle continued with the journos throwing more *grenades*; that is, questions about The Beatles. And the band threw those same grenades back with answers about Wings and the Sydney show. The battle was declared a draw; Patty Mostyn was happy – and when Patty was happy, Paul Dainty was happy.

About halfway through the PR exercise, Billy and I stepped out. He wanted to get me up to speed concerning his adventures with *his* band.

'Chief, you know when you were giving me those pre-tour tips about the importance of a client respecting their bodyguard, and the best way of getting respect was to first give respect? Well, that very first afternoon in Perth, Linda decided the family was going to have a pizza takeaway meal together. After compiling a list of who wanted what, she simply handed it to me and said: "Be a dear, and organise this for us."

'"I'm terribly sorry Linda, but I don't do pizzas." Wow, talk about indignant! I'm about to get the sack on my first day; the Chief will be impressed!

'"Well, our minders back home always get pizzas and things for us."

'"In Australia my job is to protect the McCartney family, and if anything happened to you or any of the kids while I'm off getting pizzas, or anything of the like, then I'd have to answer to this guy, who's my martial arts mentor, and if you knew him, then you'd understand why we take this minder thing so serious."

'Then without explaining the situation any further, I took her pizza list and went two doors down the corridor. This was Trudy's room; Trudy was in charge of Wings' makeup and Paul's and Linda's wardrobe. Sort of a girl Friday, she didn't mind at all, volunteering to do the pizza run after I quickly explained my predicament. Within minutes I was back in the Penthouse, nothing was mentioned until about forty-five minutes later when Trudy arrived with the goodies.

'"Heather, Mary and Stella, you all thank Trudy – and thank Billy, too. He's a lovely man."

'Paul and Linda now realised I was deadly serious when it came to my concept of *comitatus*. I'd won their respect.

'After dinner on the Tuesday night Paul told me about a recent escapade he'd pulled off with the kids as an attempt just to have a normal family situation.

'"I recently took my kids Halloween trick or treating in America. We went door-to-door to a bunch of perfect strangers in a residential area around Los Angeles. I had on a black top hat and a big rubber mask that made me look like a ghoulish goofy, and my kids were a mixture of fairies, witches and crazy clowns. No-one guessed that the dad behind the rubber mask was the ex-Beatle, creator of Wings, although a few gave me quizzical glances.

'"What bothered me most about this Halloween jaunt was the fact that I needed to be present. The McCartney kids, in fact just about anyone's kids these days, can't be sent out there alone.

'"Anyway, now we've got Billy Manne, our own bodyguard. First thing tomorrow we'll need a costume shop. It'll be into our costumes and off to that flea market down on the beach at Glenelg. No-one will know who the Hell we are, and if they do – we've got you, Billy!"

'That's exactly what they did ... and do you know what Paul said?

'"Billy, you can go dressed as a rock 'n' roll bodyguard-come-minder – those jeans and that Wings tour T-shirt make you look the part. And those callused knuckles will trick everyone."

'In Melbourne their desire to be a normal family had us staying on a farm house in the Dandenongs, complete with dogs, cattle and horses. They enjoyed riding the horses, especially Stella, who looked like she was born to ride. And Linda loved doing the cooking in a home.

'On the day of the press conference at the Southern Cross, we were coming down from the tenth floor in the elevator. At the seventh floor – you won't believe it! On gets this guy wearing a Stetson cowboy hat and smoking a fat Cuban cigar a good five centimeters long. He's that tall he has to bend down to get his head clear of the door when he lifts his head up.

'It was Paul's favourite actor, and he was direct from California, John Wayne.

'They both recognised each other.

Paul was so excited. I thought this is stupid, in less than sixty seconds these elevator doors will open, so,

"Ah, excuse me, Mr Wayne, we only have a moment, and I'd really like you to meet Mr Paul McCartney."

'"Ah, Paul, Linda this is–"

'"Paul, ar'e thought I recognised yo'all. Ar'e wasn't sure. Linda, how are you both? Ar'e love the new album of yours, it's the best."

'Everyone exploded; everyone was talking at once, like they were trying to put their lifetimes into this sixty seconds. As the "L" lit up and the doors slid open for the Southern Cross Lobby, they organised to catch up later for drinks. Thank God for pre-tour research!

'Here in Sydney, we've got this penthouse at the Hyatt, and we've got this incredible mansion down at Bondi that's owned by some movie producer friend of Patty Mostyn. He's overseas at the moment and given us access to this absolute palace. It's built into the cliffs and has these incredible ocean views. The hardest thing is getting to and from these two destinations.

'Prior to this press conference, there's been complete media frenzy. Everywhere we go, there's the media. Between them and crazy fans in Sydney, it's been total mayhem. Especially in transit: just loads of cars full of press and these over-zealous Wings fans.'

Billy was exhausted; he'd hardly taken a breath in the previous thirty minutes or so. Now it was my turn. I was about to launch into my Joe Cocker rave when the double doors of the convention centre opened and everyone spilled out.

People were giving their opinion as to how good or not so good this Sydney press conference had just gone down. It wasn't long before the positives outweighed the negatives, and the vibe took the afternoon's PR exercise into the realms of the best on tour. Naturally, Patty Mostyn and Paul Dainty were exceptionally pleased.

The energy animated the limo dialogue as Billy Manne and the McCartney's gave me a lift back to the Chateau Commodore.

'Aye Bob, you be sure to say hello to Joe for Linda and me,' Paul said as a passing gesture of friendship.

Up in my room Norm-e was watching a sports show on TV, his feet on the coffee table as he polished off the last of the VBs from the mini-bar.

'Norm-e, what's happening? Is the Mad Dog awake yet?' I'd been gone two hours and it was now three in the afternoon.

'No, thank Christ! The Mad Dog's still asleep, but Joe's up and about and he's having a shower.'

'You mean he's *sober*?'

'As a fucking judge! I told him where you were. He just wants to go for a walk up the 'Cross' to Denny's Pool Room and shoot some snooker with you and me. He said he just wants to kick back and talk to some of the locals.'

Joe could do that, without the top hat and mask.

We could just go into a local pub anywhere and within five minutes he'd be playing pool and talking away.

Just then Joe walked in. 'So while me minder's off bloody gallivanting, I coulda had me bloody throat cut!' This was Joe's brand of humour.

'So who won the war? Did those buggars give Paul and Linda tha' Beatles bullshit the whole time?'

By the time we'd walked to the 'Cross' and had our game of snooker, I'd told Norm-e and Joe most of Billy's yarns. By 4:30 we were in one of Budget's hire cars cruising up the Newcastle expressway with plenty of time to make the gig that night. Norm-e was driving one of Budget's latest 1975 LTDs. He had the driver's side tyres hugging the white lines around those sweeping bends as we cruised towards Gosford.

That landscape on dusk, the magnificence of so many different colour-combinations in the sunset, with the 180-degree rolling green and blue valleys that disappeared over the horizon – despite it all, within a few hours Joe would be performing 'When the Night Comes', 'High Time We Went', 'Up Where We Belong'.

Meanwhile, Joe Cocker was waving his bottle of J.D. over one of his Cocker Cocktails. He gave me one of those 'With a Little Help from my Friends' looks.

For a professional bodyguard life couldn't get any better than this.

Right then, everything was *shattered* as the bourbon poured over the ice, filling the long glass, leaving enough room at the top for the customary single dash of Coke. And next I saw that devilish what-are-you-doing-with-a-fool-like-me? expression in his eyes. It meant only one thing: the Mad Dog was about to come out to play.

Christmas arrived a couple of weeks after the Cocker and McCartney tours. I'd called into Billy Manne's pre-Christmas take-a-month-off-training break-up party for all of our peninsula martial arts students. Billy had this state-of-the-art Kodak camera that Paul and Linda had given to everyone to celebrate the success of the tour. (As most of you would know, Linda's family name was Eastman. With the family fame of Eastman Colour being connected to cinematography and Kodak, guess that's as good-a-reason as any, to give everyone a camera.)

Billy and I ended up talking of our tour experiences. I had a story on Keith Richards from the tour in Auckland, New Zealand. One night Stuey 'the Lifesaver' Lomax had been out on the town looking after Keith. Just as the sun was coming up, they'd pulled up in front of the hotel.

Keith had asked the driver: 'How much is the fare?'

'Six, forty, aye,' responded the Maori cabbie.

'Six, forty!' Keith winked at Stuey. 'Is that Australian, American or do you have separate New Zealand dollars in this country?'

'The lifesaver' wondered what the wink was about.

'New Zealand Dollars, aye.'

'Okay, what 'ave I got 'ere? Oh yeah, here we are. I think these are your currency. What was it again, woz it six, forty?'

'Yes sir.'

'Al right ... One, two, three, four, five ... What did 'e

say Stuey? Six, forty? Wannit? Okay, I got it, six ... six hundred, seven hundred ... Here ya are driver and you keep the change, and you 'ave a nice day!'

This had been one of my better Rolling Stones party jokes after two years full-time touring.

However, Billy came out with ...

'That reminds me of the end of the Wings tour. We were all in the Golden Wing Lounge, everybody was sad about leaving the friends they'd made in Australia, but at the same time excited about continuing on to the US leg of this world tour. Just then, Paul McCartney had said to me:

'"Billy, I've got this Australian currency – mostly notes and a bit of loose change. I can't be bothered cashing it in for American currency. The Aussie dollar is far too strong at the moment, it's about double the US dollar. So, if I put this money through the International Exchange they'll hit me with their commissions and with the devaluation they'll rip me off for half. I hate that."

'I just put Paul's spare change in the pocket of my carry bag. After saying our good-byes I went home, and I think it was the next day, or a couple of days later, when I actually tipped that petty cash out and counted it. There was twelve hundred bloody dollars and loose change, which I think really was Paul's way of saying thank you to me.'

The current Joe Cocker tour (our third together) was coming to a sad end: the band had played a great gig on the Tuesday night in Melbourne, but then after the concert the guys partied it up at the King Street nightclubs. We'd flown into Sydney late Wednesday afternoon; of course, seeing it was a day off there was a dawn party that kicked off at the Manzel room and would finish off with an escapade at Kings Cross' favourite entertainers' hangout, Benny's Bar.

After four years of touring I'd become well conditioned to staying out all night protecting the famous names of rock 'n' roll from themselves. My martial arts training had kept me sane. I was still amazed how the acts kept it together with all the pressures of life on the road. There was no exercise, no diet to speak of; just hard gigs, all-night parties, too much booze, way too many drugs and groupies everywhere, but then again a lot of these performers had paid the ultimate price.

All Joe Cocker needed was a day like this one, a no-binge day, seeing there'd be a gig that night and he'd need to pull up as good as new for it. This would then be followed with a day off and Saturday night at the Hordern Pavilion, the final show, which would be sold out.

On day's like this, I'd think how lucky I was to have shared time with one of the earth's most beautiful human beings.

Joe had tossed around some ideas that he was using for his next album. He knew of my love for music, despite my inability to play any musical instruments, but he'd always ask my opinion and I'd do my best to give him what I thought might be constructive criticism – he'd be too polite to laugh at this and from that grew healthy conversation.

That afternoon we'd set up in a bar lounge with Nicky Hopkins and Bobby Keyes. Everybody drank a variety of tomato juice, mineral water and Coca-Cola on the rocks. Was this hard to believe? Well, it was a gig day, and most times they'd tried to stay straight for the afternoon sound check, and then the gig at night.

After this gig and for the next day or two we'd be travelling to the next city, so it'd be party time. Naturally, while living on the road and out of a suitcase as much as someone like Joe had done, it was easy to occasionally mix up this tour rule of partying.

Meanwhile, Michael Lang, Joe's new manager, and the rest of the band had gone off to the Hordern Pavilion for the sound check. We weren't due until 4.00 p.m. and just as we were thinking of making the move, *enter* Bad Company.

'Woz thart you're all fookin' drinking? Hay Simon get th' lads somthin' decent 'a drink, will ya?'

I figured this was Paul Rodgers, the lead singer of the group. The taller, good-looking blond guy would be the band's drummer, Simon Kirke. They were to be my next assignment starting the following Sunday. Even though the two tours overlapped, Paul Dainty wasn't game to have anybody but me looking after this crew – due to their reputation.

Simon and Paul both wore designer bikie leather jackets and pastel-coloured T-shirts. They both wore bell-bottom flairs. And both wore those expensive Californian cowboy boots that had been made to order. Paul's were black and Simon's were brown.

Paul Rodgers must have noticed my look of disapproval as he plonked himself down at our table and brought on the alcohol – and it was right on sound check time!

'Just relax marthar farkar. Paul Dainty tol' me abou' yoo. Apparently I get you as a minder from Sundee.'

Simon, back from the bar, pulled a chair up next to his Bad Company buddy and gave out the drinks, complete with that Joe Cocker special (a long glass filled to the top with ice, four or five nips of Jim Beam, which just about leaves enough room for a short dash of Coke).

'An' nats a dubble hit of black label Scotch on tha' rocks for yoo, mister minder. Ya looks like a Black Label kinda guy. Ya know black belt an' all that.

'Little did Simon know that off tour this was my favourite party drink. But on tour, well, it just couldn't be done.

That Scotch just sat there as the two performers looked and acted more like a couple of Pommy Teddy Boys than two of the biggest rock stars on the world's touring circuit.

'Aye, wha' abou' yoo, yah fookin' old fart? I ain't seen yoo since Germany. Yair, yoo got me so fookin' drunk on a gig day, I coodn't rembare tha' words to 'arf me fookin' songs, cood I, aye?'

Joe, with a mischievous grin, sat up as straight as only Joe could do: with arms folded high on his chest. His right arm then swung out and with four stiffened fingers he combed the back of his hair (on stage this helps him hit the high notes).

Joe yelled to the bar, waving his arm with five fingers outstretched and demanding another round – enter the Mad Dog.

The performers were now in a world of their own, with a type of humour foreign to me.

'Wot's thar worse job yoo evar 'ad?'

'Gettin' lobsters out o' Jane Mansfield's fookin' arsehole.'

'Nah, I mean thar fookin' worse job–'

'Ore, tha' mustar been tha' job I 'ad countin' Winston Churchill's fookin' dandruff. Tha' wha' fell down on tha' floor. Yoo wooden know wethar you 'ad one or two bits of fookin' dandruff!'

The drinks really started coming and this question–answer routine went on with no order of who asked or responded:

'Ha, ha, ha, ha, ha, ha!' They all broke out in unison. I remembered thinking, what'll happen when Michael Lang gets back from the sound check?

At lunchtime Michael Lang was co-ordinating everyone's tickets and the gang was putting baggage through the usual Customs ordeal. Joe and all the guys had pulled up miraculously considering what they'd put themselves through during the final stage of this tour. The band was on its way to South America and Michael Lang was very concerned about its welfare. He'd first tried me, and then put the word on Paul Dainty about having me continue on those last couple of legs of the world tour, due to the political unrest and drug connotations of South America.

Paul Dainty left the decision with me but pleaded, 'I really need you with Paul Rodgers and Bad Company.'

My mind buzzed with cities such as Santiago, Buenos Aires, São Paulo and all those beautiful southern belles of Rio de Janeiro ...

Until I'd just caught my flight and flipped open the regimen that the PDC had given me so I'd know who I was about to protect.

Free was the original name of Bad Company. They'd been discovered by Alexis Korner. At the time, seventeen-year-old Paul Kossoff's blues-rock style of guitar playing had impressed him. Free caught everybody's attention after supporting Blind Faith on a 1968 US tour. Their debut album of the same year *Tons of Sobs* fell short of their in-concert prowess, but a new-found maturity was evidenced on the 1969 release *Free*. The group peaked with their third album, *Fire and Water* (1970).

The single 'All Right Now' was an instant hit throughout Europe, and with a show-stealing Isle of Wight Festival appearance, Free seemed destined to become one of the biggest rock acts of the new decade. However, commercial pressures caused internal rifts and the group split up in 1971, in the wake of the relatively disappointing *Highway* album. Ironically, 'My Brother Jake', one of the album's leftovers, gave the group a second posthumous hit.

Uninspired solo projects and Kossoff's rapid descent into drink and drugs provided the reasons for the group's reformation, at the start of 1972. But Kossoff maintained his habits for another four years until he'd eventually learn the lesson of life: *addiction is suicide on the time payment plan*. The Black Dragon would eventually take Kossoff in 1976.

Andy Fraser, the group's bassist and pianist, would depart shortly afterwards to form the band, Sharks.

In 1973 Rodgers and Kirke formed Bad Company. The lineup was Paul Rodgers on vocals, Mick Ralphs on guitar, Boz Burrell on bass and Simon Kirke on drums. Bad Company was one of the few supergroups to live up to expectations. Rodgers' soulful delivery combined with Ralphs' raunchy guitar work met with immediate success.

Bad Company (1974) was a US number 1 and UK number 3, while 'Can't Get Enough' was the band's first hit and remains an enduring classic.

Straight Shooter (1975, a US and UK number three) saw a shift to a more commercial approach. A good sign for the band was Paul Rodgers being voted the most successful male singer in Britain in that year.

Run With The Pack (1976) suggested that a formulaic approach to their songwriting was developing.

The plane had begun its descent, the flight attendant had requested, 'Okay Bob, put your seat forward please, we'll be landing in a couple of minutes.'

'Hey Leanne, are you going to the concert tonight?' It was nice to be recognised.

'Well, if some handsome bodyguard could arrange a couple of passes, you never know what could eventuate...'

Paul Dainty had sent a limo to pick me up at the airport. We went straight to the sound check. 'Run With the Wind' was thumping out of the stack of speakers and Paul's voice was evidence of why he'd been voted 'Male Voice of Britain'. After a few more songs, Paul wiped the sweat from his body and leaned into the microphone.

'Aye Simon, It's our fookin' minder an' eeze only three days late. Aye Borb did ja get that fookin' ol' fart off safe 'n soun'? If 'e ain't got good security in South America, 'e ain't gonna make it!'

I was beginning to get a grip on this special brand of *bad* humour and it made me laugh.

'Yeah, yoo can fookin' laugh now, but I tell yoo wha' – I'm gonna be a fookin' 'andful for yoo. On my tours, minders earn their fookin' money.'

I really laughed out aloud, camouflaging the fact that I was just three seconds away from punching him. However, I had to keep reminding myself that Paul Dainty didn't want any punching on these tours. There was only six weeks to go. About now, I was really thinking I should've taken the option of

South America, Joe Cocker, Rio de Janeiro and those long-legged southern belles!

Bad Company rocked a capacity crowd to the rafters that night at Brisbane's Festival Hall, and it did not take much convincing to have the whole band come back to our *dojo*-house, which was a tropic-styled timber house built on three-metre stilts whose walls we'd gutted out, which made it great for parties, particularly outrageous rock 'n' roll parties. There were well over two hundred Black Belts with their girls present. This meant the large crowd could be in the house, under the house and around the house.

Leanne, the flight attendant whom I'd known for a year, and a half dozen of her work mates had showed up, so I was happy.

I always knew that George Roumeliotis, the 'Black Panther' and my local state manager, had a great voice. He had the *dojo*-band set up when we arrived in the limos. (Bad Company was his favourite band.)

Willy Ferris was playing lead guitar and George was belting out 'Bad Company'. On arrival Paul Rodgers ran into the house and grabbed a backing microphone, and he and George and Willy sang together like they'd been singing for years. Mick Ralphs, Boz Burrell and Simon Kirke politely waited the fifteen minutes it took for the guys to finish the song. Then the real Bad Company moved in and took up positions on the instruments and we endeavored to keep as many neighbours as possible wide awake until dawn, including our neighbours, a Catholic monastery full of nuns.

Just as daybreak had the sun peering over the horizon it was back to Brisbane's Park Royal

Hotel. Here Rodgers began his Aleister Crowley 'do-as-though-will-shall-be-the-name-of-the-law' minder freak-out behaviour routine that would be commonplace for most of the tour.

'Aye, Borb, wotch this for a bi' o' fun!'

Paul ran down the corridor knocking on every door (our entourage included the lighting/sound guys, admin. and everyone of this fifth floor). Then he sprinted back to me, grabbed the fire extinguisher from the passage area at the elevators and upended it to set it off.

Almost as if this had been rehearsed, everyone opened their doors as Mr Bad Company ran past, splashing everything and everyone with white foam. By the end of his run, he was out of foam, with the whole crew swearing at him in their lack-of-sleep state of semi-naked awareness. Paul then put his key into his penthouse door and disappeared.

With an apologetic smile I quickly made it into my room, which adjoined Paul's suite, before the floor would be crawling with hotel security.

Monday 11.30 a.m. I woke to the irritating sound of the phone. Leanne had gone earlier to catch a connecting flight ...

'Hey, oh illustrious Chief, grand master of our Zen Do Kai-martial arts organisation, we await here to do training with thee. Unless, of course, thou has flown away to Qantas paradise and thou soul is floating in torment.' It was far to early for George the Black Panther's sexual harassment sense of humour, but I knew the guys would be keen to train with me.

After sixty seconds in the shower I had my training gear on. Meanwhile, new carpet was being laid outside, wallpaper was being scraped off the passage walls and painters were touching up the ceiling where it was needed. (Paul Dainty would later confide that Rodgers had done his fire-extinguisher trick at a hotel reception area in Singapore four weeks earlier to the tune of a $6200 repair bill.) The previous night's escapade would run to $4800!

George 'the Black Panther' Roumeliotis had our elite Black Belts ready to do it. We trained as if there was never going to be another tomorrow. An hour and a half later we sat around poolside having a swim and then having lunch together. Simon Kirke, Mick Ralphs, Boz Burrell and around half the rest of the entourage had come alcohol-free and foam-free to have lunch with that new minder and his crew.

When Paul Rodgers finally made his poolside appearance, he was in a foul mood: possibly the afterthought of his near-dawn escapade having a price tag of $4800.

'Oi you motley lot, we've go' a six o'clock to Sydney, two o'clock now, so we got three 'ours to pack 'n' be in reception for the bus 'n' limos.

'Good afternoon gentlemen, could you fasten your seatbelts ready for take-off?'

Paul was still in a foul mood, even though the hostess had spoken to us with the voice of an angel. He took hold of both seatbelt buckles and placed them on either side of his crotch.

'Yoo want thar belt done up so bad, well 'ere, yoo do the fookin' thin' up yourself'. He kept mumbling something about, 'travellin' aroun' thar fookin' world, fookin' Customs, fookin' limos, fookin' 'otels, fookin', fookin', fookin' ...'

'I'm sorry sir, I will have to inform my supervisor on this flight.'

Now came the bitch from Hell, wearing all the accessories that said she was the head honcho flight attendant. And she wore a look on her face that matched the mood.

'What seems to be the problem here?'

Was this an ultimatum?

'There's no problem 'ere, ma'am, I just told tha' other hostie tha' if she wanted my seat belt done up, she could do tha' fookin' thing up 'erself.'

'Look here, sir. There's no call for that type of language. With your refusal to do up your seatbelt, I have no choice but to call security from the pilot's cabin'. And off she went.

'Well where's 'er sense of fookin' humour. Matter of fact, where's my minder's fookin' sense of humour?'

Just then I think he sensed I was about to punch him out.

I had to spell it out: 'You want sense of humour, next on the itinerary after security for holding up of the flight comes Commonwealth cops and lock-up and charges for disrupting this domestic flight.'

'Well, if everybody wants the fookin' belt done up that bad, then I'd bettar do the fookin' thing up!' Paul outstretched the belt by the buckles to its full extension and he tied the belt into, I don't know, maybe twelve to fifteen knots.

Now, here came the *brigade* for one last shot. The security guy who was about to do battle with us, Colin Walters, was a long-time employee as a Qantas steward, and he was also a long-time trainee and

Black Belt student of mine. We both smiled, as at this point he didn't know what he was walking into. The flight attendant from Hell, reacting to my smile, spun and caught Colin smiling back at me. She came level to our row and could see what Paul had done: with the expression of a primary school kid he'd grasped his knotted, drooping belt, with both hands and shook the bow-tie buckles ...

'Oi, would this be wha' yoo woz wanting?'

Despite the sexual connotation, the flight attendant from Hell almost collapsed with laughter. Colin almost pissed himself, also due to the fact he'd just avoided a confrontation with his martial arts master.

Mick Ralphs, Boz and Simon were all kneeling on their seats straining to see what mischief Paul had got himself up to – thank Christ I hadn't punched him because I was now laughing as hard as I could, also as a release from how this might have turned out.

Finally, Paul calmed down.

'There, woz tha' so fookin' 'ard; all I wanted woz a bi' o' some sense o' 'umour.
Now I'm in a good mood as well!'

Seemed like no time at all that we'd checked into the Melbourne Hotel, into our usual penthouse, and my next door en-suite, and that it wasn't long before Paul was banging on our connecting door.

'Oye, its nine o'clock in Melbourne on a Monday. I woz just wonderin' wha' mischief me 'n' me minder wood be up to?'

It was now ten years since Victoria's drinking laws had been extended to 10 p.m. Most suburban hotels were now bartering midnight to 1 a.m. licences and the night club scene was negotiating between 3 a.m. and 5 a.m. licences.

Meanwhile, Dragon, one of Melbourne's top bands were playing out on the north side at the 'Croc' (Croxton Park Hotel).
On the way out in the limo, I was telling Paul that Dragon was one of the best bands around and how they'd come across the Tasman to Australia from New Zealand about the same time as Split Enz. I'd got to know Dragon at Sydney's Swap at the Bondi Life saving Club. Two brothers ran the band: wild man Marc and his brother Todd Hunter.

As we entered the lounge, Dragon was *cooking*. Their set at the time included Lou Reed's ode to outsiders, 'Sweet Jane' and some Roxy Music material.

An earlier phone call had the 'Croc' manager clear a couple of tables for us and Paul, Simon and the guys relaxed and enjoyed the show and, of course, the girls, who started to hover around.

In between pranks Paul could be fun. And right now he was having a good time. But sure enough , the *Bad* of Bad Company wouldn't be far away. Dragon had finished their set and the DJ was spinning a couple of Bad Company's numbers, as Marc Hunter and his band's drummer Neil Storrey had come out to meet Paul and the band. Meanwhile, Paul swung his leg high in the air and stomped his heel on the table, shaking glasses and bottles, and turning his gaze to me with a look of defiance.

No don't, I thought, he's just attention-seeking. Ignore it and it'll go away. There was no such luck.

Enter a conscientious bouncer with a northern suburbs' mentality and who doesn't care who the rock star is because he has to abide by the rules.

'Hey you, pop star! How about taking your fucking foot off the table?'

'Oh, so yoo want me fuckin' foot off your fookin' table, do yoo?'

Paul swung his other leg high in the air and stomped it down across the offending leg, knocking over several bottles and glasses, as well as showing off his expensive cowboy boots. He then focused his gaze of defiance back to me.

The conscientious bouncer was probably thinking about knocking Paul's feet back on to the floor. It was then that our eyes met.

If you even touch him, I thought, I'll break every bone in your ugly face.

Two wrongs don't make a right. Paul's foot on the table – that was wrong. This bouncer's attitude – that was also wrong. Whether Paul was right or wrong, it didn't matter: I was being paid to protect him.

The bouncer read my intention; it was as if I'd yelled it at him.

'Yeah, well we'll see about this!' He stormed off, either for a manager or back up.

Either way I had his number. He'd already shown his colours.

'No' as good as th' real thing, bu' it'll do for now.' Paul laughed as he sat up, swinging both feet back on the floor.

This little shit, I thought, he just wants to see me fight. That's what this is all about.

Marc Hunter and Neil Storrey invited the boys backstage. Thank Christ that got us all out of the crowd. For the next half-hour there was some pretty heavy drug-devouring.

I'd gone out front to organise the limos to go around the back of the hotel to the backstage door. Our conscientious bouncer nodded and smiled at me. Had Paul Rodgers also introduced him to his sense o' 'umour, or had the manager or his bouncer buddies told him about me?

A quick trip back into the city saw us at Russell Street's infamous Billboard, one of Melbourne's most established clubs.

Meanwhile, Martin 'Ugly' Debono knew we were coming; he'd organised a bunch of great-looking Billboard regulars, all with the standard bums and tits, in his VIP lounge, which overlooked the entire dance floor and stage area. There were drink cards for everyone. An hour later most of Dragon turned up and there was more serious substance abuse.

'Ugly' had several of my Black Belts working security at Billboard, which made me feel 'at home'.

''Ere Borb, can you help me mate?' Kirke asked.

'Sure mate, what can I do for you?'

'Well mate, I need a hooker, bu' I 'ope I'm no' out of order with a request like this?'

This was certainly different. All those great-looking babes in the VIP lounge and Simon wanted a hooker. I raised my eyebrows at 'Ugly', which was enough of a gesture for him to take Kirke's question personally.

'Sure mate, I'll 'ave one 'ere for yoo in less time than it'd take yoo to knock the top off ya dick!' 'Ugly' mimicked Kirke's accent and organised a hooker for him in less that ten minutes.

'Hi, I'm Mandy.'

'Hi Mandy, this is Simon'. 'Ugly' was always the perfect host.

Kirke and Mandy instantly disappeared.

Bad Company performed great sell-out shows in Melbourne. We'd arrived in Sydney for another sell-out performance, and because it was a gig day, it was meant to be a day off the booze 'n' drugs. The band had heard about Bondi Beach and had decided to spend the day lazing about the shore. My best mate in Sydney, Norman-e Sweeney (Norm-e by now was no longer Billy Thorpe's road manager as Thorpie had packed up and moved to the US) was like 'Ugly'; he could organise just about anything before you could knock the top off ...

By early afternoon we'd decided to wander over to the beer garden at The Bondi-Junction Hotel for some lunch. The boys figured a coupla beers would be the order of the day. Bad Company had *chick magnet* stamped all over them. Paul Rodgers and Simon and Norm-e had been playing pool, and Paul had a run in with a patron who was yelling at Paul (seemed as if this punter's girl had been showing too much attention to Paul or Simon). Norman-e figured he'd fill in briefly for me and yelled at the patron. One of the patron's mates yelled at Norm-e as Simon was asking if all the yelling was necessary.

About now, it looked as if I'd have to get to

work, which would have made Paul happy.

When I appeared in the pool room, everyone, including Paul, were holding their billiard cues by the wrong end. The whole thing could have been messy ...

'Sensei!' (In Japanese the word for a person of knowledge and wisdom.)

'Sensei!'
'Sensei!'
'Sensei!'
'Oosss!' (A sign of respect.)
'Sensei!'
'Oosss!'

All those with a billiard cue in hand dropped them, cracked their heels together and slapping their hands to their sides. The fact they were all yelling 'Sensei!' and bowing their heads as a mark of respect for me was their acknowledgement of the Master of the Black Belt (Steve Fyfield, a fifth-degree Black Belt with a *dojo* in Bondi) who'd been teaching them.

'SENSEI!'

The loudest voice of all came from the Maori bouncer I'd spent a lot of time training, both in New Zealand and here at the Bondi Life Saving Club *dojo*.

'Fook me, a bloke carn't 'ave any fun with Borb Jones as a fookin' minder?' Paul Rodgers was both impressed and depressed – he still hadn't got to see his minder in action.

The band spent another couple of hours fooling around on the beach after more drinks. It proved a couple too many ...

'Oi, Mr Minder, wot would yoo do if some fooker did throw a punch at yer?'

Thanks to the challenge in his voice I attempted the usual one-line throwaway: 'Depends on the situation.'

'Oh!' Paul replied. This wasn't the answer he was looking for.

'Hey Paul, you don't really want to see what he'd do.' Norm-e came to the rescue. 'I have. Trust me – it isn't pretty.'

Paul Dainty arrived for a pre-concert dinner. By then Paul Rodgers had had a couple more drinks.

'Oi, Paul Dainty, abou' this minder o' mine – can yoo tell me wha' 'e'd do if someone threw a fookin' punch a' 'im?' It seemed as if Paul was going to keep this up forever.

Luckily, Simon (the drummer) and Boz (the bass player) took the conversation to the running order of the set that night and if any changes were needed to improve on the last performance.

On the way to the gig, Paul kept drinking from the limo's cocktail bar.

'Oi, wha' if some fookin' idiot threw–'

'It all depends on the situation at hand.'

Backstage at the Hordern Pavilion for another sell-out Sydney show, while the support band was warming up the crowd for the main event, people from the media and the industry – Eric Robinson from Jands Sound Systems, Michael 'Chuggy' Chugg, a couple of sports stars, a handful of special groupies and, of course, the boss, Paul Dainty – had showed up.

Considering it was only a couple of hours since dinner, Paul Dainty had put a fabulous spread on; the caterers had done a real job on the presentation.

There were bottles and bottles of Dom Perignon, caviar, finger food ... Meanwhile, Paul Rodgers was leaning against the trestles with his feet and arms crossed. He asked me about those guys at the pub in Bondi: why did they all bow and what was this *sensei* thing?

As I explained, everything seemed to be goingfine until: 'Yair, but wha' thar fook would yoo do ... Wha' thar fook would yoo do if *I* threw a punch at yoo?'

Oh no! How do I get out of this one? I looked around, Paul Dainty was nowhere in sight; only my best mate Norm-e was listening.

'All right Paul, I guess you won't be happy until you find out. Maybe you should take a shot.' The *maybe* was an attempt at leaving the back door open.

It didn't work. Bad Company's Paul Rodgers came off that trestle with some serious intent and threw a 'king hit'. Had it landed, it would've done more damage to Joe Frazier than the best shot Muhammad Ali ever put on him. But, of course, coming from a leaning and cross-legged and arm's position, it really wasn't that hard to read and slip, causing Paul to lose balance and falter, attracting everybody's attention ...

'Lucky cunt! I bet yoo coodn' do tha' again!'

Paul began to bounce around like you're better-than-average-three-round amateur, so he did know a bit, but that was all. Now he'd bridge the gap and enter the void between him and me, coming at me with aggression. Men have almost died for far less!

I let him get off with four, maybe five shots – I'm sorry Paul Dainty, I really tried! On the fifth shot I slipped, had Paul really overstretch as he missed and that's what I was waiting for ... I hit him with an uppercut to his solar plexus, putting it in just far enough, then snapping it out. His diaphragm contracted that fast I felt it almost grab hold of my fist.

The shock rocked him back into and on to the trestles, right on to the lobsters and caviar and spilt some Dom. Paul Rodgers slowly rolled off the trestles, down on to the floor on one knee. Both hands were crossed over his chest and his face was bluey-purple.

I loved his sense of humour as he looked up at me and said: 'As God is my witness, I swear I'll never ask you, ever, to do thart again'. It took several minutes for his diaphragm to release so he could actually suck in air again.

Bad Company did a fabulous show, and from the moment I hit Paul Rodgers, I never had another problem with him. We'd bonded – exit the smart arse – Paul Rodgers and Bob Jones were buddies!

The backstage after-show party was full of praise for the Bad Company performance. The limos took us back to The Hilton for quick showers for the boys. Norm-e and I were sitting at the same lounge tables that had seen the undoing of Joe Cocker only a week earlier.

First to arrive was Simon …

''Ere Borb, yer know that mate of yours in Melbourne, wha' was 'is name? "Ugly", wannit? Well, yer know 'is lady friend Mandy …'

Norm-e knew what to do, even knowing how to imitate 'Ugly's' accent … 'Sure mate, I'll 'ave one 'ere for yoo in less time than it would take yoo to roon up th' stairs o' the opera 'ouse!'

Within ten minutes a drop-dead gorgeous Sydney version of Mandy had appeared and she and

Simon were gone.

Norm-e, as well as being a getcha-watcha-want kinda guy, was also quite an authority of 'who was who in the zoo'. Later, on the way in the limo to the Swap, at the Bondi Lifesaver, he'd filled Paul Rodgers in on the local scene: 'You know that band you saw at the "Croc" in Melbourne – Dragon? Well, their lead singer Marc Hunter, he's only got one rival thats any competition in the charisma stakes, and that's Bon Scott. He's the former singer of a band called The Valentines and before that he was lead singer in Fraternity. When he joined The Valentines he dug the band more than his married life, so he left his Adelaide wife for the band and they all came over east to work the club scene.'

'All right, 'ee sounds like my kinda guy,' Paul cut in. 'If 'e's on a par with Marc Hunter, then I'm lookin' forward to meetin' 'im. Anyway, tell me oo else is in tha' band?

'Sometime in mid-1974, Bon Scott joined up with a band consisting of three young brothers. Older brother George Young had been with The Easybeats, the middle brother Malcolm Young was responsible for the name of the band AC/DC, which he took from his sister Margaret's sewing machine. Malcolm hooked up his little brother Angus Young as a fellow guitarist in 1973. One year later they hooked up with Bon Scott ... Then last year their first album *High Voltage* sold its tits off. But right now, they're riding higher than ever with a brand new album *TNT* that's just been released and its explosive.'

'Explosive, aye, that's jus' wha' I want: a fookin' explosion. Jus' wha' tha doctor ordered, and aye Norm, thanks for tha local info.'

As the limos pulled up out front of the Bondi-Swap (The Swap got it's name from the idea that if you bought a girl to the swap you weren't supposed to go home with the same girl), I started to think I could've been in for a spot of bother. When Bon Scott had left The Valentines to join AC/DC he'd brought his roadie with him. This guy was about as aggressive as Paul Rodgers.

Back in 1966 I'd worked him at The Catcher. I'd never had to put anyone off from The Catcher for being too violent before – only Mick Hammer. I'd nicknamed him Hammer because when we'd have trouble he'd use one.

Mick had been adopted, and his stepbrother (who'd been one of Melbourne's best streetfighters), Wally Christino thought it much better for his half-brother to use the alias 'Christian'. Everyone was happy when I named him Hammer. As Mickey Christian, he'd been the roadie for The Valentines when he and Bon Scott had backed the Billy Thorpe Band when they'd had a hard time with the thugs at Queanbeyan, when they'd toured the ACT.

Back in Canberra, Mick, along with another roadie (one of my Black Belts) Darryl Cavanaugh, had stood shoulder to shoulder in the main street brandishing a cut-down .303 with its stock reshaped with a target pistol grip.

Now, what we didn't know about the Bondi-Swap on this night with AC/DC, was the fact that eight to ten suburban louts had been hassling Mick Hammer in front of the stage. The band was playing a great set of their most aggressive blues-rock numbers. The louts were giving Mick Hammer the finger and Bon Scott was handling Mick with the line of please leave it Mick, there's too many of them. Fuck, it's like Canberra with Billy Thorpe all over again. Mick please, fuck it, I mean no trouble ...

Enter Bob Jones, Paul Rodgers and Norman-e Sweeney. I'd just enough time to look around; it wasn't hard to pick out the troublemakers. Then it all happened: Mick's eyes met mine. They, in fact, his face lit up like the face on Luna Park. He gave me Shelley Berman's tug-the-nose trick that I'd taught him at The Catcher, then he dove off the stage, through the air on to the heads of a heap of those suburban bozos.

'Norm-e, I won't be a minute. Look after Paul here at the bar. I just have to ...' I was gone – into the brawl to help Mick out.

God, I hoped it was Christian and not Hammer; no, hang on, it could have been worse, it could have been Christian with a .303!

It was just fists and feet. Mick and I were into it. Mick was on the floor with three of them, and I was doing my stand-up routine with five to seven of those suburban brawlers, but not for long: Bon Scott was off the stage with Mick and me! Could it get worse? You know it can and yes, not only Norm-e, but wow, looking much better than your average three-rounder, and punching everybody in sight, was Paul Rodgers.

Then came a couple of bouncers to give us a hand. This made it almost one-for-one standing, with Mick's accommodating now four on the floor. I pulled up so I could keep an eye on Paul, after all that was my job.

'Now I'm 'avin' a fookin' good time!' He was whacking everybody, including a few boisterous bystanders who had bothered to stick their noses into something that didn't concern them.

As the sun was coming up, Bon Scott and AC/DC had long finished their set. It'd been a couple of hours since the brawl and it still made good conversation. Meanwhile, Paul was sounding more like a fighter than a muso, telling the others what a spoilsport I'd been up until that night.

Norm-e, Bon, the band and the Hammer, and I, well, mostly the Hammer and I were laughing about our old times together (his hammer stories are something else).

Paul Dainty had organised an after-show party for the Perth gig. Just about everyone in Perth's rock industry was there.

"Ere, well then, wot's tha worse job yoo evar had?' Simon had asked Paul Rodgers, who was seated half a dozen seats away, in between Perth's local promoter and the rest of the band.

'Fook that worse job shit!' Paul's voice was loud enough to catch the entire party's attention. 'I mean, wha' would yoo doo? Wha' tha fook would yoo doo if yoo come 'ome from tha' pub, aftar 'avin a few pints with tha' ladz? Wha' would yoo doo if you come 'ome an' there in your fookin' lounge room ... in the middle of tha' room, right there on the floor there's this fookin' huge gorilla, fookin' your wife. I mean, wot would yoo doo?'

'Well, fook me, don't really know wha' I'd doo!'

'Well, I mean, would yoo 'it 'im?'

'Nah, I doh'n suppose yoo would. Yoo know, the other Saturdee, I woz at tha football. I woz out tha' back of tha gran'stan's a' tha Birmingham groun',

an' this geeza comes up to me an' 'e says ...'
About now the whole party was laughing.
'"Yoo carnt!"
'An' I said to 'im, "Aye, yoo carn't call me tha'!"
'"Yes I can, yoo carnt!"
'"Nah, its not on. Yoo carn't call me tha'!"
'"I can, in fact, yoo are a fookin' carnt!" Well, I mean, now 'ees gon' too far, 'e carn't say tha' to me can 'e?'

'Nah, nah, 'e carn't. So wha' did yoo doo then?' Simon asked.

'Well, fuck 'im, I 'it 'im, din' I?'

'Well, so you should. Yeah, I'm glad yoo 'it 'im.'

Just about now everyone was falling about on the floor, almost pissing themselves laughing.

'But arh, 'ow come yoo did'n 'it tha gorilla?'

''it tha fookin' gorilla?'

'Yeah, 'ow cum?'

'Well, 'e didn' call me a cunt.'

Now they were in total control ...the transition from a couple of Teddy Boys to rock stars and now to being a couple of stand-ups ...

There was the old geezer that got his dick stuck in the faucet, Winston Churchill's 'one or two bits of fookin' dandruff', and that line of: 'Wot's tha worse job yoo evar 'ad?'

This *bad* company *bad* humour could break out anywhere at any time: flights, restaurants, parties like this one; in fact, I'd seen them in TV interviews and they'd tried to get that 'wots-tha'-worse-job-yoo-evar-'ad' routine going even there.

'Big' Alan Carter, the equivalent of my Melbourne 'Ugly' and Sydney Norm-e, was my West Australian 'man about town.'

"Ere Borb, y'know tha' 'Ugly' and Norm-e?' Simon Kirke was about to make his usual request.

"Ere Simon, meet Marilyn', was big Al's response, proving he could have anything waiting for Simon, even before he'd requested it.

Before we knew it, Simon and Marilyn were both out of there!

And yet another party continued till dawn ...

During another long flight from some city to another, Paul Dainty and Mick Ralphs sat behind me talking about the tour. The pressure must have practically got to nearly all the rest of the crew, who, with nothing better to do, were snoring their heads off. With Paul Rodgers and Boz asleep in their first-row window seats, and Simon and me occupying the first-row aisle seats, I'd figured this an ideal time to discover a couple of *bad* secrets.

'Hey, arr, Simon, how'd you pull up this morning? How was Marilyn? Not that I want to know the minor details, but, you know, did she fill the bill?'

'Mate, do I love Orstralya ... beautiful blonde, fiery redhead and that buxom brunette: Mandy, Maureen and Marilyn. I go' the colour of the 'air; I got the names all startin' with 'M', but don't ask me wha' city they all belong to. I wouden 'ave a clue. Especially now this tour is into its tenth month – that's a fookin' lot of cities!'

'Simon, while we're on the subject, I hope you don't mind but I've got to ask you ... how come you're off with the hookers? Here you are, travelling around the world in the role of rock star. Everywhere you go Bad Company are surrounded by band moles and groupies. Everywhere you look, there's some chick dying to meet the *bad* boys. All of these are free but you always hook up with a hooker?'

'Hey Borb, first up, nothin' ain't free. If it's free, then it's gonna cost a lot somewhere down the line. I should know. I used to be in a band called Free. Now, as for all these groupies and band moles, they're the *bad* company on this tour, all fookin' empty heads. What the fook would they know?' Simon smiled, as if he'd just shared the meaning of life with a good friend.

'Let me pu' it to you this way, Borb. When I'm 'ome off tha road, an' me tap in the kitchen 'as got a leak, well, I calls a plumber, dohn' I? If a light switch is faulty, well, I dohn' fook around, I calls the electrician, dohn' I? Well, it makes sense, if I'm on tha road tourin' and me body needs a service, I call a fookin' professional, dohn' I?'

Well, that was certainly thought-provoking, I said to myself.

'Simon, I got one more for you. You know the Derek and Clive style of humour you guys break into every now and then? You guys ran through that routine in Sydney with Bobby Keys and Nicky Hopkins and Joe Cocker. Last year some of the guys on the Alice Cooper Welcome To My Nightmare tour did it constantly. What I'm interested in finding out is what's the hook; I mean, how come that humour is so popular with all you guys?'

'Borb, Derek and Clive are dark-side personas of Peter Cooke and Dudley Moore. Whenever they're in the studio recording, and they get too zonked, too out of it to continue their legitimate tracks, then they fook around and ad-lib a bunch of the good gear about the "worse job" an' "what tha fook would yoo doo?"

'It's basically a very Cockney thing, Borb. It's Peter and Dudley's way of communicatin' with their roots. Yoo know, that characteristic East End of London, traditionally within the sound of tha bells of St. Mary-Le-Bow Church in Cheapside. They really play up the dialect or accent of the East End Londoners', especially getting' a feel for the uneducated, yet pretentious city person, or in our case, the fookin' pretentious rock stars. Before we were rock stars we all 'ad a worse job. Hangin' with gangs in the early days we all often faced the challenge of "wot tha fook would yoo doo?"

'Then in typical East End ways Derek and Clive really like to send up the superstars. You know, Winston Churchill, Jane Mansfield, Kirk Douglas and the whole fookin' crew. Look 'ere Borb ...' Simon rummaged about in his flight bag.

'O yeah, just as I thought, 'ere's a whole set of Peter Cooke and Dudley Moore bootleg tapes, especially for me minder mate, Borb Jones.'

During the tour Simon Kirke and I bonded, due to the fact that all my life I was somewhat of a frustrated drummer. Whenever we got a chance I'd trade Simon a lesson in self-defence for a lesson in drumming. He was too polite to tell me that my drumming sucked. Simon's street background made him way better than average at martial arts, plus all the drummers I'd taught had a rhythm co-ordination of hand to foot far superior to most of my students with our self-defence empty hand manoeuvres.

The plane began its descent into Adelaide, the famous city of the Joe Cocker bust ...

Suddenly my thoughts were back here with Peter Rudge during The Rolling Stones tour. He'd wanted to see some good local bands, and I'd taken him down to Hindley Street, to the number one club of the time, 'Countdown'. On this particular night a good mate of mine was performing his guts out.

Hey Barb, this guy really rocks; what's his name?'

'Jimmy Barnes! He's good, eh! He really needs to get his arse over to Sydney or Melbourne.'

We were at a table with a bunch of local promoters, record people and the usual pool of *damsels de choice*. It was one of those Hindley Street, Adelaide club-scene stinking hot nights and Jimmy had cranked his system up to heaven.

I really needed a break. 'Peter, I gotta go suck up some air.'

'Hey cool. Take five, but then I'll need ya.'

I was standing on the door of the club, looking every bit the friendly bouncer as I'd done for a decade. Then out of the club waltzes Cinderella. I swear to the good Lord himself, she actually stopped my ticker for about three beats. She was right on 150 centimetres tall; 160 with the heels. She had moderately long blonde hair, the brownest skin colour ... Covering one of the cutest bodies I'd ever encountered was a high-neck, no-sleeves-with-narrow-shoulder-straps snow-white cotton jersey dress that reached to her ankles. She had the cutest bounce as she walked, which made not only her snow-white blonde hair bounce against her shoulders, but it had her breasts bouncing in rhythm with the tap of her heels. She had too much going for her to be part of the rib of any man.

'Cinderella, what are you doing after the show?'

How corny can a guy get? I thought as she passed right on by.

That's when I saw the split in her dress from the heels to just below the curve of her bum, and the shoulders dropping into a deep 'v' at the very bottom of her back. There was definitely no bra and from the smooth shape of that bum, maybe no knickers. (I was keeping the exterior so cool, but inside it was like ten rounds of sparring with Richard Norton.)

Right then, twenty years before Michael Jackson had ever thought of moon-walking, she back-peddled four or five steps until she was eye-level with me.

'I'm not sure, but I'd certainly settle for anything you might have in mind.' Off she strutted down the end of the lane and spun into Hindley Street.

It had all happened so fast, I was left standing there stunned. Maybe I should've chased after her, but that wasn't me. Maybe I should've grabbed hold of her, now that was me!

My five minutes was up, seeing that Peter's last word was 'need ya'.

About an hour later, Peter Rudge had, with some minimum backup from me, put the SA – Adelaide leg of the upcoming Rolling Stones tour to bed. We were all shaking hands and acknowledging a very successful meeting when I felt the softest lips in my ear whispering, 'It's your Cinderella here, I hope you won't be disappointed but my name is ...' She paused, then purred like a very sexy kitten, 'My name is Ursula, and what ever you have in mind is fine by me, as long as its back at my place. My car's out the front with the motor running.'

Peter Rudge was forever the maximum Mr Astute. 'Well Barb, I guess I'll be seeing yo'all at the airport at 10.30 a.m. for that 11 o'clock flight to New Zealand.'

I was really getting into this reminiscence thing when the tyres started squealing on touch down. It was back to reality and Mother Earth.

'Oi, where we all fookin' been?' Paul Rodgers had just broken out of his deep sleep with a gleam of *bad* sparkling in his eyes.

'Hey guys, this is Adelaide, the city of churches. It's been four years since the *big* occasion. Whatever you do, be real careful smoking joints and as long as you're here – no homosexual jokes!'

Perhaps the fondest memory I have of the Bad Company Australian tour was that night in Adelaide after an outrageous concert at the Apollo Stadium. It was close to Ursula's twenty-first birthday so we made the occasion her special celebration. After the show we went back to a bar called 'Bogarts', which was as simple as its name. Humphrey Bogart's photos hung around the walls, but the feature of the place, in one corner and exposed by a single light, was a beautifully in tune (I know coz Paul and Simon told me) highly glossed white-enamelled grand piano: one with a huge lid up on a stilt, exposing the piano's interior, showing the cords that created the melodies.

Simon was with a hooker (courtesy of Big Mick, my 'Ugly', Norm-e and Alan Carter of South Australia). I couldn't remember her name but it didn't start with 'M'. Paul was talking casually with someone whom he thought was the best of the backstage *sexual smorgasbord*. However, what had been so memorable on this night of nights was Simon supporting Paul, playing percussion on a set of bongo's while Paul 'Mr Bad-guy' Rodgers exposed a side of his soul that showed the humane realm of a real nice guy. In front of a capacity crowd of about 120 patrons they played some of their hits, ballads and love songs just for Ursula. It was four years since that first encounter, when we'd gone back to her place. This whole relationship was a two-way sexual gratification trip.

There were no inhibitions, only the experience of total exploration and experimentation.

Paul Rodgers sang to Ursula for three hours and later swapped his penthouse for my suite. The evening was one of the most consummate events of my life.

The tour with Paul Rodgers, Simon Kirke, Mick Ralphs and Boz Burrell had come to an end, but what would Paul 'Bad-boy' Rodgers do for an encore? That last show in Sydney had been a blast: 'Straight Shooter', 'Bad Company' and 'Shooting Star' had bought the capacity crowd to a frenzy. Their latest hit 'Run with the Pack' brought the house to its feet, the crowd screaming for more.

Paul Dainty, as was his tour signature, had put on a totally extravagant party at 'The Bourbon and Beef'. Sally, my favourite Sydney lady of the night, had, of course, taken the night off. Simon had disappeared with Maureen, since she had the meter ticking over.

We were back on the twenty-second floor of The Hilton (made famous during The Rolling Stones tour), and it looked as if this tour was going to have a peaceful ending. Seeing it was all quiet I switched my attention to Sally, whom I'd known from Melbourne since she was a teenager. She was now a professional lady of the night in her mid-twenties.

Sally was serious to the point of being stern but when she smiled at you, she could make a hard man melt. On this particular night we were undressing each other one piece of clothing at a time. Suddenly, Simon's spiel about plumbers, electricians and professional services made sense.

Sally had got the shower running and once we'd got each other's gear off, the whole place was full of steam. She flashed me one of those Sally smiles. I swear to God I almost melted; well, almost ... She began to climb up me like a ladder and wrapped herself around my neck and chest with her arms and legs; her feet crossed and locked at the ankles with the ball of her foot digging into my lower back – now Sally's was about 170 centimetres with, I mean, a long lean body, long arms and long legs with close-to-zero body fat. I had no idea how she'd climbed and compacted her way around me. Her thighs jammed up under my armpits, with her elbows on my shoulders and her heel in the small of my back.

We entered the en-suite, Sally still hugging me in python-fashion. Christ, I could hardly breath. When she began slithering, thanks to the sweat of our bodies and the steam of the shower, she manipulated her body until she was upside down and crushing my back with her arms, my neck between her thighs.

As I carried her to the shower her python assimilation became more interesting ...

Half an hour later we rested on the bed and Sally asked, 'Would you like to experience my spider impersonation?' This is when Sally ...

Just then the phone rang. It was 5 a.m.

'Hey Borb, 'ow yoo doin' mate? Listen man, I need yoo out in tha corridor, fookin' right now! Man, I'm whippin' up a righ' fookin' storm!'

'Oh no Sally, he's done it!' I slammed the phone.

We threw on this special 'twin set of his 'n' hers' Hilton bathrobes and ventured into the corridor. Sure enough, there was *his* storm: water pouring out of the ceiling fire extinguishers, water pouring down the elevator shafts ...

Jesuz, when I'd been here with The Stones, that bitch Mrs Richards had been screaming rape right here and now Paul had a burnt newspaper in hand, with smoke marks on the ceiling around the censors. He had that stupid mischievous kid-like look on his face.

So what next?

I just hung out my 'Please do not disturb' red card on the door knob and closed my door. For the next thirty minutes we could hear firemen, cops, hotel managers and hotel security. Everybody seemed to be there, then it grew quiet, dead quiet.

'Now, would you like me to show you my spider-woman impersonation?' Sally asked. This was the last fond memory of my *bad* company experience.

David Robert Jones came into the world at 9.00 a.m. on 8 January 1947 at 40 Stansfield Road, Brixton, London. He shared his birthday with hero Elvis Presley (1947 was also the year that another mentor, Aleister Crowley, had died). David was an only child and a product of the marriage between Soho club-owner-turned-publicist, Haywood Stenton Jones and Margaret Mary Burns, a theatre usherette.

Haywood, a divorcee on the grounds of adultery, had two children from this previous marriage. Thus, David Robert Jones had two siblings, Terrence (or Terry) and Annette, and behind them was also a family heritage fraught with insanity.

Terry, his older stepbrother (by eight years), had introduced him to the books of the Beat Generation, jazz and philosophy. His stepsister Annette was said to have gone to Egypt with a millionaire businessman and was never heard from again, despite several exhaustive attempts to locate her.

Unfortunately, Terry suffered from schizophrenia and was prone to long, fitful bouts of unexplained weeping. After Terry (now in his early twenties) had returned from his stint of service in The Royal Air Force, younger brother David (now fifteen) could only watch as his stepbrother gradually shut out the world, eventually ceasing to talk. After several years he was discovered in a mental asylum where he remained institutionalised. In 1985 Terry committed suicide.

Many other close relatives had been prone to sudden, mysterious disappearances: aunts and cousins had been hospitalised after being found wandering in the streets.

As a reaction to this home life the Jones boy had become withdrawn, almost a recluse. Terry had earlier turned him on to Franz Kafka's 'Metamorphosis'. This solitude only served to heighten David's innermost emotions, accompanied by the vivid nightmares of grotesque human insects, and the often seeing himself as an unrecognisable monster. David tried to distance himself from these images and, aware of the lunacy that had afflicted his family and that could afflict him, it became imperative that he protect himself by developing new sides to his character.

At Bromley Technical School David had two good friends: art teacher Owen Frampton and his son Peter, who'd eventually be lead singer in the band Herd. George Underwood would become a close friend, although he'd be responsible for the Jones boy's famous odd-coloured eyes. An altercation over a girl had developed into a fistfight, George punching him in the eye, thus hospitalising David. When he returned to school three months later,

David's left eye was stricken with aniscora, paralysis of the pupil, which left him with a permanently dilated pupil that gives the impression that one eye is darker than the other. Their relationship was put under more pressure when they each formed competing rock bands: George and The Dragons and The Konrads.

After graduation from Bromley, David took a job as a 'junior visualiser' with a commercial art company. Then for six months he was employed by a London ad agency. In 1963 he and George got together as the King Bees with Underwood.

In June 1964 seventeen-year-old Davey Jones and the King Bees released their first single 'Liza Jane'. (The recording company was the Vocalion Pop Label – Vocalion had also been Robert Johnson's record label. Robert Johnson from the era of World War 1 and the depression years was the inspiration of almost every rock 'n' roll guitar player.) In November 1965 David had an early taste of national exposure. He was invited to take part in a TV program to defend the rights of young men to grow their hair long, which turned out to be a debate titled 'The Prevention of Cruelty to Longhaired Men'. Later that year he'd record singles with two other bands: The Mannish Boys (which featured Jimmy Page in the session) and Davey Jones and the Lower Third.

David Robert Jones had become hooked on fame at an early age. Like so many of his contemporaries, his first heroes were Elvis Presley and the flamboyant Little Richard. It was not surprising that he'd make a career of reinventing himself. Among his many incarnations and styles of music, this most conspicuous mannequin has been a pop star, a glam queen, an alien, a Warhol devotee, an artist and also an actor.

David gained notoriety for his sexual ambiguity. He'd declared himself gay, then bisexualand played the part of the androgyne to perfection. He was also a married man and father who found himself surrounded by groupies of both sexes. This was acceptable to both he and wife Mary Angela ('Angie') Barnett, the couple agreeing to an open marriage (from March 1970) that would accommodate unrestrained infidelities and Bowie's bisexuality.

At times it appeared that he'd be in danger of being engulfed by his creations, but then he'd pull back from the brink to re-emerge in a different guise. It was during those early years of experimentation that many of his acerbic critics accused him of hiding behind these different personas, attributing his success to a triumph of style over the quality of the performance.

But for this performer, style was always more important than the outrageous costumes and the bizarre makeup. His desire was to elevate stage performance to the status of high art.

In January 1966 David Robert Jones created the major character of his artistic persona. On his nineteenth birthday he deleted Robert Jones from his life and created the nom de plume from his schoolboy fascination with the Wild West – from a popular hunting knife, named after the US' frontier legend Jim Bowie, an almost mythical hero of the Alamo. Thus, David Bowie was born; the media branded it an attempt to avoid confusion with the similarly named member of the US supergroup of the time, The Monkees, who'd found success through their long-running TV series.

My time with David Bowie comprised four tours over more than a decade. I worked as a bodyguard for him as he ventured around the South Pacific. The first of these tours included the 1976 'Black and White' shows, then two years later came the Live on Stage tour. This was followed with, in 1985, the Niles Rodgers-produced Let's Dance world tour. Finally, eleven years after our first meeting came the Glass Spider Tour in 1987.

During my time with David Bowie I used to joke that the press didn't know what they were talking about – of course he had to change his name! How could David Robert (Bob) Jones go on tour with a bodyguard of the same name?

It was always good for a laugh at parties.

Before the Australasian leg of the Black and White tour, when Paul Dainty had wanted Richard Norton and me to protect David Bowie and his entourage, I didn't know much about David Bowie or his music.

Paul Dainty's office had given me the tours' rap sheet with the basics. I'd saved some articles from *Rolling Stone*. The Aussie press prior to him arriving ate up the whole media release thing about his bisexuality. Plus, there was the rock tour gossip scene, but after three years of touring, and the Bad Company experience, I thought I'd be ready for anything.

The gossip grapevine had said that Bowie, at this stage in his life, was doing drugs as if drugs were about to go out of season, that he took even less sleep than Keith Richards (I'd found that hard to believe), and that he and Mick Jagger had a *thing* goin' on.

My first mistake was to listen to the gossip.

The *Rolling Stone* articles I'd kept told of his recent collaborations on 'Golden Years' and 'Fame' with John Lennon, and of his feature in the movie *The Man Who Fell to Earth* prior to landing here in Australia for the Black and White tour.

At the national press conference in Sydney, I'd met his two bodyguards from the world tour: a heavily perspiring overweight ex-New York copper and a sly-looking supposedly ex-Mafia foot soldier (probably the reason his mate was an ex-copper).

Often there can be friction between the tour and the local bodyguards. And from up front this *fat* ex-copper wanted it to be known: he was in charge.

Richard Norton was my constant backup. He was a lot younger than me, but one of the best martial artists in the fighting arts. (As he is even more today, a quarter of a century later.) He'd done almost every tour with me since The Rolling Stones, and taught at our main martial arts school every time I was on the road. He wasn't the violent type at all – there were no street fights or any thing like that. Instead, Richard was the perfect partner to have covering my back.

From the moment he and David were introduced they shook hands, accepted each other and were instant friends. However, when David and I focused eyes, the experience proved daunting. His paralysed and dilated eye told me nothing. His right eye gave an impression of being in a maze. As we shook hands I'd begun to feel intimidated; certainly, not a physical intimidation. I could've crushed his effeminate hand grip or more than dilated his one good eye. He'd challenged me psychologically, even though he was pissed (not that I'd hung out my machismo security blanket); no, he was pissed that I'd made mistake number one: I was judging David Bowie and this was his challenge. My intimidation was a full-on confrontation with his *intelligence* (one whose outcome would lead to an increased personal awareness of my Yellow Dragon).

Within days he'd test me again with a second challenge. It was the night where he and I had gone to Sydney's Kings Cross Manzel Room, a club where industry people hung out on evenings when they weren't working gigs. Richard Norton and the *Mafia* and ex-copper bodyguards were due to meet us some time later, with the rest of the gang. One of Bowie's road crew, I think his major lighting guy, was already there and he'd fitted right in with the local scene – he was off his face and loving it! He sported a long bushy, grey-streaked black beard and black shoulder-length hair and was suddenly engulfed by a Bowie headlock after David had run over to him, leapt on to his lap and passionately tongue-kissed the guy – my first vision was that of Bowie's bright pink tongue slithering into that guy's mouth among his black and grey whiskers.

I'm sure this was Bowie's second challenge to me. However, this time there was no-one sitting in judgement; there was no intimidation. Instead, I swung my attention to my Sydney Black Belts, who were working the door. Our conversation centred on training and nutrition, and which strippers weren't working that night.

The Australasian tour was nothing short of spectacular. David Bowie was and is the total consummate performer and the Western Springs Arena in North Island, New Zealand, along with Wellington, were sellout shows.

That last show down on the South Island at the Christchurch Rugby Football Stadium was noteworthy for two reasons: for the first time I'd gone out front of the house to specifically watch the first three or four numbers of the set. For the entire stage everything was black, then as they announced David Bowie he'd come on dressed in white shoes and socks, white satin trousers and a white satin dress shirt. Then he was floodlit in radiant high-voltage spotlights by his kissin'-buddy lighting guy.

The second noteworthy moment occurred about halfway through the show. Had I not been so fit, I could've easily been killed or at least wound up in hospital on that last tour night.

I'd just done a check of all security areas, and started on the sound mix and lighting console. They had good security. I'd checked the ticket boxes and the front of the house was fine, likewise the car parks. A quick look at fence security saw about 120 personnel and another twenty pit crew, with half a dozen around backstage. All up there were around 160 people doing a reasonable job.

Richard Norton was at his security point, at the left-hand side of stage, keeping his eye on David Bowie. Oh, and the world-tour Mafia boy ex-copper bodyguards who were totally in charge ... of drinking any excess alcohol in the back of the stage area. They were at their posts.

'Oh Bob, I've got a real problem, and I'm relying on you to take care of it for me.' This was an unusual request from my real boss, Paul Dainty.

'What's the problem Paul, I've just done the entire circuit; everyone's doing a reasonable job–'

'I wish it were that simple. No, it's a much more pressing problem than that ... come and look at this! Right in front of the stage: that guy, right there. He's upsetting David so much, that if we don't do something, David's threatening to walk off the stage.'

It was about then that I'd thought of informing the chief of bodyguards before he and his mate drank all the alcohol.

'Hey boys, there's a 120-kilo, two-metre Maori bikie from ... probably the biggest rebel bike gang in New Zealand. He's in front of stage really pissing Bowie off. It might even stop the show if something's not done'.

Talk about pants-shitting! The stutter and the sculling of the Scotch confirmed the response I thought I'd get from the head of security.

By now Richard had come over from the side of stage where he'd been keeping an eye on Bowie. He needed to find out whose job it was to solve the problem of the belligerent bikie.

'Paul, there's two of us here. Richard and I can't count on the New York ex-cop and Mafia bodyguards. There's more than 160 local security personnel, can't any of them talk to him? What about the dozen or so uniformed Christchurch coppers floating around? Our contract states our obligation is to protect David Bowie, and we can't do that if we're both fucking dead!'

I rarely swore in front of Paul Dainty, but this time it was to make a point.

Paul got this real disappointed look on his face ...

'I don't know – I just thought you ...' He turned and walked off.

There was no choice as the words that Ron 'the Con' Blackmore said to me during that first Stones gig came back: 'Hey next week – same venue, same tour managers and promoters – but different bands!'

'Richard I guess it's up to us. Go back to your spot; I'll go into the crowd and make our bikie an offer he won't be able to refuse.' I'd watched the Godfather movies so many times that *offer* routine actually builds my confidence.

Richard, if anything goes wrong, I'll need you with me. I don't wanna die on my own!

My attempt at making some sort of gag of the situation didn't hide the fact that Richard had zero street experience. However, this was our third year of touring together, we'd been in spots before. We never got perturbed, neither of us!

By the time I'd thought this out, I was down in the crowd of around 22,000. I'd worked my way around the far side of the clearing where this overzealous bikie stood. He was just on two metres, with a frame well in excess of 100 kilos, and in full uniform: Cuban-heeled Harley Davidson Biker Boots, black jeans and a no-sleeves blue denim jacket with several hard-earned patches and an emblazoned club-name patch across the shoulders. Wouldn't you know it? He was from one of the three most notorious clubs in New Zealand. Street-smart tells me it's smarter not to mention in print his *family* name. His thick shoulder-length dark hair dripped with sweat. The one accessory he was wearing, the reason for the three- to four-metre circular clearing around him, was the thick-linked one-metre-plus chain bolted to his right wrist, with an actual padlock.

For some time he'd been swinging his body in time to the music, and this chain had followed the arc line of his circular rhythmic motions. After clouting a few heads, he'd created his own magick circle. And the bad news was that he wasn't alone.

The spotlights coming from the sound and lighting console lit this biker up as much as Bowie. No wonder David wanted him out. These spotlights also lit up fifteen to twenty of the same family patch members, mixed in with other David Bowie fans – on average they were about three to four deep between him and the security barrier fence to the *pits*.

My plan was to get a good run at him. I'd need full speed, taking three to four metres, to punch my right fist between his legs, to cradle him up on to the crux of my arm bridged against my bicep. I'd have to lift slightly with this, to elevate him to his toes while reaching up and pulling his hair back and down with my left fist.

During all this I'd have to avoid his chain, while slamming my body into the back of his, so that I'd lose no momentum, to create a self-perpetuating inertia of both our bodies to crash through his mates. My intention, if we were still standing, was to pivot him on his own axis and tilt him over the security fence and follow him into the safety of the concert security pit crew.

Positive visualisation can be a great aid to a martial arts-trained bodyguard, particularly in times of stress, and this was one of those times.

My plan worked like a dream, but then came the nightmare ... As the both of us sprawled over the pit fence, having fallen to the ground, I'd managed to land mostly on top of my adversary. All I needed was the pit crew guys to get the both of us to our feet, and give me a hand to escort this *Mongrel* to the backstage area before his buddies jumped the fence.

But right then I was punched in the back of the head, and was being kicked in the body and the legs. I was meant to be home-safe. Those *Mongrels* in white shirts and bow ties had taken off their colors – they were working as the pit-crew and were getting paid to see the show!

Meanwhile, the bikie underneath me was doing his best to roll over and bite my face off. A couple of his mates came over the fence and several more of the white shirts headed my way.

Richard, please appear with the coppers, and the army and airforce …

I looked up, protecting my head as best I could, to see that the stage was over two metres in height. No-one was visible on stage. All the white shirts close by contrasted with the front of the stage, which was covered in black hessian.

About twenty to twenty-five seconds had passed; until now I'd controlled the bikie by using my centre of balance and natural gravity to pin him under me. But one of his buddy's had got me by the ankle and started to leverage himself to drag me clear, thus making me a better kicking target. I forcefully shifted my forearm to the bikie's wrist with the chain attached to it, and grabbed the chain and ran my hand over the links until there were only a couple left. I rotated my hand three or four times, wrapping the chain around my wrist and hand until there was only about ten centimetres between my hand and his. I lunged with my hips and kicked the guy holding my foot, smack in the face with my free leg.

The sidekick position of my foot ensured that the

edge of my heel and instep busted his cheekbone wide open; there was blood splattered everywhere all over his face and shoulders.

On landing next to the original member of my newly formed chain gang, I slithered across the pit to the edge of the stage, lifted the hessian, rolled under, using every ounce of strength, and dragged my bikie counterpart under the stage with me.

It was pitch black. I had no hope of seeing the enemy but knew damned well that he was on the other end of the chain.

We'd both stood quickly; at 1.8 metres I just banged my head against the floor support beams of the stage. At just over two metres he yelped with pain, shrieking,

'Fuck me!'

I threw a solid shot with my free fist in the direction of his voice, pulling the chain with my other hand. And my fist landed right on the spot that had spoken those words. My next thought was to unwrangle myself out of this *bondage*, but the links had knotted us together like a dog and bitch that needed a bucket of water thrown over them.

With not a drop of water in sight, my intention was to drag him to the back of the stage, which I'd figured was in the same direction we'd come from. While moving backwards in that direction, and dragging Mr Fat Lips with me, after four steps, I tripped over an iron pipe, that caught me behind the legs at the top of the calf muscles. Flat on my arse and shoulders, I instinctively did a back roll, stood up into a crouched position and pulled the bikie into that same iron pipe, except that it caught him across the shins.

'Fuck, mmm!' he tried to yell as he fell on his face and took in a mouthful of dirt.

We now fought tooth and nail in this meccano of a zillion iron pipes holding up the stage, all parallel, horizontal or crossed at 45-degree angles. We punched, kicked, spat and tripped to more than halfway through the under-stage area. Having tripped once, I knew now to backslide – feel the next bar press against my calf, step over it – and repeatedly drag him quickly, shins first into the same bar. Before we'd got to the halfway point he'd lost it, being so full of drugs and half-full of grog he was out of puff. By now I'd had several 'second winds' and was getting stronger by the minute.

Richard had been looking for me, and was I glad to see him. I stood over my prey like one of those rodeo riders that had just dismounted and was about to tie together the legs of the calf he'd run down. I had one foot on his thigh, hoisting the chain high above his head and stretching his arm before wrapping it around his neck, and then wrapping the chain around his face, across his eyes and back down under his ears. When I ran out of chain, as I tried to unhook the links, the New York duo appeared, punching and kicking my now-defenceless captive. I swear to God I nearly lost it. If I hadn't been chained to that bikie prick I'd have possibly killed the both of them.

I screamed obscenities I hadn't used since my gang days. Everyone gathered backstage, they must have all been wondering at that moment if I was in or out of control of this situation. On centre stage Bowie was happy; he'd recaptured total audience attention. Right at that moment in space I thanked my lucky stars for whatever reason that gang had not followed us under the stage.

Paul Dainty (the promoter), Michael Barnett (the accountant), Eric Barrett (Bowie's US tour manager) and Michael Chugg (Paul Dainty's Australasian tour manager) stood around open-mouthed as those New York weak-as-piss bodyguards had backed off from my blitzkrieg and my Maori POW, who was blanched out, almost white. I figured I'd better drop the verbal diarrhoea. No-one had any idea of my level of adrenaline flow, and the high I was experiencing – having just been to Hell and back.

'How ya' doin' buddy?' I'd asked, helping 'the almost cause of my death' to his feet, and as we walked towards the backstage gate. I'd finally unhooked those links and stuffed them down the back of his neck.

'Hey, you ain't half bad for a fucking white boy!' This was his attempt at establishing some sort of rapport between us.

'Yep!' This was mine.

Richard opened the backstage gate.

'Richard, there's those twelve coppers and take a look at the condition this sucker's in!'

'Thanks Bob!' was all that one of the cops had to say as they surrounded 'the life of the party' and marched him off into the night.

'Thanks Bob' was more than I got from David Bowie. It was as if the situation had never happened – there was no 'thank you', or 'Are you okay? Glad you're not dead, kiss my arse, Bob's your uncle ...'

The reason may have been that some time prior and up to the time he'd played in *The Man Who Fell to Earth*, David had experienced a drug-induced relationship with the Spiders from Mars and the bizarre insects that entered the Dreamtime of his inner sanctum. He quite possibly saw that bikie and me as indescribable monsters. It would have pleased him no end to see us simply disappear.

After the Australasian leg of his Black and White World Tour David Bowie returned to the US and his LA pastimes: more drugs; spiders, insects and monsters; and forever, much, much less sleep. Eventually he entered a wipeout period in his life of being totally washed up, emotionally and physically. He was hallucinating twenty-four hours a day.

Late in 1976, while journalist Cameron Crowe was interviewing him for a feature article, David suddenly interrupted, claiming that he'd just seen a man falling from the sky! He ran over and pulled down the window shade and Cameron noted that on the shade 'AUM' was scrawled on a star. Bowie then lit a black candle, claiming that this was a regular occurrence.

At the time he'd been living in a rented house that had been renovated with Egyptian décor. This suited his more-than-passing interest in Egyptology, mysticism and the Cabala. David also had some hodgepodge spiritual guru hang-about who's crux Bowie'd long forgotten.

Then suddenly he awoke and realised everything about this LA lunacy was inherently misleading. It was time to exile himself back to Europe and to get himself back on track.

Thus, it was on to Germany and from 1977 there were two years of convalescence from his LA-aggravated mental traumas.

This exile to a Spartan apartment on the first floor above an auto shop in Berlin had Bowie commenting in 1979 to Cameron Crow that he was 'slowly gaining control over *me* again'. In 1977 he'd collaborated on the first of the so-called Berlin trilogy with Brian Eno (ex-Roxy Music synthesizer wizard), the result of which was *Low*, an accurate reflection of Bowie's mood at the time. Relying heavily on strange, atmospheric instrumentals conceived by Eno (the story goes that Bowie simply ran out of new songs for the second side of the album) the result baffled many, not least RCA and Bowie's manager. The most commercial track, 'Sound and Vision' was a single hit, but *Low* can now be seen as a prelude to the electrifying *Heroes* album. Recorded in the Hansa Studio, a mere 350 metres from the Berlin Wall, this was Bowie at his most ambitious, confident and inspired.

Heroes was an artistic triumph, as was the third Berlin recording, *Lodger*, which retold the age-old myth of the figure condemned to wander the world for eternity, summed up in the track 'Fantastic Voyage'.

In late 1979 David Bowie and Brian Eno had moved on to Switzerland to complete their trilogy. While in Switzerland, David finalised his divorce from Angie and acquired custody of their son Zowie, now eleven years old, and known as Joseph.

Bowie re-emerged in public halfway through this two-year self-imposed cleansing period; first, to play keyboards on Iggy Pop's US and UK Tours; and second, to undertake a tour of his own. This was documented in the live album set, *Stage*. Prior to this Live on Stage World Tour I was determined to learn as much as I could about the history of the act I was about to protect once again.

This time the tour security liaison was a large African-American. He was real easy to get along with and made life much smoother than the previous so-called bodyguards from the earlier tour. Although he also did nothing, he didn't even bother to look busy.

After the show at the Melbourne Cricket Ground (MCG), Bowie and his guard, and Richard and myself, had gone to one of the King Street strip's most established nightclubs: The Underground.

Brian Goldsmith, a good friend of mine, was the originator and at this time still-owner of the club. He'd bowled over to our table, looked at Bowie and his African-American security chief and asked, 'Which one of you guys is David Bowie?'

'Why, he is of course, you silly thing!' Bowie had answered, pointing with the index fingers of both hands at his tour security boss.

'Now come on David', Brian fell for the ploy, 'buy this nice man a drink before he gets confused and thinks our bodyguard Robert Jones is David Bowie.'

That night was about as life-threatening as it got on this tour and David handled it admirably. Plus, between his earlier security entourage and the present security chief, I'd learnt a lesson from the three of them that I would never forget: to try and do absolutely nothing. This way any little thing you might have to do will be noticed by everyone. But, then again, I don't think that'd be me.

The Let's Dance tour of 1983 got us all back together for the first time in five years, and this tour was the best acceptance David Bowie had given me. Finally, I'd felt that I was looking after a good friend.

On another of those long flights from one city to another we got to talking about rock 'n' roll and one of its once-familiar names.

'David, whatever happened to Bad Company's Paul Rodgers? I was touring with him just before that very first tour with you, and I haven't heard anything at all about him lately.'

'Well Bob, just last year Led Zeppelin's Jimmy Page, after several years of terrible misfortunes, including his drummer's choking on his own vomit, consented to provide the film score to *Deathwish II*. Early this year he formed a completely new act: The Firm. And he did that with former Bad Company lead vocalist Paul Rodgers.

'Paul Rodgers and his hit single 'Shooting Star' is the epitome of what happens at the pinnacle of any rock star's career. I hear you're building a martial arts empire here in the South Pacific. If you keep expanding, possibly even around the world, you'll have to be careful not to become a shooting star. In my industry, and it's the same in any business if you have one hit after another, and you just get bigger and bigger, you become a shooting star, and pretty soon you explode and disintegrate. To build longevity you need to come in waves, establish highs and lows in your career. What I try and do is alternate my writing style: I do one album purely from a commercial standpoint – that is, mass sales – then I do my next album for my diehard fans. It's not as commercially successful, but it keeps my base strong. And I can keep building from a strong base. If you can adapt that principle to your self-defence schools, you'll probably go around the world.'

I'd take much of this advice on board. It formed one of my many business strategies learned from these years of touring.

Back in 1967 Bowie had spent some time in contemplation. His pop career had faltered and he was left wondering whether he should become a serious actor – and pursue his interest as an artist – or carry on with his music. In 1994 he had his inaugural art exhibition.

Over the years Bowie's love of self-expression and creativity has developed with his passion for art, which he now sells on the Internet at www.bowieart.com. During his peak in the 1970s, Bowie was a hugely influential artist: his restless spirit, sexual ambivalence, effortless cool and unwillingness to settle into one image or style of music inspired thousands of younger musicians.

By 2000, David Bowie would float himself on the stock market as a public company. This would help him to become one of the wealthiest men in England. He would release a dual-interactive new album and a CD game with a downtown raunchy French theme. More concerts would ensue. David Bowie just keeps on keeping on ...

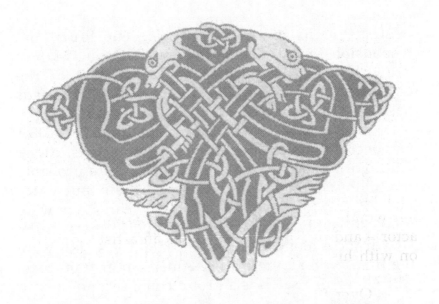

> Sydney (KvP) Torsdag 3.3.1977 Medan ABBA och resten av Australien sover vilar ett par bla argusogon pa dem, de tilhot **'BOB JONES'** som ar, om han ursaktar att jag sagger det, den mest osannolika **'GORILLA'** jag nagonsin har sett. Det kan man knappast sagas om Bob Jones. Han har valborstat tjockt rott har som hanger till axlarna.

The above Swedish extract was part of a full-page write-up. Its heading read as follows;
>   ABBA'S DYGNET-RUNT-VAKTER:
>   KARATEDEMONER I POPKLADER!

The article, from Sweden's leading daily, was an attempt to keep its readers assured that the four members of ABBA would be in safe hands in the South Pacific. The article described the two Australian bodyguards as well-muscled martial arts experts, one of which had shoulder-length flaming red hair and the protective instincts of a *gorilla*. The journalist responsible for this description was Sweden's Monica Braw; she'd flown to Australia as part of the entourage. Her job was to report home to the fans news of ABBA's life on the road in Australia.

By the time they'd toured down under, ABBA had become one of Sweden' big three exports. Along with Bjorn Borg and Volvo cars, they were probably the biggest money-spinners. From their tour dates in 1977, and for the following three years, they were unquestionably the most popular performers in the world, and along with Australia's Bee Gees, they were the first to break the British–American grip on rock. ABBA's record sales as a group come second only to The Beatles.

The name of the band was devised by taking the first letter of each of the band members' first names. The first 'A' was Anni-Frid (Frida) Lyngstad Fredriksson (vocalist), the fiery red-haired siren. She was strong-willed and extremely forthright whenever the occasion demanded. A conscientious mother, Frida was always concerned about the whereabouts and welfare of her fourteen-year-old son and nine-year-old daughter who'd come to Australia for the tour.

Next came Benny Andersson (keyboards), the placid one, who was almost totally relaxed all the time. Out of all of the band members, Benny was the most at home on the road. When it came to Richard's and my martial arts physical training, he much preferred to talk about fitness. He was extremely good-natured and the joker of the troupe.

Benny had also brought his twelve-year-old son with him.

Frida's and Benny's three children were from

previous relationships. On this tour Frida and Benny were an item and within a year they'd marry.

Bjorn Ulvaeus (guitar), although very well-read, seemed the worrier, prone to uptightness offstage. And yet, he always knew what he wanted and was very precise in thought and action. His relationship with Anna was very close and loving, and for the most part he was the unofficial spokesman of the group.

Agnetha (Anna) Faltskog appeared almost fragile, but not as quiet as we'd assumed. She had a very well developed sense of fun and was very feminine, affectionate and liked to relate to others – even to the extent of touching during a conversation. Her three-year-old daughter Linda had stayed at home with family. Anna missed her constantly; she was also a couple of months pregnant with Christian.

After the tour, by the time Frida and Benny would marry, Anna and Bjorn would separate. By 1982 both couples would be divorced.

Before ABBA had come together as a foursome, all the members had established themselves individually in the Swedish music scene by the early 1970s.

Frida was born in Norway but raised in Sweden. She'd arrived in Stockholm in 1967 at the age of twenty-two, and had been having some success with her solo singing career.

Benny (born in Stockholm) was playing with a band called the Hep Cats. Meanwhile, Bjorn had led a successful band called The Hootenanny Singers during the late 1960s. Finally, a seventeen-year-old Anna was also starting to make hit records at this time.

By 1970 Benny was living with Frida and in July 1971 Bjorn had married Anna. This had become something of a national event in Sweden as both were now well-known identities and thousands of fans were at the wedding.

Each of them had been unhappy with the lack of direction and progress within their respective groups. Unknowingly, both of the guys, within a short time of each other, had quit what they'd been doing and joined Stikkan (Stig) Anderson's record company, Polar Music. (Stig would go on to become the manager of the band.) It was here that they learned the art of production while composing material for themselves and others.

During the cutting of the album *Lycka*, both girls were brought in to add some backing vocals. A fun atmosphere developed among the four of them, which led to some live gigs. Eventually, as they all contributed more and more to the recordings, they came together as a group, and between 1971 and 1973 they worked on and polished their stage act. The intention, although premature, was to then represent Sweden in the Eurovision Song Contest as a means of gaining some international recognition.

For the 1973 contest they sang 'Ring Ring', but in 1974 in Brighton, watched by an estimated TV audience of 500 million, even against very strong opposition, they were declared outright winners with 'Waterloo'. Thanks to such exposure this jaunty, catchy single instantly made the top of every national chart in Europe, and reached as high as number six in the US. They became household names in Australia, with both 'Waterloo' and 'SOS' (1975).

Bjorn's and Benny's production on these songs was backed up by an attractive and wholesome group image. Their act was now superbly professional and their material had hit a winning formula. It was very tuneful, easy on the ear with its pleasant harmonies and had appealing hooks in the melody. And above all, it was all so sing-along and danceable.

For all these reasons the hits just kept coming. In 1975 they produced 'Mamma Mia' and in early 1976 came 'Fernando', followed by their trilogy of chart-toppers: 'Knowing Me Knowing You', 'The Name Of The Game' and 'Take A Chance On Me'.

Due to the fact the boys had taken the production to such a superb level, the band was reluctant to play live. However, in 1977 they undertook a world tour, complete with a seventeen-piece string orchestra, two drummers, two extra guitarists, an organist, a moog synthesizer keyman, and a small army of technicians.

'Richard, is that you? Richard we've both died and gone to heaven. You're not gonna believe this!' I'd called Richard Norton at the Immigration Department.

'Mate, I've just spent a couple of hours with Paul Dainty and he's booked us to bodyguard the two girls from ABBA.'

'You're right, died and gone to heaven! That's us!' Richard's initial response was followed by, 'It's an even better deal if I get to look after Anna and you Frida. That'll make a couple of blondes together, and a couple of fiery redheads together!'

Funny thing was, that was exactly how Paul Dainty had said he'd wanted it ...

'Bob, it sounds like Frida and Benny are the extroverts who like to party and are prone to occasional outbursts. I figure you'd be more suited to them. Bjorn and Anna are a more introspective couple, perfect for Richard's personality. Plus, this way we have the coincidence of a pair of blondes and a pair of redheads, classic match-up security'.

It turned out that none of us could have been more off-centre. Although Paul was right on with his concept of matching us up (when it came to our appearances on TV) it'd only been a year or two since Australia'd got colour TV, it was still quite a novelty for a touring band as spectacular as ABBA to be presented in full colour, and *we* did all stand out!

On every international tour that Richard Norton and I'd worked on together, we'd had this friendly contest to see which of us could get any members of the crew (for example, sound and lighting guys) or of the band, its leader, or everybody, to train in the martial arts with us. There was an unofficial grading points system or simply *feathers in our cap* if we would get them interested in training in the shortest period of time from the commencement of the tour dates.

Since poor diets, a lack of any form of exercise, or of normal sleeping hours, plus too many cigarettes, too much alcohol and copious amounts of drug-taking were so prevalent among almost all the bands we'd looked after, Richard and I both figured we were doing them a huge favor if we could get them *hooked* on our routine, even if it were only for the time they'd be with us. Any break from such negative social activities for any amount of time would be feathers in our caps in the eyes of the promoters and the bands management.

ABBA arrived in Australia for a summer tour, in a time of dismal overcast skies and tropical storms that threatened with strong gusts. The band had managed a good night's sleep to combat the jet lag they'd suffered after such a long flight. I'd introduced myself to Bo Norling, the band's tour manager and suggested a drive around the traps, including the venues. As we drove around Kings Cross, and then on our way out to the venue, I made small talk about the tour with Paul Rodgers and Bad Company, how on that last night the sprinkler system had flooded the entire floor. That mishap had got all future touring rock 'n' roll bands barred from staying at The Hyatt Kingsgate up the top end of Darlinghurst Road, where Kings Cross invites everyone into Sydney's flashing bright lights and sinister dark side. Instead, we now all stayed at the downtown bottom end of Darlinghurst Road at the Sebel Townhouse.

During the last half a dozen tours everyone had gotten quite used to the Sebel and its reputation of having almost zero staff turnover. After a while we knew everyone on a first-name basis, of its inhouse 24-hour limousine service with Maxs' Limo Service where even Max the owner would stay out all night looking after us if need be. The Sebel was a smaller hotel than most five-star complexes. That way, no matter who we were looking after, between the corridors, lobbies, pool, gym, foyer and famous club bar, we'd forever be bumping into the Elton Johns or Rod Stewarts, or anyone else staying there.

It was just like one big family, with an unwritten law that no-one should muck up such a good thing – and most times, everyone abided by this rule.

When opened by businessman Harry Sebel in 1963, the owner of the Sebel and his manager Henry Rose were to as rarely as possible say *no* to any request; that is, anything and everything that most (almost every) other hotel would consider as unreasonable, the Sebel considered a normal part of customer service. Hence, if somebody wanted a typewriter and a glass of freshly squeezed orange juice at 3 a.m., then it was a typewriter and orange juice with a smile that was promptly delivered.

Accepting the bad with the good, The Sebel always had celebrities on board: this meant it was often a gathering place for fans as well as stars. The staff always worked in well with us bodyguards, helping to keep autograph-hunters at arm's length, or at least on the opposite side of Elizabeth Bay Road from the hotel. ABBA and The Bay City Rollers were just two of the acts that caused hundreds of fans to mill around the entrance for a glimpse of their heroes. However, a simple request from the *maître d'hôtel* would have them line up across the road in an orderly fashion.

Former general manager Nick Truswell had started as duty manager in 1971. He'd had more than his fair share of rock 'n' roll excess to deal with.

'Led Zeppelin were a wild lot,' he recalled. 'Not because they were all that difficult, but because it was during the time of everybody being into the sex, drugs and rock 'n' roll thing.'

Nick could recall only one TV set being thrown from a window during his lengthy reign and he couldn't remember who threw it.

But he does recall, however, the England Cricket team, including Ian Botham, dressed in drag, using water-filled balloons as ballast. They'd flooded the dance floor as a result.

Everyone from Frank Sinatra to Tori Amos has been seen balancing on the barstools in the Sebel Club Bar. Nick had been best man at a handful of impromptu weddings in the hotel's lobby and Shirley Maclaine liked to cook her own porridge in the kitchens.

During its thirty-seven years the Sebel had been home to all major acts and celebrities passing through Sydney. Elton John had married there, as had Mark Knopfler, and towards the end Sheryl Crowe, Art Garfunkel and U2 had been guests. The traditional post-ARIA Awards in October 2000 were the last major hurrah party for the hotel that had been witness to some of the most eccentric guests – and had always done its best to accommodate even to their most bizarre eccentricities and requests.

By 2000 the Sebel Townhouse, as it was known to all of us, would be torn down to make way for a block of luxury apartments. A very rich part of Sydney's heart died that day. The entertainment industry will be hard-pressed to find a new home with customer service even similar to the once-legendary Sebel of Sydney.

Bo Norling, ABBA's tour manager, was impressed to have learned so much local goss' and to have had such a quick look around the traps, simply by the time we'd gone with Max and his longest stretch-limo (still a big thing for me) to the venue and back.

But then Richard Norton had me impressed – while I was away he'd broken all our tour records for minimum time–maximum performers training in our martial art.

Bjorn Ulvaeus had woken from a good night's sleep; Anna was still catching up on her beauty sleep, as were both Frida and Benny. Bjorn had showered, donned his tracksuit and rang for his bodyguard to accompany him on a morning run. One of Max's other drivers had taken Bjorn and Richard down to the Reg Bartley oval in Rushcutters Bay Park. When they'd got there, however, it was pouring with rain; of course, this created the problem of Bjorn catching a cold, losing his voice. The morning jog was abandoned.

'See if you can find an indoor swimming pool,' was his next proposal.

Richard and the driver tried, but the torrential rain had set in solid. Besides, many of the leisure centres around Sydney were closed tighter than a clam. It was decided, thanks to Richard, that it'd be better to give the rain and traffic a miss.

However, Bjorn really wanted to do his morning exercises. This in itself was something totally new to us – someone in the rock 'n' roll industry actually wanting to work out!

Now ABBA hadn't even been in the country twenty-four hours and Bjorn hadn't even been out of bed an hour yet!

'Why don't you let me run you through a martial arts warm-up?' Richard was really hopeful.

Bjorn was agape. 'Why not? I'll try anything once – long as it doesn't kill me.'

They'd been working out for about ten minutes in the aerobics area of the Sebel gym next door to the pool when the girls arrived, complete with music tapes, tights and leotards, all set for one of their daily jazz ballet routines – their way of keeping in shape.

Anna and Frida watched for a couple of minutes. Seeing how different it was to anything they'd been used to, they asked, 'Mind if we join in?' Richard had created an all-time record: 75 per cent of the group in just on twenty-four hours!

Benny heard the noise and had wandered up to the gym with a cup of coffee. He sat on the bench press and watched the proceedings with great interest. (That was as close as Benny ever got to our exercises, but he used to laugh, pat his stomach and always promise to get in with the action soon.)

As already mentioned, Paul Dainty's tip for how Richard and I should fit in with the band wasn't so clear-cut. As it turned out, our first night in Sydney pretty much set the format for the whole tour. My couple, Frida and Benny, had three children with them. We would all eat at the hotel restaurant at night. After dinner the family would settle into their penthouse for an early night. I'd leave the door of my suite next door to them open, just in case, and kick back to watch a bit of television.

Meanwhile, Bjorn and Anna had said to Richard, 'We've heard all about Sydney's Kings Cross, we want to see it from top to bottom.'

At about 5 a.m. Richard had come up to my

room. 'Man, I had to take them to every place in town. For a couple of rock stars who don't do drugs, they sure have got some energy! "Take us here, take us there, take us everywhere!" They never let up. What did you get up to with the outrageous couple?'

'Oh, we just kicked back, had a lazy one. Watched a bit of telly. That was cool.' I had to lie through my teeth about it being cool.

The next afternoon saw the holding of the national press conference at the Sebel's Convention Centre. Paul Dainty had certainly whipped up a storm with his pre-tour marketing strategies. Everyone was here, as well as several international journalists, media from every state and by the look of it from just about every major country centre. ABBA were sitting up on stage behind a large trestle with a microphone each. All of them looked very sporting, all decked out with their new Bob Jones martial arts uniforms, giving them the appearance of being really comfortable. They were pleasant, answering questions about drugs and the trivia that they were just not into. I kept hoping for some researched questions about their backgrounds, music and song-writing. Instead ABBA explained how, since arriving in Australia, their bodyguards had put them on this fantastic fitness regime of martial arts training. The press, all of them, ate it up. (By halfway through the tour, press articles and pictures of Richard and me getting ABBA fit and teaching them self-defence had been beamed all over Australia and Europe.)

About halfway through the press conference, without any warning and totally unexpected, a very poor-imitation Elvis Presley appeared, complete with brushed-back black hair, ear-lobe-length side-burns, black suede shoes, black-flared bell-bottom pants and, wait for it, a purple shirt with the pointed collars turned up, buttons undone down far enough to expose a hairy chest and at least a dozen thick gold-plated theatrical chains. Plus, of course, not dark but black thick-rimmed extra-large sunglasses. Not that the shades are out of character in rock 'n' roll except that it'd been overcast with a torrential downpour for most of the day.

Rather than instantly move in and evict this Elvis clown out on his arse into the middle of Darlinghurst Road, I thought I'd better check with somebody, just in case Elvis was a simpleton Kings Cross cronie who'd conned his way in.

By now, Elvis was strutting up and down, right in front of the group, and telling some of the television camera crew that they were working far too close to the band.

Just then I saw my mate, Patty Mostyn (Paul Dainty's Sydney publicist).

'Patty, who's the walking gold mine in the black glasses? I'm thinking seriously of bouncing him on his arse out of here.'

'Oh no, Bob, don't do that, that's Tom Oliver, the actor. You know Tom, from "Number 96" and "Bellbird". Someone said he's moonlighting as a security guard. I even thought he was a third bodyguard working with you and Richard.'

I couldn't believe it; I'd known Patty for a few years and that smile, or something in her body language, said that something here was out of whack.

About an hour after the press conference we were all back at the Sebel Club-Bar. There was an air of excitement, thanks to the success of the afternoon's media meeting. Suddenly, in came Elvis, a.k.a. actor Tom Oliver, who'd bowled straight up to Frida and

Anna and commenced laughing and joking like he'd known them since high school. Eventually, he asked both girls, in quite a loud voice, loud enough for the whole bar to tune into the conversation, 'Well, Frida and Anna, what did you both think?'

'Oh, the whole thing was fabulous,' Frida replied.

'Tom, you were the best – you trick everyone!' Anna's positive reply had everyone in the bar nodding and murmuring about how well *it* had gone down.

'Ladies and gentlemen, can I have your attention? There's one man among us whom I really respect, therefore I really value his opinion about this – and that's Mr Bob Jones. Bob, tell me, what did you think?'

What did I think about what?

Patty Mostyn hadn't told me anything, neither had anyone else. I could've told her what I really thought about Elvis and his stupid outfit that almost got this actor's arse kicked earlier that afternoon. But judging by the reaction of everyone there so far, I went along with the flow.

'Well Tom, the girls were right, you were fabulous. And you definitely did trick *everyone*.'

'Ladies and gentlemen, did you hear that? Straight from a *real-life* bodyguard, the best, and he thinks *it* was great! Christ, now I do feel like a real bodyguard. I know we *got* all those journalists, and they all thought I was moonlighting by working as a bodyguard for ABBA!'

A couple of hours later, after several opportune questions, I finally learned that there was going to be a full-length movie of ABBA in concert. The idea was the brainchild of Reg Grundy, who put up 25 per cent of the deal, with ABBA, who were to be 75 per cent partners in the venture. Bob Caswell wrote the film, and it was to be directed by Swedish film whiz kid Lasser Hollstrom, who'd been labelled as 'the new Ingmar Bergman'.

The basic plot was Ashley Wallace (played by actor Robert Hughes), a resident DJ at a not so well-known country radio station, worked a dead-end midnight-to-dawn shift. This station's only executive got the bright idea that the station's failing ratings would definitely soar through the roof if only their all-night DJ could get an exclusive interview with the hottest band in the world, ABBA, which any reporter would know was a downright impossibility.

Armed with a tape recorder and a lot of guts, Wallace followed the four Swedish singers around Australia, bursting late into press conferences, pushing through crowds and always trying to outwit the bodyguard (Elvis a.k.a. Tom Oliver).

'That's it Bob, and as well as the bodyguard I also play a very gay butler, an ocker taxi driver, a golf caddie, and a dirty old barman in a wild west saloon. It's quite challenging for me, playing these different parts. It's a ridiculous comedy, but we're all having humungous fun doing it.

'The film is going to include a lot of scenes from this tour as it happens, including concert appearances, backstage scenes and press conferences. As we go, the footage is mostly shot secretly for an air of realism.'

'That's a great way to catch realism on film,' I said, thinking how real it would've been if I'd kicked his arse and bounced him across the bitumen out front of the Sebel.

Tom continued: 'The DJ will annoy ABBA

during a picnic at a beautiful outdoor setting, during a game of poker in a smoke-filled room and while they're trying to relax on their boat. Robert Hughes, the DJ, will be the only media personality to get aboard. At another time he will share their picnic, with Anna and Frida tempting him with berries and wine. In his dreams he'll be seduced by the girls.'

On one of those long flights from one city to another we'd taken up all the first-class, business-class and about the first twenty seats of economy.

The talk about a movie of ABBA in concert, and the relationship of the group to Tom Oliver, *their* bodyguard, had me thinking back to my American tour, and the guy that had started all this celebrity body-guarding and movie stuff: Bruce Lee, in his role as The Green Hornet, himself a famous martial artist playing the bodyguard to a celebrity.

It was also Bruce Lee who had inspired me in 1975 to develop the idea of Richard Norton and Bob Jones getting *their* own TV series called 'The Bodyguards'. This was three years before 'Miami Vice' (1978) and four years before the British version, 'Minder' (1979).

It was only during these long flights that I could find the time to dream up thirteen one-hour episodes, commencing with a two-hour feature pilot called 'The Final Twist'. Toshiro Mifune, in our correspondence, had been impressed with my idea of two expert martial arts Western bodyguards fighting crime and evil forces while at the same time adhering to the Asian concept of Bushido (martial arts valor). He was the most famous actor in Japan at the time (he'd just completed *The Red Sun* with Charles Bronson), due to his involvement in *The Seven Samurai*, a Japanese epic that was remade in America as *The Magnificent Seven*.

Meanwhile, my earlier exchange with Tom Oliver now had him working out with Richard and I during our routines almost daily.

In between tours I found time to work with a well-known Melbourne journalist, Jim Simmonds. Jim also was a practitioner of the Korean martial art Tae Kwon Do (the first style that I'd trained in with Jack Rozinsky). Jim, sympathetic to my cause, had worked with me on the first three episodes, including the two-hour pilot. The second episode was titled 'The Bakers Dozen'. This was about a sinister gang of twelve of the most notorious bikies coming together from different gangs, to form one powerful and impenetrable gang. Of course, I would gain acceptance into this inner-sanctum; hence, 'The Bakers Dozen'. The third show was to be called 'The Missing Link' and Jim did a great job on this screenplay. The story line had Richard and I training with Masutatsu Oyama at his Kyokoshinkai-Kan (his headquarters in Tokyo). Mas Oyama, a tenth-degree Black Belt, the highest achievable level and depicted by the wearing of a solid red belt, was the highest profile martial arts master of the time. His empire of karate, with multiple millions of students, was spread around the globe. Like Mifune, Oyama was excited about the concept, and its potential to market the martial arts to a broader audience. This episode also had Richard leaving me in Japan to train with Oyama, while he went to Okinawa to save a damsel in distress. This would see him fighting in a death match in an Okinawan Buddhist temple in the mountains.

We couldn't get the series off the ground. The powers to be reckoned it would be too much of a risk committing money to an unknown concept that starred a couple of unknown martial arts bodyguards. As it turned out 'Miami' and 'Minder' broke all ratings records. It also turned out that Richard by 2000 had acted in more than sixty movies worldwide.

Just as the Qantas jet started its descent, there was a cry of, '*Eear – yuk!*' It was the blood-curdling scream of our newest martial arts student – movie bodyguard, Tom Oliver. He'd sprung out of his seat and leapt into the aisle in a Ninja stance (I don't even know who taught him that one) to ward off actor Robert Hughes a.k.a. country DJ Ashley Wallace, who was simply heading up to the first-class toilets.

'Oh no you don't!' was the strict command of ABBA's so-called *bodyguard* as he requested the DJ to use the toilets at the back of the plane and not to go anywhere near the group. With this, everyone present broke up with laughter.

The more shows ABBA did the better they sounded. And that wasn't an easy thing to do – the first show was near perfect. Swedish journalist Monica Braw kept interviewing me for behind-the-scenes snippets of news to send back home. I kept flirting with her as if she had a bounty on her head.

Before every show, as ABBA were about to go on stage, Anna would ask: 'Oh Richard, where are you taking Bjorn and me tonight?'

Whereas, when it came to Frida it was, 'Oh Bob, where are the kids? Promise me you will look after them while I am on stage.'

So much for the two fiery redheads together.

The next clash with the bodyguard, the DJ and the film crew didn't happen until we hit Melbourne for three packed-out shows at the Myer Music Bowl. Naturally, every time Tom would appear to play his part in the movie, either Richard or myself, or the both of us, would be there.

At the first show in Melbourne, down on the right-hand side of the stage, with all cameras strategically out of sight, there was Tom the *bodyguard* hassling Ashley Wallace, that conniving DJ still busting his arse to get to ABBA for his interview. Again, the *bodyguard* had a problem with all of this – according to the script, of course.

In the name of realism, no-one had told my Black Belts on backstage security. (Why should I tell them – no-one bothered to tell me?) They figured Elvis to be a part of the whole travelling circus; after all, he was wearing his access-all-areas pass. The aggressor, Ashley Wallace, certainly did look like your average country DJ trying to con his way backstage (thanks to good casting agents). Robert Hughes, in his capacity as actor, kept trying to explain to my Black Belts as they bounced him off the stage and continued to bounce him over to the side exit of the Myer Music Bowl perimeters; never to be allowed entry for as long as he would try.

'Listen, it's this movie deal, you know we're pretending,' he'd insist. 'Oh, you know Bob – Bob Jones! Well, I know Bob. If you could just ask him, he'll tell you I'm not just a DJ trying to get backstage, I'm really this actor, and it's my ...'

'Yeah, sure man, we'll tell Bob Jones. He's got

nothing better to do than listen to a bullshit story like this. It's not like you're the only one that wants to get backstage and, you all know Bob Jones.' Frank Chick, who looked after backstage would then inform the exit gate security, 'Hey, Tum Joe, this guy's not a DJ, he's a movie star!' *Wink, wink.* 'It's Mel Gibson! Will you make sure he never gets in here again?'

All the bouncers around this exit gate would laugh their arses off.

However, there was a problem in Sydney. Each day's shoot was being filed and sent there for previewing, before going on to Sweden with the band after the tour. The producer, director and the editor viewed the rushes daily, and every time ABBA appeared there were these two guys that looked like they could be related to the group, or they at least look like they were really serious, real-life bodyguards.

'Who are these men? What are they doing here?' the producer would ask; after all, he was paying the bills.

'They're the real-life bodyguards. What a pity we didn't pre-plan this into the script!' the director, as any director would, replied.

I could just see Richard and me, with those black glasses, turned-up collars and purple shirts, and all those gold chains hanging around our hairy chests. What hairy chests?

'What if we write them into the script? Have them do something that makes them look like understudies to Tom, the boss of the *bodyguards*?' The editor knew that if he edited out Richard and me every time we appeared on film, instead of a feature movie, he'd wind up with a ten-minute documentary.

'When they come back to Sydney for the finish of the tour, we'll think of something.'

The third and final show in Melbourne at the Myer Music Bowl drew by far the biggest crowd and it was the most spectacular of the shows. Thousands of fans roamed the exterior's perimeters. They either couldn't get tickets, or were there because the sound was great (never mind not being able to see the band).

After the show, Frida, Benny, Bjorn, Anna, Richard and I bailed into the limo in the security compound at the rear of the Music Bowl, and proceeded to head back to our hotel. Unfortunately, thousands upon thousands of fans had milled around the rear access road that would take us back to St. Kilda Road. The driver had, for safety reasons, slowed right down, to a point where he couldn't continue, and actually had to stop the car. The fans couldn't see the group through the tinted windows, so they started yelling and pounding on the car. I could see the boys were coping, but Frida started to look concerned. As she looked at me I could feel her thinking, oh, Bob will fix it all up! The biggest problem was that Anna was not only showing signs of paranoia, she was petrified!

'Richard, stay in the car, make sure everyone's okay. I'm gonna get us moving again.' I found it hard to force my way out. Richard and I both had to put our shoulder weight against the door. Then I had to get out while around a hundred ABBA fans were trying to get in. Once out, I had to edge my way along the length of the limo until I'd positioned myself to the front of the car. Now it was merely a matter of encouraging people to shift to the sides, and we slowly got the momentum of the crowd and the car moving at a slow walking pace. Unknown to me, the episode was being filmed by the ABBA film crew with their strategically positioned cameras.

The ABBA film was released several months later. One of my Black Belts, who was living and working in London, had called. Excitedly he'd said, 'This pub I'm working at in the East End showed the ABBA movie on the big screen the other night. The whole pub was going ape shit over all of ABBA's music, and I kept screaming out over the melee, "*Hey!* That guy with the blond hair, that's Richard Norton! And the red-haired guy is Bob Jones! And they're my martial arts instructors and that's the Myer Music Bowl, Melbourne! That's where I live! Where I come from!" It was great to see you guys so far from home, in a downtown pub! And Chief, that thing in front of the stretch limo with that mass crowd, fuck that looked real!'

We were back in Sydney for the last gig and back at the Sebel Town House. The group was resting while Richard and I were watching a report on ABBA on 'A Current Affair'. The show host had been interviewing Tom Oliver about his role as the bodyguard, and asked Tom what he thought of the ABBA girls.

'Anna and Frida are beautiful. I find Swedish girls very charming, very conservative and so hospitable.'

European women seem to combine sophistication with femininity and individualism.

'Australian men haven't learnt how to treat their women properly,' said our local English-born *bodyguard*, Tom.

Richard and I agreed, Tom couldn't have said it better, until he blew it when he got to the bit about Australian men ... But then again?

Meanwhile, Paul Dainty had organised a spectacular end-of-tour dinner at a major Sydney restaurant. After that we'd all gone back to the Sebel Club-Bar and everyone was enjoying the spirit of the moment. Each of us, in a way, was a little sad that the following night would bring the curtain down on the tour. The vibrant nightlife of the previous weeks had Anna looking a little tired, and she may have had that one drink over her limit. Bjorn had asked Richard to see Anna safely up to their penthouse as he was in a busy rave with Benny and Paul Dainty, Michael Chugg and Keith Bradley, the production manager, about specifications of the following night's spectacular finale.

About twenty minutes later Benny and Frida decided that they'd had enough. While I was taking them to their room, and as we came off the elevator on ABBA's floor, we could see Richard and Anna at the door of the penthouse.

'Bob, what's that your best friend's doing with my best friend's wife?'

'Well, maybe he's teaching her some *stand-up* grappling techniques for self-defence ... *Maybe!*'

Christ, what else could I say?

'Wouldn't they be more comfortable laying down?' Benny asked as we walked past.

It'd been over six weeks since we'd been in Sydney. At around 10 a.m. Sebel management had sent up to my room a variety of accumulated presents for the band. Most were for the two girls, and a lot were for Linda, Anna's baby daughter. I'd rung Richard to give me a hand. Before we could pass the gifts on to the group we had to be quite meticulous and search for any narcotics or crank messages that could offend. This proved to be tedious as we had forty-three koalas of all shapes and sizes, twenty-eight boxes of chocolates, fourteen nicely wrapped gift boxes and twelve large bunches and displays of flowers. Finally, Richard and I joked about which one of us would open a box, about twelve centimetres square, with a slow, quite audible ticking noise coming from within ...

'Good morning guys, how's the bodyguarding business going this morning?' asked the movie star bodyguard as he entered our room.

'Great mate! We were just going through all these presents before we give them clearance to ABBA. You know, the usual, checking for cannabis among the flowers, any plastic bag substances among the koalas, *cool* cookies in those gift packages, and *crank* offensive love notes among the flowers ... Stuff like that ...' To me it was as if this were an everyday occurrence.

'Oh man, that's perfect! Bob, the director, Lasser Hollstrom says he has this dilemma in the cutting room. The editors keep asking, "who are these two guys who keep appearing everywhere? One has blond hair and the other has red hair, and they are fucking everywhere!" He's sent me to work something out with you and Richard where we could film something that would make it look like you two are my understudies. Like you know, I'd look like the boss of the bodyguards.

'What you just said before is perfect, we could film you two checking all these goodies on camera and I could be sort of overseeing the whole thing'.

'All right Tom, let me see if I've got this thing right. Richard and I are to look like understudy bodyguards to you – you're the boss?'

Tom nodded.

I looked at Richard and tugged at my ear lobe with the thumb and bent index finger of my right hand. I then wiped my chin with my index finger.

Richard read my Shelley Berman hand language: Are you tuned in: the bullshit's about to flow!

'Hey Richard,' I joked. 'Can you pass over that gift box for Linda, Anna's daughter? You know, that one on top of the television; I think our boss should check it out.'

Richard brought it over, as if he were carrying a full-to-the-brim bowl of hot soup. I took the brightly packaged box off him, as if I'd just taken a name card off an Asian entrepreneur, and looked square at Tom Oliver, as if I were trying out for a Logie for best supporting actor.

'Tom, Richard and I have opened two of these this morning, but I think we were lucky. Listen to this,' I whispered, 'can you hear that slow ticking inside?' I handed him the box.

Tom held it ever so gently with his fingertips. Slowly, without a word from anybody, he leaned down and ever so carefully placed it at his feet. There was fear in his eyes as he left the room as quickly as he'd come in.

I went over to the box, tore the gift-wrapping off: inside was a small statue of a cute kangaroo with boxing gloves on, standing on a plaque in the shape of Australia. In the middle of the plaque, which read 'ABBA we love you', was a clock:

Tick, tock, tick, tock, tick tock …

Richard and I both fell about laughing and laughing, and then we laughed some more.

It's now more than twenty-five years since ABBA's debut mega-global hit, 'Waterloo'. Their music is still revered and has a new generation of fans, thanks to the success of *Muriel's Wedding*, 1970s nostalgia and a revamped enthusiastic following among the gay community. ABBA may have broken up many years ago, but in a sense, they've never really gone away.

Now, in the new millennium, as Sweden's biggest earning export after Volvo, the band has sold in excess of 350 million albums worldwide. Recently, they received the ultimate accolade when *Mamma Mia!*, a stage tribute to their music, and written by Benny and Bjorn, opened in London's West End and received rave reviews.

There were more rave reviews as *Mamma Mia!* made its mark on the Australian stage.

As our Qantas flight landed in Japan, the whole band broke into spontaneous laughter. Everyone had left their seats and were tripping over one another to peer through the aircraft's porthole windows to a banner that read:

FREETWOOD MAC

The message 'Welcome to Tokyo' was printed in small letters across the top of a large horizontal canvas banner, which hung off the side of the airport lounge, in the distance, as we taxied alongside on the runway.

The Japanese promoters had no problem linguistically with the 'L' in 'welcome', but the spelling of the band's name had been a serious attempt at Western humour. It'd worked, not only on the band, but on everyone on the flight. Everyone was laughing as cameras flashed from one end of the plane to the other.

However, many tourists entering Japan may have been laughing because they'd thought *Freetwood* was a spelling mistake.

This had been a very special day for both Richard and I. That's why, even though we hadn't reached home until after 5 a.m., we'd got up really early (with less than two hours' sleep). We'd done our six-kilometre run, hit the gym for a quick circuit of weight training and then headed down to the hotel restaurant for breakfast. As arranged, John 'Colonel' Courage (Fleetwood Mac's tour manager) had arrived. I'd picked up Tamiko, this drop-dead gorgeous Japanese Mac fan (we'd taken a natural shine to one another at the band's press conference), from our suite and the four of us were enjoying each other's company and breakfast.

It had been four days since our Freetwood Mac introduction to Tokyo. That night was to be the band's first gig in Japan. The reason for the early breakfast was that John 'Colonel' Courage, or JC as most of the crew referred to him, had wanted most of the bodyguards to do a dry run to the gig and back to familiarise themselves with the Tokyo traffic flows (it's the same twenty-four hours a day) and the general layout of the venue: the famous Budokan. Those that couldn't do it on the morning would in the afternoon during the band's sound check.

'Well, today is the big day for our two Aussie bodyguards. This would have to be the pinnacle for a couple of martial arts minders protecting the world's biggest rock circus in what must be the *summum bonum* in the world of the martial arts: Tokyo's Budokan!' JC was right on the money.

Richard was excited, but as for me it was definitely going to be one of the highlights of my career: both as a martial artist and as a bodyguard. We were going to be using the philosophy and principles of these arts to protect. Shit! Shit! Shit! We were really going to be doing our thing at the Budokan!

Then along came Fleetwood Mac's lead guitarist, Lindsey Buckingham, and his offsider Richard Dashut, and several of the sound and lighting guys, including Curry Grant and James 'Trip' Khaulf.

Lindsey, who was a very competent songwriter, could also be a very aggressive lead guitarist. This certainly bears out on the *Rumours* album, with songs like 'Second Hand News', 'Never Going Back Again' and his super-aggressive playing on 'Go Your Own Way'. Off stage, Lindsey is no recluse but he is very private.

Richard Dashut had been given the job of co-production on *Rumours* (supported by Ken Callait), and as I quickly learned, his heart was an open book. He and I became great friends from day dot.

'Everyone's looking super pretty and super handsome this morning!' Richard Dashut would use his Dale Carnegie *How To Win Friends and Influence People* attitude. 'Especially you Tamiko! You look as pretty as a Tokyo rose in the spring.'

H e gave me a wicked wink and asked Tamiko, 'Did you have a good night's sleep?'

'*Hai!*' she answered demurely.

This made Richard and me laugh our heads off.

As I soon learned, *hai* was Japanese for *yes*. The Japanese regularly say *hai*, the concept of *no* being such a negative, they avoid it like the plague. Therefore, more often than not, whether it's even applicable or not, they answer in the affirmative. Also, *hai* is spoken by contracting the lower abdominals. This way the speaker expels just enough air to accompany the word, which is always pushed directly at the speaker by cupping the back of the tongue against the back of the rear teeth, with a general nodding of the head, again for the affirmative.

Now, those keen readers with a desire to experience a little oriental culture may want to check this out in front of a mirror. Breath normally a few times and look into the mirror with a positive attitude. Now, concentrate and cause a contraction of your lower abdominals from your pelvis. Push the air upwards and outwards, and, at the same time, say *hai* quickly but firmly. Make sure you lock the rear of your tongue against the back edge of your rear teeth and nod your head! Perform this exercise at least ten times; no matter what size your breasts, or pectorals, when you say *hai*, your nipples will bounce upwards and forwards at the same time.

(This is possibly the reason Richard Dashut and all rock 'n' rollers have conversations with Japanese women, always prompting questions that allow them to answer in the affirmative!)

Just then, in what was fast becoming a Fleetwood Mac intramural breakfast extraordinaire, the belle of the ball, Stevie Nicks, and her bodyguard, joined our gathering. (Well, he wasn't really her bodyguard, he was more one of the Mac's cocaine couriers, but he looked the part.)

Perhaps already, or if not at that moment,

Stevie would become the most prolific songwriter in the group. Her love of fairytales and fantasy had been instilled in her by her mother. Stevie's original route to Fleetwood Mac was the same path as Lindsey Buckingham, as members of a band called Fritz and then together as Buckingham–Nicks. They'd joined Fleetwood Mac after Bob Welch had exited two years earlier. This incarnation of the band had recorded their first album *Fleetwood Mac*, toured, then after twelve months of traumatic studio time had produced *Rumours*. And here we all were, having breakfast together in Japan.

Stevie on this particular morning was bouncing along. 'Good morning everyone! Okay, okay, last night you guys were all so cool! You know, after dinner and JC ushered all of us band members into our limos? We got back to the hotel for an early night; luckily for an early night coz we don't have any bodyguards, do we? That's cool, I just want to know what a bunch of Fleetwood Mac bodyguards do in downtown Tokyo, when Fleetwood Mac's home in bed, or maybe, breakfast is not a good time?'

Stevie had read it exactly like it was. Fleetwood Mac, all the bodyguards, Mr Udo (the promoter) and some local record industry people had all gone to a celebration dinner. The *Rumours* album was selling as well in Japan as it was anywhere else in the world, especially since the band had hit town. Anyway, at about 1.30 a.m. (as Stevie had said, this was an early night for the band, they'd just finished dinner), Mr Udo had fixed up the dinner's humungous tab, and as we were saying our goodnights, JC had organised the limos ...

'Mick Fleetwood in this one. Mr Udo and you record people, this is your car. Stevie, over there.

Lindsey and Dashut, that one. McVie, this one. Christine, that one.'

As the limos drove off there we were, five bodyguards plus JC and Kenji (an interpreter organised for us by Mr Udo. Yes, there we were, just like Japan's original *Magnificent Seven*, *The Seven Samurai*. Now, which way was downtown?

Back at the breakfast table, conversation picked up thanks to JC. 'Did anybody see how much that fucking tab at the Kobe restaurant was last night? That Udo picked up for the lot of us!'

'But wasn't it a beautiful meal, the whole menu was absolutely kosher! I thought the tab would've been over the top, every steak listed was from $US120 up to $US180! And you all know you wouldn't pay twenty dollars for a steak in California!' Unknowingly, Stevie had taken the conversation away from the previous evening downtown.

'But man, what a steak!' added Richard Dashut. 'It just seemed to melt in your mouth, and afterwards I felt sort of comfortable, no feeling of nausea like the twenty-dollar steak back home.'

'There's a reason for all of this!' JC wanted to milk this steak thing for all it was worth. 'One night, on a long flight from some city to another, Bob Jones had given me a little piece of martial arts insight. He'd said the Japanese believed that Western culture got a lot of its stress and health problems from eating meat. Our meat is slaughtered, with the cattle coming off the trucks being prodded to leave through a chute, down ramps. Then they're herded single file down narrow corrals, at the end of which "Bop!", they're hit between the eyes with a high-pressured bolt gun, sometimes more than once, until they're

dead. This sense of death, along with the horrific death sounds that each one makes, is constantly felt back through the lines of cattle, until the very last one to come off
that truck suffers the same fate. Now all this stress and death is skinned, boned, packed, sold and delivered in almost no time. It's a twenty-dollar steak right around the Western world!'

'Jesus Christ! JC, what's this got to do with that steak melting in my mouth last night at the Kobe restaurant in the Ginza?' said Richard Dashut, on behalf of everyone at the table, acting as if they'd been scripted into a horror movie.

'That's the point to the whole fucking story, i'n' it? All the beef at the kobe restaurant comes from this little island off Japan called Kobe Island. Now, here on this island there are very old and wise cattle-carers, and on the day in question they put alcohol, not a lot, but just enough to relax the cow, in its feed. They have a special Japanese technique for massaging the cow ...

'While they relax the cow with alcohol and massage, they play very soothing Japanese traditional music. When the cow is all soothed out, "Bop!" right between the eyes, and no ones any the wiser. And that's why, Kobe beef just melts in your mouth, with none of the stress attached.'

Stevie Nicks, totally bewildered, stared at JC. I wasn't even sure if she enjoyed the first, or the second part of the story.

'Bob Jones, is that a true story?'

Stevie's question spun me out. My brain had to race through its memory tracks to find out where I'd picked up a story like that. Was it three years earlier in 1974, when I was bodyguard to his Divine

Grace A. C. Bhaktivedanta Swami Prabhupada (the guru of a famous Indian religious sect)? He'd told me so many stories, that hundreds of by-products came from the cow (the cow was truly a holy being), that it should be worshipped and always protected, never killed for only its meat! In fact, he said we should not eat meat.

Then there was the guru of a famous martial arts style (Kyokushinkai Karate-Do Association). In 1975 I was attempting to put a television series together, and that was the reason I'd spent some time with its leader, Masatutsu Oyama. One day, his interpreter had told me that it hadn't been much more than a decade since he'd gained notoriety as a 'killer of the bull'. Mr Oyama would actually challenge a bull to a duel as a public spectacle of his inner strengths. Television, radio and the press would be present as the bull would charge. Then 'Bop!' right between the eyes. Oyama would deliver his fist, the bull would be dead, and everyone knew about it! I didn't know what they did with the meat (probably sold it to the West!).

Just as I was trying to decide from which of the two gentlemen the story had come from I was saved.

'Good morning!'
'Good morning!'
'Good morning!'
'Hi!'

Enter the reason why this great band had its name. At the Windsor jazz and blues festival of 1967, Peter Green had named the band after his favourite rhythm section, consisting of our two main men: Mick Fleetwood (the drummer) and John McVie (the bass player) a.k.a. Fleetwood Mac. With them entered the third bonding force of the 'Mac', Christine McVie (married to John McVie since 1968, but they'd separated a couple of years earlier in 1975), and another of the Mac's full-time bodyguards (well not really a bodyguard, he was more like one of the Mac's full-time cocaine-snorters but he looked the part).

Mick, John, Chris and the bodyguard drew in their chairs; we had to shuffle some extra tables around. Then Mr Udo and those record people arrived. We had to repeat the process to accommodate the newcomers, who by now were conversing with everybody, mostly about this the first gig night at the Budokan.

This was as good a time as any to go back to that jaunt downtown ...

It was 1:30 in the morning, JC had just shuffled the band into their limos. Suddenly, there were only five bodyguards (Richard Norton and myself and the three full-time 'Big Macs'); JC made it six and our mediator, supplied by our promoter, Kenji, was the Seventh Samurai.

'Now, that takes care of the band, Udo and everybody. Kenji, you take me and my boys to wherever those beautiful Japanese girls are,' JC commanded.

'Ok, I know, Mr Udo awready exprain to me. I take you meet many Japanese rady. I take you cabaret.'

'Fuck the fucken' cabaret,' JC wouldn't hear of Kenji wasting any time. 'If we wanted to see Tom Jones or Frank Sinatra, we'd have stayed in fucking California, and spent the weekend in Las Vegas. You take us to where the girls are *now*!'

'Ok, thank you, I understand. I take everyone to cabaret.'

It wasn't hard to see that JC and Kenji were having a slight misunderstanding.

As we walked nine, maybe ten blocks through the Ginza (we were definitely downtown) we passed a constant array of clubs controlled by the Yakuza (the Japanese criminal element): the usual strip joints, this ones topless, this ones bottomless, we feature live sex on stage. These descriptions flashed at you via mulit-coloured fluro signs, across the front of each club. At each doorway lurked your usual, almost any-language, spruikers. Their backs were being protected by a couple of typical Yakuza-type associates, standing either side of a reception area that housed those cute young Japanese girls, ready to take your money.

'Fuck! I don't know about you guys, but we just passed at least a dozen joints! Hey, you, Kenji!' JC bellowed. 'Kenji, where the fuck are you taking us? What we want is real simple: club, bar, drinks, girls, in that order ... Have you got it, or should I fucking well spell it?'

'Ok, thank you, I understand: I take you cabaret. Rook here Mr JC, this is cabaret. This one!' He was right, there was the sign *Les Cabaret* across the top of the doorway.

The spruiker took one look at Greg Thomason (at 193 centimetres this American was the tallest of us) and tried some German but it had no affect. He focused on Dwayne Taylor (at 188 centimetres, the second tallest) and his Dutch spiel had the same affect as his German: none. The third bodyguard from the US and JC, Richard Norton and I were all just a whisker over or under 183 centimetres. Kenji, at 163 centimetres, was the same height as the spruiker. They spoke briefly in their own tongue; the spruiker smiled a lottery-winning smile and said,

'Wearcome gentremen, wearcome to our cabaret! Come, you have good time.'

We followed JC and Kenji into *Les Cabaret*, without being quizzed about cover charge or who we were. I figured Kenji through Mr Udo must have squared any entry fees with the spruiker during their brief exchange. Of course, they knew who we were: we all had our Freetwood Mac Rumours tour jackets on.

Every lady in the place probably thought *we were* Freetwood Mac. On came the dancing girls, wearing nothing but big smiles and the smallest G-string pelvis covers, two each just to start. Then came the drinks (of course, Richard and I couldn't drink, we were on tour, which meant we were working). The US minders' self-control drinking rules were about as good as their self-control drug rules (plus they didn't train).

The *Les Cabaret* had a good crowd, there were girls everywhere for everyone, but something didn't seem right: no-one, including us, was paying for anything. Girls, booze, food, more girls: it just kept getting laid on. JC was letting off steam and getting outrageous, so my work was cut out for the rest of night: making sure he'd be okay!

Meanwhile, Big Greg was the typical *town crier*, the Mac circus clown. He was always being funny, and as a large-framed 109-kilogram (or 240-pound) mass on the dance floor in some state of bardic revelry, he entertained the tourists by setting a record of how many Japanese bar girls could stick their near-naked bodies against one bodyguard. There were seven of these bar ladies hanging all over Greg; JC argued that there were nine.

Les Cabaret had been playing the hit singles off *Rumours* and the occasional blast from the past. Most people knew the words and sang along. As one more bar girl attempted to mount Greg, he sang along to the song Peter Green (the ex-Fleetwood Mac blues guitarist) had penned around ten years earlier: 'Rattlesnake Shake'. Big Greg then began to scream his own version, as if he were trying out for world champion karaoke.

> *I'm a bodyguard for a band called Mac.*
> *I have this boss and his name is Mick.*
> *We're on the road and he ain't got no chick.*

Without even missing a beat Greg continued ad-libbing his own words to the song:

> *So it's the occasional shake he gives his dick.*
> *Fleetwood calls this his rattlesnake shake.*

I doubt if any of these punters rolling on the floor laughing at big Greg's karaoke show would've been aware that Peter Green, actually had written 'Rattlesnake Shake' about Mick Fleetwood and jerking off.

Close by, Dwayne was having an argument with some German or Dutch businessmen at the table next to us. They'd been aggressively rude to some of the girls. Richard Norton was at the other end of the table from me, smiling like a Cheshire cat. It wasn't because of the karaoke floor show. By about two songs earlier Greg had toppled on to the dance floor like a deck of cards with all the girls on top of him. I gave Richard the old double palms-up sign for, 'what the fuck?' He gave me the double-index fingers jabbing down sign, meaning, 'take a look under the table'.

I leaned back but could see nothing, so I asked JC would he mind moving his chair slightly. I guess he thought I'd dropped something. It was damned dark down there, but pretty soon I could make out that Richard's trousers were down around his ankles and two of the cutest bar girls were giving my best mate some lip service he'd never tell his mother about. I just fell back in my chair in uncontrollable laughter.

Looking under the table makes you laugh? JC thought to himself. One quick look and he was in the same state as me. Then JC surprised me, despite his laughter, and after a couple of hours of some serious drinking, he leaned across and said with a very serious sober voice, 'It really is time that we got the fuck out of here.'

Suddenly, what I'd been worried about all night materialised at the front door as we were preparing to leave ...

'What the fuck? Someone's got to be fucking kidding!' JC thundered. 'Hey guys, if we thought last night at the Kobe beef restaurant was expensive, take a fucking look at this, the *Les Cabaret* account, it's more than fucking double!'

It turned out that *Les Cabaret* was using an Asian concept that had not reached America yet (and it'd be three years after that before it'd reach Australia): the cover charge (admission fee), drinks and every whim of every hostess (as we found out, that was what the bar girls were called) were all tallied throughout the night.

'Yes gentremen, this is the account we need to settre' before you can reave,' the receptionist affirmed.

Nearby, the Yakuza associates took a pace forward and folded their arms. Richard Norton moved off to the left of JC and had Yakuza number one in his sights. Richard gave me a quick eye line and casually rubbed his ear lobe to let me know he was tuned in and ready. I wiped my chin with my thumb and index finger, stating that the drama was going down and may not be coming back. It was good that we were communicating. Richard would never lead off in a situation like this, he respected my experience but knew that if I pinched the tip of my nose, that was the signal for the both of us to explode.

Then I noticed Yakuza number two, a little older, more experienced, maybe the boss and he'd picked up on Richard and my conversation. He couldn't understand what we were saying but he knew we were gesticulating. Now it was his turn to pick up on a different kind of trademark. During our Shelley Berman conversation, he'd noticed our calloused knuckles (this is where the face of the index and centre knuckle become enlarged and discoloured as a result of many years, and many legions of push-ups; even though we were Westerners he knew we were martial artists). He hadn't been concerned that there were two of them and seven of us, he'd shown some concern at the size of Greg and Dwayne but that didn't detract from his confidence. However, our callouses, that had him lean back and appear to rest his left hand on the reception desk. He and I both knew his thumb was pressing the regular old bouncer buzzer, that old bouncer buzzer for back-up.

He may have been worried about Richard and I, but now I was worried about him, not because he'd just called for back-up, but because the pinkie of his left hand had two joints missing, and his third finger had the first joint missing – these guys really were the Yakuza! Finally, we all knew who the players were.

The spruiker and receptionist were trying to make sense of Kenji's interpretation of JC's English and why we weren't going to pay the bill.

The Yakuza back-up began to appear in the shadows. Just as I was thinking I was in good company and that it was a good day to die, the head Yakuza and JC had come to a compatible arrangement of payment. Thank God for tour managers and their unfaltering gift of the gab.

'Bob,' I heard from the distance. It was that beautiful English, sometimes American, and sometimes international, accent.

'Bob!' All we needed was Christine McVie in the middle of all this …

'Bob, this is the third time I've called! I hope you're not back at that bloody *Les Cabaret* at five o'clock this morning, are you?'

'Ah, I'd just wandered off there briefly, but I was following your conversation. I agree that those penguin ice carvings were truly spectacular.' Mick, John and Christine had been discussing the press conference on the night of our arrival in Tokyo.

Six years earlier, in 1971, when Bob Welch and Danny Kirwan were out front (doing what Stevie and Lindsey do now) they'd just recorded *Future Games*, released in September of that year, just in time for another Fleetwood Mac US tour. Sally, Mick's sister, had shot the album cover. Interestingly, she'd used this shot to symbolise the band's aspirations of this album on its future. Sally photographed her two children, Kells and Tiffany, playing in the River Nadder near Salisbury. Perhaps John McVie's personal aspirations were to give the band a new theme. Since the tragic loss of Peter Green and more recently Jeremy Spencer, the band needed a fresh look. On the back of the album were photos of the five musicians, except for McVie, who'd switched his picture with a shot of a penguin. This was because, a few years earlier, during their romantic years, John and Christine had lived near the London Zoo where John was a member of The Zoological Society. Here he became fascinated with photographing the resident penguin population. He'd studied everything he could about them. Thus on *Future Games* he'd said, 'I'm out, my penguin shot is in.' Then he went out, got extremely drunk and had a penguin tattooed on his right forearm that dances every time he plays bass. This was the beginning of all the Fleetwood Mac penguin iconography. From this time on it was commonplace to have them plastered on album covers and most other available surfaces.

What had been unique about the press conference was the spectacular sight that Japanese artists had carved out of ice: five penguins, each life-size characters of the five members of Fleetwood Mac. The likeness of each of the five penguins to the band members was remarkable. The carvings were set on long trestles among a beautifully manicured arrangement of all styles of Japanese cuisine. They were all carved as if this copious smorgasbord was an art deco food festival.

As I watched these works of art melting away, Kenji noticed my concern, 'Bob San, you are on journey of martial arts?'

'Kenji, the warrior way is my passion.'

You read book of most famous samurai warrior, Myamotto Musashi?'

'Kenji, all my Black Belts read *Five Rings*.'

'Then think about what you see. Expranation come easy'.

Then I saw the huge container running down the centre of the trestles, which was where the melting ice was draining to. These massive life-size carvings were the spirits of five penguin warriors, which were, in turn, representative of the fighting spirits of the five individual members of Fleetwood Mac. This, in turn, was symbolic of Musashi's five rings: earth, air, fire, water and the void – the five elements of nature's universal laws, the importance of each one being equal with the source. With the melting of the penguins, the purpose of the chameleon would be complete. Along with the grandiose presentation of the meal you had the denouement of the warriors' concept. With the combining of the fighting spirit of Fleetwood Mac, the Japanese were saying, the band would experience long life, good health and much fortune along the way.

'You see, and now you understand.'

'*Hai, domo arigato* (thank you very much), was my response to Kenji San.'

Back at the Tokyo International Hotel breakfast scene with almost thirty people, somebody produced photos of our Fleetwood Mac banner and everyone was either talking or laughing about something. These moments were typical of the time spent with Fleetwood Mac; we all felt the Mac was a large family. And each of us was made to feel as if he or she were extended members of this family. For me this continues until the present day.

After breakfast, we braved the Tokyo traffic. On any good tourist invasion day, the population of Tokyo can hover either side of 30 000 000, so eventually we arrived, complete with goose bumps, at the martial arts capital of the world: the Budokan. It was everything I expected and more. Its huge complex dome, of a typical Japanese oriental design, displayed a simplicity. Richard Norton and I wanted to get in there and do some serious training. However, on this particular day it would not be possible.

'Look here guys, make sure we all walk on the plastic. Don't you dare step on the bare floor with your shoes on the ... Bob and Richard, what do you call the floor?' JC's question was sincere.

'*Dojo*. Actually this is the Honbu-Dojo, meaning main school,' Richard replied.

'There you go, don't stand on it, otherwise you might be struck dead or at least you might suffer a hundred years of bad luck, for you and your offspring.' JC was now sounding like an authority on the subject.

Everyone laughed, except Richard and I. The laughter echoed around the magnificent old Honbu-Dojo.

The contract for hire stated that the only way the Budokan could be used in concert was if the entire floor was covered and taped down, with large rolls of very thick plastic. Members of the public could never set foot on the actual floor. This had been the law since the first time the Budokan had been used for anything other than the National Martial Arts Championships, where everyone competed barefoot.

(This was only a decade ago when The Beatles had performed five sell-out shows there in 1966.)

The above-ground area of the Budokan was a huge auditorium surrounded by tiered seating, that for a live concert like Fleetwood Mac's, with extra floor 15 000 per show. The underground area held the most fascination for Richard and me: more than a dozen large *dojo*, each one specifically catering for the different arts: Judo, Aikido, Jiu-Jitsu, Kendo, Karate and so on.

On stage that afternoon Fleetwood Mac were magic as they did their sound levels and Curry Grant highlighted different songs with his lighting arrangements. This great Budokan had come to life with samples of that night's show like Lindsey's 'Never Going Back Again', Christine's 'Don't Stop' (a song written for John) and Stevie's 'I Don't Want to Know', with the sound adjustments being done by Richard Dashut.

While the band continued their sound check, JC called a meeting backstage of us bodyguards, and laid down the law, as he'd also done with the crew after lunch.

'Guys, the touring circus is out of control, we are spending far too fucking much. It is the prerogative of the members in the band to spend what they like, when they like. But the rest of us, from here on in, I'll need signed dockets for everything. Any money you spend on behalf of the band: keep the dockets.'

But what if I were out with any of the band members like the day before? I'd gone with Christine while she'd done some shopping, down to Roppongi. We'd taken cabs and had lunch at the centre's restaurant. How could I get cab and lunch receipts, when Christine would never stand around. She was always on the go, especially when shopping.

In no time at all, the touring circus grapevine filled me in: JC's diversion was not about cabs and lunches, it was a 'who's doing how many drugs?'

Sometime earlier (during the studio recording sessions), JC had taken it on himself to protect the band from downtown questionable ingredients via junky drug suppliers, set-up busts and the like. He'd become the buyer/supplier of the circus. That way, he'd take charge of both quality and financial control, and risk management.

Now, in Japan drugs are almost impossible, and when they are encountered, you can bet on triple-up on the cost. Thus, for the bookkeeping session, JC figured he'd be answerable to the accountants back home wanting to bill the right people for their usage on this around-the-world tour. Besides, this was what a good tour manager does: he watches the ins, outs and balances everything, including the finances. Keeping the whole circus in line requires the occasional making of loud noises and sometimes jumping on toes.

Actually, the previous night's outing had been at the suggestion of Fleetwood Mac, who'd stated that JC should treat the boys to a night on the town and that was why JC finally went on the alert: something at *Les Cabaret* wasn't right. But more important, this could be costing Fleetwood Mac unnecessary money. Hence, the refusal to pay the rip-off tab. We never did find out how much JC paid that night. It was rumoured (excuse the pun) to be less than half; anyway, it was enough not to have to go to war with the downtown urban Yakuza samurai.

The show that night at the Budokan was our

third trip for the day. The traffic was constant: as always it was traffic bedlam.

Backstage, during the countdown for Fleetwood Mac to present themselves and their album *Rumours* to their first Japanese live audience, every one was up and in good spirits. However, there did seem to be something missing: that *break-a-leg edge* as they say in the business. John McVie was pumping and in great spirits. It made sense why: he'd drunk his normal bottle of pre-stage pick-me-up. For John this was normal, except for the rest of the band: we were in Japan and JC hadn't scored yet. That meant the band hadn't had any drugs for more than four days! Thus, that missing edge. However, the show had to go on ...

Lindsey, the girls and John ran on to the stage. The lights went up and that Japanese audience roared like the best of them. I remember looking at Mick and thinking, come on man, you can do it! You don't need any damned bullshit drugs!

Mick was devastated; he'd sometimes have a problem with severe hypo glycaemia (not enough sugar in the blood). He was straining and ranting, but then I saw a craziness in his eyes, brought on by a neo-Falstaffian consumption of alcohol, and four day's drought from any drug. Suddenly, it was as if Mick had received direction from the Devil himself: he'd rushed over to the half-nibbled smorgasbord, grabbed a straw, and begun snorting first through one nostril, then the other, copious amounts of caffeine straight out of a two-kilo can of coffee. His eyes had grown as big as the duo stage balls, which he wore dangling between his legs, as he ran past Richard and me, giving us the thumbs-up with both drumsticks and with the biggest smile on his face (sadly the smile of a little kid). As he streaked on to the stage that crowd roared louder than any Japanese quake. Mick then put his foot on the bass peddle, like an Olympic shooter puts his or her finger on the trigger just prior to firing off, and beat his drumsticks together four times as he counted in that opening song 'Say You Love Me'. That was when the Fleetwood Mac magic became a reality at the Budokan and everybody exploded. For almost two hours the Mac would take this audience down memory lane with the top singles off their previous albums. This audience, 90 per cent of whom could not even speak English, not only understood the meaning of every song, they actually sang along, especially the songs off *Rumours*.

Well into the show, 'Station Man' had John McVie take centre stage and punch out his classic bass line, proving that Peter Green had made a wise decision with the name of the band. On drums, Mick was pulling the most ghoulish crazy faces, trying to break John up, but to no avail. John was right there with the sounds of his guitar joining forces with the drums and producing the powerful rhythm they were famous for.

Christine then took the limelight with her 'You Make Loving Fun' and brought the house down with her new single 'Don't Stop', just released from the *Rumours* album. During this time Stevie had gone into her on-stage dressing room to change costumes, to prepare for a little Celtic antiquity.

After Christine it was Lindsey's turn. He was dressed in jeans and a cream-coloured kimono top. Lindsey had been filling in with his usual sparkling folkish riffs. As he took the lead, Richard Dashut, from the sound console, cranked Lindsey's guitar up a couple of decibels, which was about the fourth time during the set. Lindsey's guitar was virtually screaming, and at this volume it would be a real competition for Stevie's howling voice to match. The crowd loved Lindsey's playing as much as he did, and they applauded every lick.

Suddenly, everything went quiet, the Budokan faded to darkness. Richard Dashut, in control of sound mix and volume, and Curry Grant, with his fingers on the buttons controlling darkness, then created some Celtic magic: a single spot showing Stevie as a 'celestial figure'. She was about to launch the Budokan and its audience up to another level with the rites of the Welsh witch: the dance of 'Rhiannon'. The audience could sense she was a believer in ghosts and witches, a devotee of the occult whose favourite night of the year is Halloween. Hundreds of Stevie's adoring Japanese fans, as had fans all over the world during this tour, had come dressed in Stevie's style of chiffon and witchy hats, all with varying Halloween-painted fairy faces. By the time the song ended, the screaming guitar and howling voice would be declared a draw, and the audience exhausted yet, exalted.

Then, from the back of the stage came what this small-statured Japanese audience must have thought to be a gangly giant, as tall as the heavens. It took control of centre stage. Meanwhile, Christine had stepped out from behind her keyboards, playing maracas and singing the chorus with Stevie and Lindsey. Then with his eyes still bigger than the phallic duo balls dangling between his legs, Mick's lurching 198-centimetre string-bean frame was an eerie vision. The audience swirled and swayed with the same rhythm Mick set with his own oceanic dance, stamping his lead foot, making the talking drum rumble and squawking in time to 'World Turning'.

Fleetwood Mac next concentrated on all the hit singles that had been lifted off *Rumours*. 'Go Your Own Way' set off the encores. This show finished off with the popular hit, 'Songbird'.

Prior to this magnetic performance, while the band had been relaxing in the dressing rooms, long before the actual stage entrance, JC had invited Richard and me to pop downstairs. 'Everything's happening down there, hundreds of people doing your thing ... Tell you what, you got thirty minutes. If you ain't back by then, I'll come looking for ya!'

Down to the *dojo* we went. The energy and atmosphere rivalled that of upstairs. At least that was what Richard and I'd thought. There were five instructors and sixty-four students on the floor in the Kendo-Dojo. The floor was so spacious it was only reasonably crowded, but the class had me in awe. It was so mystical with everyone dressed in full correct *Gu*: *men-do-kote-tare* (traditional body armour protection for the head, chest, wrists and groin). The quilted tops and *hakama*s (baggy pants) were in full flight during the one-step sparring with clashing *shinnae*s (a bamboo version of the traditional *katana* or samurai sword). The sound of the bamboo contacting echoed around, thanks to the natural acoustics of the *dojo*. The friction of this contact also gave the air a strong smell of burning bamboo. Years later (during late 1980s), I'd reproduce this with many more than sixty-four students with a children's Kendo class (at the new Plymouth High School, North Island, New Zealand).

Just as Fleetwood Mac were ready to take the stage, JC had to come and get us, otherwise Richard and I would still be there.

After Tokyo it was on the very-fast-for-its-day (100 to 120 kilometres per hour) Bullet Train for concerts in Kyoto, Sapporo, Osaka and Yokohama. Naturally, you could not go to these cities without visiting the true heritage of Japan. What was probably the let's-do-that-touristy thing for the members of Fleetwood Mac and their entourage was for Richard Norton and me a notch up on the Budokan. This was the chance to visit those historic castles that are suffering the encroachment of today's world, yet at the same time managing to preserve the power of the shogun's bygone era.

Kyoto, the second city Fleetwood Mac performed, introduced me to bathhouse 'A' and bathhouse 'B'. The Japanese are fanatical about cleanliness and hygiene, and they often connect cleanliness and sexuality (it doesn't matter whether you're married or single, when you're in Japan, you can go alone or take your partner – as long as you go!)

So, bathhouse 'B' is where you are cleansed by prostitutes, but they are great at cleaning. Bathhouse 'A' is where the modern-day Geisha girls are trained for years in the art of pampering while cleansing. They say that the tradition is still practised according to the old-school ethics.

The whole bathhouse thing came about because, it appeared, Mr Udo was embarrassed about what had gone down at *Les Cabaret* a few days earlier. Wanting to make up for it, he'd offered the same crew a night out at a bathhouse (he must have felt he had a lot of making up to do). He'd treated us to an 'A', which is five times more expensive than a 'B' (Geishaversus hookers). Plus, he gave each of us fat envelopes: fat as a week's pay cheque.

'You give for Geisha. When you meet, say from Mr Udo. Then Geisha, special for you, understand?' Mr Udo sounded like he was in a scene from one of the Godfather movies.

That night, after a sold-out fantastic Fleetwood Mac performance, Mr Udo sent a limousine with his most faithful smiling driver/interpreter. And off we bodyguards went, on what would turn out to be quite an adventure. After about twenty minutes of driving through the city limits of Kyoto, we eventually parked outside a gargantuan oriental-style building set in an area characterised by Western architecture. For such a worldly lot, we were noticeably silent during the trip.

'I wait here for you; come back rater,' Kenji remarked.

'You will wait here or you will come back rater?' This was Big Greg's only attempt at comedy so far.

We all laughed, though picking on Kenji's accent wasn't really that funny at all, but the steam had to be released somewhere.

Bathhouse A's are by invitation/booking only; you can't just walk in off the street like you can at a 'B'.

On entering, we found ourselves in a large foyer with highly polished floorboards, and Japanese lanterns hanging from the ceiling. At the bottom of an extremely wide staircase of about thirty stairs, up to the first floor, there was a sign, which actually stated 'Please Leave Shoes'. Neatly paired in pigeon holes were these leather slippers, made to almost fit all of us except Big Greg, who just managed to get his toes under the leather instep. This time, without even trying, he did look rather funny.

Then, through an intercom a hushed and very feminine voice spoke authoritatively, 'Now gentremen, won't you prease come upstairs?'

I remember stepping off the polished floors; how those slippers felt on the plush shag-pile carpet! At the top of the stairs, there was a large reception area with a full-size billiard table, a cocktail bar and soft leather couches. The large television screen (well it was large for 1977) telecast Gridiron live from Boston. But, best of all, of what caught Richard's and my eye was the security guy: he was either a current, or not long retired Sumo wrestler. He was the same height as Greg, but he had at least 50 per cent more bodyweight. He stood most of the time, with arms folded, wearing a very elegant white satin kimono and matching white satin *hakama* with white socks, with that sleeve they have that holds the big toe. His hair was shaved down the centre, the sides were grown long and tied back into a topknot at the back of his head. Next to him, leaning against the wall, were two samurai *katana*s. No, it was one *katana* and one *wakisashi* (one long sword and one shorter sword), which I'm sure were only there as part of the effect...maybe!

Greg, our town crier, was as quiet as a mouse, and so were the rest of us. He was first cab off the rank when this absolutely stunning Japanese Geisha appeared. She was dressed in a long black kimono from a high neck down to the floor, and wearing the same, though smaller, white socks as our samurai security man, they too with the toe sleeve. A wide elastic waist band accentuated both her tapered hips and breasts, her hair was drawn back in a round bun, to emphasise the white face makeup that featured a thin black eye-line. Richard and I looked at one another, and I'm sure we both thought, which one of us has died and gone to heaven?

The Geisha took Big Greg by the hand and they both disappeared. Just as Richard and I were about to lapse into a state of manic depression, twins appeared, looking exactly like Greg's better half; in fact, they could've been triplets. Then I remembered the years of training that went into becoming a geisha, and the sameness of appearance that came with the intricate application of traditional make-up.

I may have been looking cool on the outside, but Darwin's Cyclone Tracey was blowing on the inside ... And then it happened, they both took Richard and me by the hand and off we went. Richard and number two went off down a passageway to the right. Number three turned me to the left, let my hand go so she could hold her kimono, as we had about ten stairs to walk down to a passageway that was lined with that white rice paper set in   natural timber-grained squares. Once off the stairs' carpet and back on to polished boards, I followed my Geisha very closely, looking around for any more samurai security, or whatever!

It just seemed like one of those times I should've looked around, but I damned near fell over number three. She'd dropped in a huddle, right in front of me on to the floor.

What do I do now? With her fingertips she slid the rice paper wall with the grained squares, which was really a sliding partition. Then she looked up at me and looked inside, inviting me to enter. What do I do now? I stepped in, she stood up and stepped from the passage on to the bamboo mat inside the room. Then she dropped down again huddled on to the floor and with her fingertips she slid the partition very gently, until it closed.

What do I do now? I thought as I looked at the surroundings. We were in a clinically clean snow white medium-sized room, on my left was a very comfortable looking white kid-leather couch. On my right was a very comfortable looking white massage table. There were shelves with stacks of very white towels and a shelf with a variety of oils and lotions and, I guess, perfumes. Then there was the weirdest sight: through the middle of the room from another of these rooms on the right to also one on the left was a running water creek. It was a miniature creek, actually it was more like a miniature brook with water running over rocks. There were two small pond areas that had numerous oriental fish swimming about. Amazingly, two trees grew on either side of the brook, and up and out of holes through the ceiling.

I couldn't tell if any of it was real, but it conjured a mood of surrealism. In the middle of this all white room, and the brook, there was a miniature red and black *Tori* bridge that straddled the waterflow. On the other side of the room, and the brook, on the right there was a sauna room, all glass, set in the same-sized natural timber-grained squares as the walls. This sauna reminded me of those old glass and red timber squared telephone boxes; they were built exactly the same way. In the opposite corner on the left there was a matching all glass bathtub (with the same grained squares). Everything matched. The same as in the sauna. The bath had a bench to sit on, the whole thing was about a metre square and looked like a giant Rubix-cube. In between the two cleansers was an intriguing object of oriental art: a round whiteplastic stump set into the white-tiled floor. It looked like it could serve as some sort of seat, except that it was just this flat top, a half-circle on either side down to the floor with no centre.

Another interesting piece of décor was the shower hose and nozzle, which hung out of the ceiling, directly above the odd-looking stool. The far wall behind the bath and sauna was entirely mirrored. I could see my reflection and that of number three Geisha. She was sitting upright on her knees, just looking at me, giving me time to absorb and I guess to get comfortable. Then she grabbed my trouser leg and gestured for me to lift my foot. She then took off my slipper and sock. She repeated the process on the other side, now both my feet were bare.

I then remembered the Godfather movie. 'Ah, this is for you, from Mr Udo, do you understand? I handed her the envelop.

'Hai, domo, arigato.' She sounded like Tamiko. Oh God, I'm in heaven went through me as she took off my Fleetwood Mac tour jacket and hung it on a hanger next to that comfortable couch. She continued, one item at a time, until my body was stark naked. Then she bought me one of those fluffy white towels and wrapped it around my hips, securing it with small Velcro strips. She then took me on this little journey to the brook and over the *Tori* bridge and across to the sauna.

I almost felt like I was about to make a phone call to GOD and give him my personal thanks and ask how I could repay...

Man it was hot, and getting hotter as I endeavored to adjust. Geisha number three didn't make it any easier. She'd retraced our journey back

across the bridge, gone over to the massage table, knelt down on the floor again, in front of a long mirror, and began to remove her white face makeup. On completing the task, she reached up and removed two sticks and a clip from her hair, which tumbled down across her shoulders and continued down to the small of her back. Now she stood up and I had no idea how she did it: she just stepped out of her kimono, looked at me and smiled. The only thing
she was wearing was that smile and a pair of white briefs. Then she took a white jacket from a shelf near the towels, it now hung loosely just covering her hips. As she came across the bridge she swept her hair free of the jacket, buttoned up three buttons and rolled her sleeves up to her elbows. This had taken around five minutes and I was *cookern'*.

Next thing she'd got me out of that hot sauna, unclipped the Velcro strip at my hips, and had me sitting on this intriguing oriental art object while hosing me down with cold, very cold, no, bloody freezing water. I had goose bumps all over my body, which had nothing to do with the cold water. But matter of fact within a few seconds the water had turned to warm. Feeling much more relaxed, I'd leaned forward with my elbows on my knees and let my head hang down. I was being covered with more soapsuds than I'd ever seen before, and this bloody stool I was sitting on felt like the most comfortable chair I'd ever had the pleasure of sitting on.

The design shape, with its central schism, was the comfort zone. That no-centre section allowed access to every part of my body, to be soaped down and sudded up, without me even bending a finger.

After maybe ten minutes, Geisha number three

hoisted me under the arm pits, took two steps and she tipped me into the bath. There I sat through another five minutes of washing and facial massage.

Between the phone box sauna, the sexual fantasy satisfaction stool (maybe I should copyright and trade mark that) and the Rubix-cube bathtub, and just about the quickest hour of my life ever, geisha number three had put me through that cleansing process three times. Man, I was cleansed.

Each time after the bath, she towelled me down and patted me dry before re-entering the sauna. However, on this third time I was taken, all patted dry, over the bridge and laid out on the massage table with my head comfortably wedged into the face-support hole. Then I was gently covered in several layers of towels and left in silence, for about fifteen minutes. I'd lost all sense of time, it was as if I were floating in a void. I then felt the towels, one by one, sliding off my body until I was bare. Then I heard the splashing of oil, the softest brush applying the oil to the back of my legs. At about that time she got to my backside muscles; there was this weird feeling as the softest brush delivered oil over my body. I felt her inner thighs and finally realised that she was oiling me down with her shortly shaved pelvic hair.

For the next hour my mind wandered and my body levitated in a swirl ...

I was dressed and soon at the bottom of the stairs on my way back to the samurai security man. However, I couldn't lift my foot on to them. How the hell was I gonna make it up those ten stairs? I tried holding the banister with one hand, and lifting either leg up on to that first step. Nope, I couldn't make that work either. How about sort of laying about, on the banister with as much of my upper body as I could, and sort of rolling my hips and one leg at a time to drag them up those stairs? Then bingo it happened, one leg at a time and eventually I made the ten steps, straightening myself up and hoping to God nobody had noticed me on Mount Fuji. Most of the guys were back at reception, lounging around. Was I the only one that had to contend with those bloody stairs? A couple of them were having a drink at the bar; there was only Richard Norton to come.

'Ah, how was it for you?'
'Who me?'
'Yeah.'
'Oh fine.'
'Hmmm, yeah different'.
'Me too!'
'Would you come again?'
'Who me?'
'Yeah you!'
'Oh yeah, I think so.'
'Yeah, me to!'

Such worldly men, this was the extent of our conversation. We all needed to be cool; you know, macho-minders, world travellers who'd been there, done that, seen it all ...

Pretty soon, they'd wandered off, saying they'd wait in the limo with Kenji. I had to wait for me Aussie mate! Just then, Richard came in with that big smile. The kind that told me he'd just done a few more tricks he probably wouldn't tell his mum about.

'Hey Rick, how d'ya feel?'
'I never felt better. I feel like I'm on top of the world.'
'You're it man, all the guys are downstairs,' I'd said as we both gave our samurai a courtesy bow.

He smiled back and bowed. Richard was just

ahead of me at the top of the stairs ...

'Richard,' I yelled, 'It might be better if ...'

It was too late. As I was about to tell him he might have needed the banister for support, without an ounce of resistance in any muscle of his body, as he stepped off that top step his supporting leg collapsed. He was very lucky to be completely relaxed. He never felt a thing while rolling down those thirty stairs and sprawling all over the polished floorboards at the bottom.

One good thing came out of that tumble, he was now in a good position to put his shoes back on.

Moments later, I'd found going down stairs much more pleasant than climbing. Like the rest of the guys, I'd made it one step at a time, supported by the banister.

While sitting on the floor with both his shoes on, Richard looked up at me. 'Hey! How come you held on to that banister coming down the stairs? What are ya, a woos?'

After some crazy laughter, and after I'd put my shoes on, we both took an oath with our fists over our hearts: hope to die, you know, serious pledging. This staircase scenario would be our dying secret; that is, until now.

On the way back to the hotel, it was as if there'd been a death in the family. A little bit further along, then suddenly the tension of silent excitement became too much to bare.

The cry of 'Yeehaaa, Yeehawww, Yeehaaa' came from the front seat. It was all too much for the town crier, 'Big' Greg Thomason, who came to life. 'Man I was out there, layin' on my gut. I'm driftin' out into the stratosphere. I'm that relaxed I'm visitin' the other world. She's massaging me, she's relaxing me. Then fuckin' *boom*, she grabs the lever that's steerin' my fucking space journey, snaps it back between my legs, up between the cheeks of my arse ... God-damn, I thought she'd broken the fucking thing. But hey, how about when the little head can't get no blood supply, ain't that something else!'

Then Dwayne joined in ... 'How about that fuckin' vibratin' pelvis brush massagin' all that oil over my–'

'Yeah and what about ...'

'Yeah, but did yours ...?'

I was sitting in the backseat on the driver's side behind Kenji. I'd gone within myself. There was an early morning sunrise about to break that line of horizon, and the skyline of the city in downtown Kyoto. Some things were better left unsaid, left to the imagination ...

In about ten minutes I'd be home. Tamiko would wake up and want to know everything. Yeah, some things were better left unsaid.

Man, this Silver Bullet, sure is something else ... We were on our way to Sappora. The speedometer was right there on the wall next to the bar. Normally, the needle sat on 100 KPH but today our driver must have been making up for lost time, as he'd had it steady on 120 for ages. I was at the bar with Richard, we were both drinking orange juice. The glasses sat steady on the bar and there was no sense of movement, except when you looked out the window at everything flying by. The band members and the crew were kicking back and hangin' five, especially the bodyguards – all with filthy big smiles on their dials.

I'd spent most of the trip sitting at the windows with Tamiko. We'd *talked* about the picturesque scenery; she'd told me about the agriculture, export industry and discussed the differences in lifestyle and attitude between Japan's big-city dwellers and here in the countryside. We watched together, as one by one, the rural townships sailed on by. I'd reached out and taken her hand ...

Knock, knock; knock, knock ...

'Bob, hey Bob! C'mon, get that bloody partner in crime of yours! Get that bloody Richard Norton and you guy's meet me down in the coffee shop in five. I want to go into town and pick up some tit-bits.' By the time Mick had said tit-bits, he was already down the corridor.

Tamiko was in the shower. I didn't know what they did in there, but Japanese girls stayed in baths and showers forever.

I stuck my head into the steam. 'Gotta go babe, you be all right for a coupla hours?'

'*Hai*', she answered in the affirmative, making me laugh. Tamiko gave me a kiss on the forehead for my trouble. She was embarrassed, not because of her nakedness, but because I'd laughed at the sight of her nipples bouncing.

Richard and I went down, had a coffee with Mick, who had the address for the speciality where he wanted to go.

'Sorry to rush you guys before, it's just that we have to be back at the Sappora Hotel by one o'clock for a luncheon–press thing with Mr Udo and the media.'

'Mr Freetwood, this, your premises you ask for, up on seventh froor. Here you can get tit-bits!' That bloody Kenji San, he was everywhere!

Fifth, sixth, seventh ... Richard and I were full of anticipation, then the elevator doors opened. Holy shit, an entire floor of magic, tricks, practical jokes and oh yes, tit-bits – as far as the eye could see. Mick, the medieval magical magician, loved to play the practical joker; inside there he was, this little kid that didn't want to get out.

'Richard, Bob, over here, quick! You guys gotta see this!'

Oh, oh, what was he up to now?

'Look here, this store and those Japanese godfathers must have a deal going on. Have a look at all of these Yakuza apologies.'

The Yakuza, or Japanese Mafia, offer finger joints as apologies for any wrongdoing in the eyes of their warlords. Maybe Mick was right, here were these boxes full of cotton wool, and lying there in a sorry state were human fingers, cut-off and complete with blood. They looked so real, worse still, I picked one out of the box and felt it. The texture actually *felt* real, so real it gave me a cold sweat.

'Richard, Bob, over here quick! You guys gotta see this!'

As Richard and I approached him a second time, Mick had his back to us. He turned, holding something against his forehead. 'I see it all from up here, my meditation shows me the secrets of the universe. I am the Devil's deity.'

There was Mick, head and shoulders above Richard and me. He was head, shoulders, chest and some more above every other person in the store. Nearly everyone in the whole store had stopped to stare. This mad-man with his insane laughter, laughing at his own brand of humour, pressing a third eye against the middle of his forehead.

Just like the fingers, now there were boxes and boxes full of bloody eyes. I had to pick one up, just to see if it felt as real as that finger. There were also human tongues, hands, feet and ears; in fact, there was every human body part imaginable around the store. And, yes, there was a display wall full of them too, all shapes and sizes. There was no way I was going to be seen, standing there with one of those in my hand, trying to see how real it felt!

'Ok, I'm done, we're outta here.' This store was Mick's pleasure palace and he'd compiled bags and bags of goodies.

At street level, Richard went off to get Kenji and the car and I stayed with Mick. It was lucky Richard and I had our tour jackets on and Mick had on a long black, down-below-his-knees English tweed double-breaster. The city of Sappora had turned nasty, with dark clouds, wind and a biting cold with a capital B, which believe me is never as good as a capital A.

Kenji dropped us off at the front of the hotel and went off to park the car. The rest of us walked through the entrance, headed for reception to pick up our keys. Meanwhile, Mick pulled out a Star Wars (the movie was real big at the time, I mean real big) space invader galactic Bren-gun from his tit-bits.

'Richard, catch this!'

'Now run for your life you Aussie bodyguard bastard!'

This Sappora Hotel entry foyer reception area was surrounded by very high ceilings, probably ten metres up. The area has half a dozen huge floor-to-ceiling support pillars. So, as Richard caught Bren-gun number one, Mick rearmed himself with a second Star Wars space invader galactic Bren-gun.

Mick handed me the rest of his tit-bits shopping bags and I moved right out of the way.

Mick and Richard had taken up positions behind pillars, right in the lobby, right in reception and right in front of dozens of Japanese tourists and business identities who were either signing in or out. When the trigger of one of these galactic Bren-guns is activated (not squeezed, activated is the operative word) a strong red laser beam becomes a red laser dot on anything solid. That includes reception desks, walls, doors, or even the odd houseguests or hotel manager's foreheads.

Both Bren-guns were activated and making more noise than the Tokyo traffic and with more lights flashing than the 5 a.m. downtown cabarets. Red dots were bouncing off the pillars as both Mick and Richard tried to win this battle. Suddenly, both men stepped into the open for a stand-off. Either Richard was too fast, or Mick too slow, either way Mick bore a big red dot right on his heart, and Richard wanted everyone to know about it.

'You're dead Mick Fleetwood, dead!'

Mick's laser wound was fatal. He was dying on the floor right in front of reception, right in front of everyone. (About a decade later, Mick would do a couple of movies, but what I saw here was real academy award material. No-one could be more convincing in a death scene.) Mick's arms and legs twitched, his whole body gyrated, contorting every which-way. When this all stopped, the only sign of life left was the quivering of the eyes. Richard Norton, the survivor, grabbed our keys and shoved both Bren-guns back into the tit-bits bag I was carrying. Richard then helped his adversary back to his feet, who now was only badly wounded, and the three of us staggered towards the elevators.

Japanese people, particularly in crowds, don't generally laugh like Westerners do. When they think something is funny, they laugh by placing one hand over their mouths, and bouncing their shoulders up and down. Mick and Richard must have been really incredibly funny! Everyone had a hand over a mouth with shoulders bouncing, including the Sappora Hotel day manager! Thank God.

We'd come from the lobby reception with its ten-metre-plus ceilings and we were about to enter an elevator with a two-metre ceiling. As the doors opened six Japanese, three men and three women, had boarded from the lower lobby or car park level. Richard and I had entered and, like all good body-guards, stood with our backs to the wall, though I was more at the rear corner. Due to our height, Richard and I were a little uneasy with the two-metre ceilings. And poor old Mick had to first bend over to get under the archway. When he was actually in the elevator and stood up, he banged his head against the ceiling. I was momentarily embarrassed for him as he turned his back on all of us, and stood right up front.

Richard pressed *hachi* (number eight). The Japanese were impressed: they must have known this was the floor of the deluxe penthouses. They kept looking at Richard and me, observing how close our heads were to the ceiling. In turn, they'd look at Mick, who stood there with his knees bent and still his head jammed against the roof.

Each one of them must have been thinking, ohr, I wonder what has gone wrong with eravator; this man does not fit!

'Ping!' The doors started closing.

'Ping, ping!' They closed and sprung back open again. Richard pressed the 'close' button.

'Ping!' The doors closed again.

'Ping, ping!' They opened again.

Richard again jabbed his finger on to the 'close' button, this time angrily.

'Ping!' The doors closed for the third time. This time they stayed closed.

Mick turned around in that long black English tweed double-breaster, his head still jammed against the roof. He started screaming in excruciating and agonising pain. He used his left hand to grab the right wrist of his English tweed, but his right hand had been chopped off! It was wedged in between the elevator doors, with blood all over the doors and dripping off his fingers.

The ploy worked, he'd scared the absolute daylights out of me. Richard was as quiet as a stunned mullet as *go, roku, shichi* (five, six, seven), the needle followed the numbers ...

'Ping!' The doors opened at *hachi*, Mick's bloodied hand had fallen to the floor. He'd bent down and picked it up with his left hand, while being very careful to keep his right fist clenched, with his elbow bent and shoulder slightly raised, giving the vision of a handless right sleeve. As we all got off the elevator I thought, holy shit, what about the Japs? They were all hanging on to one and other, huddled in the corner, but it was all right. They had their hands over their mouths and their shoulders were bouncing. Whew! Thank God.

Mr Udo, the promoter, entrepreneur of Japan, did nothing by half measures, and this day would be no exception. He'd put on a lavish, no expense spared *table d'hôte*. He'd invited the who's-who of Sappora. Thus, business identities, Sappora sports stars, local media and all his local staff celebrated the success of the Fleetwood Mac world tour.

The band were enjoying themselves; people talked mostly about that night's show at Sappora Stadium. Meanwhile, Mick had politely stood up to look over at Richard and me. It looked like he was going to the rest room, for which he didn't expect us to accompany him; but, one of us always did anyway, it was so much a part of the job we didn't even think about it. If the client moves, we move.

'I'll go, you stay and keep an eye on the others,' volunteered Richard.

Moments later they returned, just as the caterers were serving soups.

Though Mick and Richard had disappeared briefly, they'd never gone anywhere near the men's room. Apparently, Mick had cooked up a deal with some guy in the kitchen ...

'*Eeargahh!*' Response number one.

'What the fuck?' Response number two.

'*Waarreee!*' Response number three.

'Who the fuck?' Response number four.

The deal Mick had cooked up was that there would be plenty of eyes and ears and other such niceties for almost everybody – in their soup!

Should anybody ever ask me what I remember most about Sappora, I'd have to say Mick the magician's really funny, just funny and definitely not-so-funny practical jokes.

Knock, knock. Knock, knock.

'Bob, hey Bob! C'mon, get that bloody partner of yours. In four weeks it's bloody Christmas, and I need to get the pressies for Jenny, Amy and Lucy and everyone. Coffee shop in five, okay?' By the time he'd said Jenny, Amy and Lucy, Mick was already down the corridor.

Tamiko was in the shower. I'd got my usual *'hai'* and one of those cute kisses on the neck when I'd told her I'd be gone for a coupla hours and asked if she'd be okay until I got back.

Richard and I went down and had a coffee with Mick. So far, this first day in Osaka was an exact replica of out first day in Sappora.

'Good morning, my formal honorary members of the Fleetwood Practical Jokers Society. Today is another shopping day. After the Hawaii and Maui concerts, we will be back in California just before Christmas. Everyone says Osaka is a great city to do some shopping. Nowhere near as crowded or as expensive as Tokyo, and there's this one thing I gotta get myself for Christmas.'

Hmm, I wondered, what could that be? I wasn't game to ask.

'Kenji, Kenji San, how are you today? So, you're taking us shopping again ...' I was trying to think who Kenji reminded me of. This funny little Japanese man was the jack-of-all-trades for Mr Udo.

'I am very good, domo (thankyou). I understand

shopping today. Mr Udo San awready exprain.' Kenji had opened the rear door of the limo for us. He stood with his feet together, stooped slightly forward and with his hands clasped.

The sight cracked me up.

'Richard, Mick, look we've got our own Japanese Manuel from Tokyo's 'Faulty Towers'.'

Kenji was really worth his salt when it came to shopping. Japan is not like Bali or Bangkok, or so many other Asian countries that love the barter system. It's a very expensive country, and for a tourist it's hard to get the prices down, unless you have a Kenji San.

Mick, as usual, was like a big kid, shopping for Jenny and their daughters, Amy who was seven and Lucy, the little one, who was four and a half years old. It was also going to be Amy's birthday a couple of weeks after Christmas, and Mick was asking the sales lady what could he get for an eight-year-old girl going on fifteen. The reason Mick was like a kid without shoes on a hot tin roof was that just over a year ago he and Jenny had divorced. And six months later, in true Fleetwood Mac tradition, they'd remarried. However, getting married again had been the furthest thing on both their minds, it was a marriage of convenience to get their Green cards and, just as important, to give their two daughters US citizenship. This way Fleetwood Mac could continue living and working in the US.

Mick had bought this lovely house high up over Topanga Canyon, which was very secluded and had stunning views. He was looking forward to a special Christmas with all the Fleetwood's together, and after around two hours of shopping, he had a heap of goodies in the carry bags.

At the time Richard Norton had had a problem: a very special lady called Beverly Pinder. Well, it wasn't really Pinder, it was De Silva and she was an Aussie Sri Lankan. Beverly Pinder was her modelling name and with that name she'd won the Miss Australia Beauty Pageant. Very soon Ms Pinderwould place third in Miss World. On top of all this she had a desire to change her name to Beverley Norton: Mrs, that is! She'd worked with Richard at the Immigration Department, and they'd been in a serious relationship for quite a while. So, Richard would have to solve his dilemma of finding that one special present. This didn't give him much choice, not even in Osaka, but he would keep searching ...

'Well that's me, I'm done. I have something for everyone, except for yours truly.' Mick was keen to get a present for himself.

Kenji knew the place where we could all get something for ourselves.

Back at the car we piled all Mick's presents into the back seat. Within thirty minutes Kenji had us somewhere in the middle of Osaka, at one of the biggest department stores I'd ever been in. Up on the third floor was a department that sold only the latest and the most expensive radio-controlled toys, gadgets and knick-knacks. The department next to that was for Bob and Richard to die for: it had everything from samurai swords, helmets, armour and a huge selection of Japanese doll characters depicting ages as far back as the Edo period. There were Ninjas, Sumo, everything conceivable: Kenji had done well again.

Being an avid weapons collector I picked up a one-only-in-stock incredibly decorated white Japanese sword. This blade was truly amazing. It was estimated to be of World War I vintage, and was an extremely rare find. In time it would become a valuable collector's item.

Richard took the same time as me to spot what he wanted: complete in a glass case, set on a crimson cushion was a really magnificent samurai helmet, alldone in black, red, gold and silver. Good things come in threes ...

Mick was ever anxious. 'Hey, that's good guys, I'm done, too! Let's get outta here! I've got a sound check at 3.00 p.m. and tonight's the big Osaka show.'

There we were, Mick, Richard and Bob, all with presents in three cardboard boxes. I was carrying mine in one hand, it was the same size as a pack of cigarettes, except about one metre in length. Richard carried his in both hands, it was the same size as a portable TV set, except it only weighed three kilos. Then there was Mick's *mystery box* present to himself: he'd held one end and Kenji the other. It was lucky enough to fit in the boot of the car. Meanwhile, Richard and I had to squeeze ours in with Mick's other presents for everyone.

'Kenji San, you did very well today, I got myself a very spectacular white *katana*.'

'Orh, thank you. I see orso Richard get very nice samurai hermet in grass case.'

'Well Mick, now you know what the two of us got for ourselves. I'm dying to know what you bought, what's in that *mystery box*, or is it some sort of national security secret?'

'How did you know that, that's exactly what it is! It's my own personal national security secret. But I can tell you guys, as long as you never breathe a word of what I'm about to tell you.' Only Mick could do this the way that he did. His words were delivered as if they'd been scripted, and the facials, contorting of the body and so on, it was all very bardic, like in an incantation.

'Yes, I can tell you guys, you can be trusted. I bought a totally radio-controlled helicopter. They wanted US$2800 and Kenji got it for me at a bargainfor US$2500. It has a two-metre wing span when it's fully assembled and will fly at up to 100 kilomtres per hour. It also can't be picked up by any radar, so no-one will know it's even flying around. The actual carry space inside the cabin is about as big as a shoebox, and it's capable of flying five times the distances I need it for. Just to fly any little secrets that might need to be flown around, or I might just take it down the canyon and entertain Amy and Lucy.'

This was then accompanied by laughter, which helped to confuse, perhaps expose the garrulity of the whole conversation.

Perhaps we'd never learn what was in Mick's *mystery box*.

Fleetwood Mac's final gig in Japan was in Yokohama. We arrived in the morning, and after lunch we had the usual local media meeting. That night there was a plan to attack downtown Yokohama. This was Tamiko's hometown. She was spending the day with family and later would catch up for dinner with Mr Udo and friends, and then would show us around the traps. On the following day, there'd be a sound check and in the evening the Mac's final Japanese performance to another sold-out show.

On this particular day I couldn't remember who

I'd gone into this city with. Kenji drove us, and it was to do some more Christmas shopping. It may have been with Christine or John McVie. I think it was John sussing out some maritime supply company, for any new technology he could take home. (At this time John had been living on his ten-metre boat in the LA marina.)

We were in the city square, which had a large rectangular pond that was packed with marine life. Seated around the pond, almost shoulder to shoulder with others standing in line, hundreds of Japanese businessmen were fishing, complete with rods and reel. They hooked and reeled their catch on to dry land, and unhooked the fish and threw them into a large basket on wheels. This continued within a void of any emotion connected to the pastime. And when the baskets were filled, a couple of Japanese elderly aqua-attendants took the baskets, replaced them with empty ones, then at an allotted pond-side section, they tipped the fish back into the pond.

As Kenji would later inform us, this lunchtime meditation came at a very expensive hourly rate.

Further down from the park we came across an entire ground floor of a high-rise office complex. This was the Japanese version of an amusement parlour. Instead of hundreds, there were thousands of businessmen and women. All of them were dressed in the familiar colours of black, navy and grey (Japanese business uniforms in 1977 had no vibrant colour). All of them were expressionless as they fed coin after coin into these machines. There were thousands of machines, each clanking with it own sound effects, and each with it's own maze of lights.

'Kenji San, how much can these people win on these machines, considering the fervent pace they're pushing those coins down the chutes?' I'd asked.

'Orh, no Bob San, this not rike Western gambring, Japanese business persons just pray for score. Come back again tomorrow, try and beat score.'

Well, that's two stupid pastimes that would never work in Australia. However, twenty-five years later, there'd be the same money-sucking machines everywhere. Would the same meditation fish ponds start to appear in the central city malls, complete with elderly aqua-attendants?

The next characteristic of the Japanese business class was the coffin motels. To stay near work during the week (thus avoiding traffic-congested journeys of many hours each way) people would rent motel rooms the size of a large coffin. They could no longer buy a car without legal proof of a car space; hence, no space, no car.

Property values in these cities had sky-rocketed to such an extent, the banks had introduced triple-life mortgages; the average business person that spent his or her lunchtime catching fish, or feeding metal boxes, or who was sleeping in a coffin, or using public transport because of no car space, had to secure a triple-life mortgage to pay for a unit.

More scary, this fish-catching/metal box mentality was a result of supposedly one of the highest standards of living in the world. The only problem was that this had resulted in such high levels of stress, the Japanese have one of the highest (and with much less drug consumption than most of their Western counterparts) rates of student suicide.

On top of all of this the Japanese can't let off steam the way Westerners do, their language does not possess profanities as we know them. Despite the high standard of education, the attitude to personal cleanliness and hygiene, this pales in light of the hierarchical levels of respect for all other members of society; hence, the Japanese lack of comprehending Westerners' stress-release through personal denigration, or us swearing at one another!

Three of their major values – education, cleanliness and personal respect for one another – affords them really only one word of an offensive nature: *baka*. With this one word they can deflate all three major values in one hit. The word *baka* is used to insult the intelligence. It literally means *silly*.

One late night, on a long flight from some city to another (actually on American Airlines from Tokyo to Hawaii), I was checking our itinerary for what was coming up: Fleetwood Mac had two sold-out shows at the HIC Stadium and our stay at my favourite resort in Waikiki for five days, the Ilakai Hotel. Then it would be off to one of the larger Hawaiian islands, Maui, where we'd stay for three days at the Royal Lahaina Hotel. The reason for this trip to Maui was John McVie, who when he wasn't living on his ten-metre yacht, lived in this great house on the island, where he wanted the Mac to do a concert for his neighbours.

The flight attendants had served dinner, Richard was sitting next to me. He was fully reclined with his black-eye patches on and with this contented smile on his face.

As usual, first class on this flight was occupied by our party, which also took up all the early rows of the economy class. Christine sat opposite me and next to JC.

'Chris, that Backgammon lesson you promised me, is that still on for this flight?' I asked, hopeful.

'You bet. Though straight after dinner I'm planning forty winks. When I wake up, it'll be upstairs for Bob Jones Backgammon lesson number, how many is this? Oh yeah, lesson number three.'

Mick Fleetwood and John McVie were in the front row. After dinner John went upstairs for a drink. Christine had gone to slumberland and JC had moved up to sit with Mick to discuss some tour business. Mick, as manager of the band, listened to JC intently. To help pass the time he'd also got some gaffer tape off one of the road crew, cut it into very thin strips and was, with quite a degree of artistry, applying a set of dinner plates, saucer and cup, and a full set of cutlery on to the wall in front of his seat. When completed some time later, it was definitely artistic enough to warrant the equally professional photo shoot Mick provided: from laying on the floor, leaning over the seat from the second row, and kneeling all over Lindsey Buckingham and Richard Dashut, to standing on his seat with his giant frame hunched over and pressing himself against the overhead lockers, and not missing a beat of JC's business rave. He'd wound off a full roll of film from his newest toy, the latest model fully automatic camera he'd picked up while passing through Tokyo's Duty Free.

Stevie, close by, had on a headset and was listening to somebody else's music.

I'd given dinner a miss. Instead it'd seemed a good chance to grab forty winks and revisit the Australian leg of the tour with the *big* Mac.

Richard Norton and I'd picked up with the circus (thanks to the Paul Dainty Corporation) on the South Pacific leg. Australasian audiences were right up there in their reaction to Fleetwood Mac's new sound and presentation. There were capacity crowds in Perth, Adelaide and Brisbane. People came out in New South Wales in force: 48 000 Fleetwood Mac fans turned out at the Sydney Showgrounds. Stamping, whistling and screaming dictated encore after encore. This went well into overtime and contrary to a city by-law that disallowed any noise pollution created by amplified music after 11 p.m.

Melbourne must have set some sort of crowd-drawing record at the Calder Raceway: 60 000 wanted to hear and see the new Fleetwood Mac. Paul Dainty had sent the 'dozers in a month early to rearrange the shape of the Calder Raceway property. He'd wanted to build this huge mound that would work as a natural amphitheater, while affording most of the fans a better view of the stage – and he did! Six large portable, self-generated lighting towers were erected to help police with the dispersion of car parks and the kilometres of cars parked on both sides of the highway. More than 100 buses provided a shuttle service from 8.30 a.m. between Flinders Street Railway Station to Calder, giving country and interstate fans easy access to the site.

Australian, UK, US and Japanese flags flew above the stage. A 70 000-watt sound system surrounded the stage, and on either side, huge screens could carry the images on stage, clear to the boundaries.

The show was billed as *Rockarena*, it headlined Fleetwood Mac. On the same bill were Santana, Creation (from Japan) and Melbourne's home-grown superstars, Little River Band. Added to all of this was The Kevin Borich Express. If Kevin wasn't *the*, he was definitely *one of the* best guitarists bred in Australia.

Paul Dainty's publicist had released the catering statistics, allowing this Circus to be well catered for. On the day food would be sold by at least 150 staff from thirty stalls at ten points around the grounds. Caterers had ordered 1500 dozen hot dogs, 1000 dozen pies, 500 dozen spring rolls, and an equal amount of hamburgers, 300 dozen packets of potato chips and, depending on the weather, 5000 to 6000 dozen soft drinks and 1500 to 2000 dozen ice-creams.

Two marquees were set up, one serving breakfast, lunch and dinner to 200 Bob Jones security personnel and the many police and first-aid officers on duty throughout the day and night.

The other marquee would be for backstage people: all the bands, road crews and publicity teams. Fleetwood Mac, for example, was treated to an elaborate buffet of ham, beef and *chook*. One of the officers in charge, Chief Superintendent K.J. Carton, said fifty police members would be on duty at the show. A considerable amount would cope with the traffic outside.

St. John's Ambulance brigade had called several times for extra members to cope with people suffering from heat exhaustion, lacerations and the combination of drugs and alcohol. The Brigade treated more than 600 people at the concert, including one case of a dislocated shoulder and one man with a broken ankle being taken to hospital.

Backstage, such details and events seemed a world away as performers, road and security crews and publicity teams gathered in their marquees and caravans, enjoying all varieties of Aussie ice-cold beers and soft drinks, lavish amounts of food, pinball machines and even a pool table.

A fleet of cars – a couple of Mercedes, a Rolls Royce and a Jaguar – stood by to taxi the band members as they arrived by helicopter.

Press reports stated that tight BJC security made

it impossible for anyone outside the industry/media and groups to get backstage.

Fleetwood Mac did a fabulous show. Everybody excelled and the support acts all outdid themselves. Little River Band's harmonies were as usual 'when only the best will do'. Creation did well, but the size of the crowd possibly intimidated them. One of the magic moments of the entire Rockarena Concert was when Kevin Borich jammed with Carlos Santana, who is one of the world's finest guitarists.

If you were there on that night in 1977 when Santana did Peter Green's 'Black Magic Woman', well you know, don't you?

This whirlwind tour around Australia and New Zealand culminated with yet another spectacular show in Western Springs, Auckland.

The message 'Welcome to Tokyo' was printed in small letters across the top of a large horizontal canvas banner ...

'Bob,' I heard from the distance, that beautiful English, sometimes American, sometimes international accent.

'Bob!'

Oh no! It's Christine McVie's voice ...

I was waking up just as we were landing in Japan. In a few hours of real time, I'd be about to meet Tamiko for the second time. The memories were flooding back ...

'Bob, this is the third time I've called you. You said you wanted that Backgammon lesson. Meet me upstairs in ten minutes.'

Just ten minutes more sleep ... back to FREETWOOD MAC and the melting penguins ...

'Bob San, this is Tamiko, she very interested for meeting you.' That's funny, I'd only met this Kenji character moments earlier, and already he was introducing me to this drop-dead gorgeous ...

'Tamiko, this is Bob San.'

She extended her hand as a courtesy of friendship. To reciprocate I took her hand. That was when lightning struck: I'd been smitten.

'Well Tamiko, you're a very attractive young lady, and I really hope you're aware I'm not one of the band members?'

'*Hai!*'

'Did you know that I'm only one of the bodyguards?'

'*Hai!*'

Two out of three, not bad. Let's try for the big one. You know, my room has two singles, perhaps I should have reception change that for a double?'

'*Hai!*'

'Kenji, Kenji San, help me!'

He came over and I explained my dilemma: I couldn't speak any Japanese, and by the sound of it, maybe Tamiko couldn't speak any English. Kenji explained that *hai* literally translated means *yes* in English. But as she didn't understand English, she had no concept of the meaning. For her, using this word was an expansion of the subject. It could have several interpretations, such as: I understand, that will be fine or if this is what you want.

I told Kenji I didn't get it.

'Orh, Bob San, you have to think first. Then you speak about subject. Then Tamiko understand.'

'Sorry Kenji, I don't get it!'

'You don't get it? Orh, Bob San when Freetwood Mac sing songs they sing about *subject*, yes?'

Of course, I understood that.

'Okay, Japanese audience cannot speak any Engrish. But when they risten to *subject*, they think, they think about the matter of this subject and then they understand. Then they can even sing songs in Engrish'.

This was the first of many times that Kenji would be of great assistance. With a little more of his help, just until I got the hang of this *subject* thing, he'd help me find out that Tamiko was twenty-two years old and studying journalism at the Yokohama University. She was also doing some work experience for the largest daily newspaper in Yokohama. She'd been sent to Tokyo in the role of like, a cub reporter, and told by her editor to do a story from a totally different perspective: she was to try and get the scoop of the tour above all opposition. This was another story I'd heard somewhere before, but Tamiko had pulled it off much quicker and easier than that reporter Ashley Wallace in the ABBA tour movie.

Bodyguard to the Stars, I could see it all. Pretty soon, I felt I was getting the hang of this form of conversation about subject matter. For the next three weeks Tamiko and I'd have many, really lengthy, stimulating conversations. That night we'd begun by discussing the press conference in detail, including the melting penguins. While travelling by Silver Bullet across Japan we discussed its scenery, politics and religion, and made each of the Mac's concerts a favourite *subject*.

During what I'd thought to be the opportune romantic moment, in the middle of making love, that night in Yokohama I'd asked Tamiko, 'Do you ruve me?'

But the only answer I got, and the last word I'd ever heard Tamiko say was, '*Hai!*'

'Bob Jones, where the hell have you been?' Christine woke me from a deep sleep.

I'd certainly blown my Backgammon lesson: about an hour had slipped by and Christine and everyone – Richard Dashut, Richard Norton, Mick, JC, John and Christine, Lindsey and Stevie – had all got into full party mode. I'd slept on, missing even the party.

Back in those days upstairs was always the party room (now it's business class) for first-class travellers to play games, watch videos, have a few drinks, join the mile-high VIP club, or whatever. Downstairs was for the most part meals, movies, meetings and sleeping ...

We arrived late in Honolulu, in this very Japanese-orientated tourist attraction capital of Hawaii, a harbor-side city in the south-east of Oahu.

In Japan, due to the population and hectic traffic, the limos were more your standard five-seater sedan, with a non–English-speaking (except for Kenji) Japanese chauffeur, who always wore white gloves and sometimes a white medical health mask over the mouth. In Hawaii, the limousine companies had bought up all the old 1950s and 1960s Californian limos: Rolls Royces, Chevrolets, Cadillac's and so on. These were the biggest, longest and most stretched out limos seen anywhere during the 1970s. They had all the luxuries you could possibly think of: black, I mean, really blacked out windows; and two, sometimes three sunroofs. Once inside these immaculate cars, the leather seats still smelled brand new. The Hawaiian owner-drivers would polish them inside and out, you could see your reflection in any of the chrome work.

When the last of us had cleared the cadre of Customs, there was this long line of gargantuan Mafiosi black automobiles waiting to shuttle us off to Waikiki, and what had to be the most grandiose of hotels in Hawaii during the 1970s: the Ilakai Hotel. The hotel overlooked the ocean and its sweeping sandy beaches and crystal clear water. On entering, the driveway led to the bottom end of the beachfront in Waikiki.

The band had had a reasonably late night and would be sleeping off the serious jet lag in the morning. Richard and I were up at sunrise to do our martial arts meditations on the beachfront. The later luncheon press conference went without a hitch. It was there that I met a very good friend of John McVie, who would eventually become a very serious martial arts student of my organisation and one of my most loyal friends.

John had introduced Wayne Cody as a personal friend, rather than as a friend of the band.

'Do you work as a bodyguard, Wayne?' I'd asked, considering he was 190 centimetres tall and physically bigger than the town crier, Big Greg.

'No-ho,' he laughed. 'I'm a lover, not a fighter, but John is always saying I should come on the road as a Mac-minder. Maybe one day.'

It turned out that Wayne's American accent was something he'd acquired after living in Hawaii for the previous couple of years. He was actually born in New Zealand. After spending time catching waves in Noosa, he'd arrived at the surfing destination of Hawaii. A chance meeting through a friend from Maui led him to John McVie. John made Wayne one of those offers he couldn't refuse: a job as a live-in house-minder. Plus, because he was a carpenter by trade, Wayne was put in charge of renovations.

Time to begin'...

The Bob Jones third-time Backgammon lesson in the penthouse of tutor Christine McVie was refereed by John 'JC' Courage and witnessed ringside by John McVie, Richard Norton and Wayne Cody.

We'd shared the roll of the dice about three times each, when the annoying sounds of bang, thump and scrape came from against the adjoining wall between Christine's and Mick Fleetwood's penthouse.

'Ignore it and it might go away,' Christine suggested.

I soon learned how, when she won a battle before I could advance all my men beyond the first six points, Christine could score triple points – and she often did!

More banging, thumping and scraping ...

'Eegarhhh, fark! Help me!' This time it was the cry of a voice in need; Mick Fleetwood sounded like he'd done himself harm.

First, one needs to conjure Mick's lanky, extremely elongated physique, his thinning straggly shoulder-length hair, and his very skinny, very white textured skin. Now, picture him in nothing but a multi-coloured, baggy, down-to-his-knees pair of board shorts.

Apart from smoking a couple of joints that had made Hawaiian plantations famous, after his dry stint in Japan, Mick had felt the need to snort several lines of cocaine. Also, on his penthouse floor lay an almost empty bottle of Jack Daniels. Thanks to all these substances Mick had thought he was on the opposite side of the island, the north shore, with its infamous five- to fifteen-metre waves.

Now, due to the five-metre-high ceilings of his penthouse, Mick had gathered every movable item of furniture and had arranged them in a rolling three-and-a-half-metre-shaped wave. This gave him a cramped metre and a half to mount his ironing board (the adjustable legs had been dismantled), kick off the peak of the wave (which was a single-seater divan) and ride down its face (the full length of the dining room eight-seater table).

Mick had wanted to turn off the table, ride the wave across his divan, on to his queen-size mattress, but his ironing board nose-dived off the end of the couch and sent him sprawling over a variety of dining chairs, the sharp edges of the coffee table and, at a guess I'd say, all the white bed pillows acting as the foam of the breaking waves ...

The Maui tennis courts were a hive of activity on the day of the concert held for John McVie's neighbours.

After an early morning training session, Richard and I had wandered over to check out where we'd be protecting our protégés. Trucks, ramps and packing cases had been unfolded and equipment transformed into stage, lights and sound-rigs right before our eyes. These international road crews had no peers when it came to having it together for that all important mid-afternoon sound check.

We'd done two shows in Honolulu at the HIC

Stadium and Mick didn't appear to be carrying any life-threatening scars from his hotel surfing prank.

It was then that I noticed a dozen men, all as big as Wayne Cody or Big Greg. They were all Islanders, dressed in slacks and white shirts with ties. They were moving around the venue, doing what I normally did: that crucial venue-check as regular as clockwork.

'JC, who are the rockapes running the security check-list?'

'Friend not foe!' he answered with a grumpy voice, which meant he'd either had a late night or a knock-back, or perhaps both. 'John McVie had a meeting with the mayor of Maui yesterday. This tennis court concert is getting a lot of media coverage on the mainland, all over the US. With all this attention on Maui, and its ever-growing tourist industry, the mayor don't want no trouble. That's the reason he sent down these guys. The locals call them the Maui Mafia, I call it a little bit of neighborhood nepotism myself. Anyway, they're on the team. John told them about you two guys and our American Fleetwood Mac minders. But, fuck man, this show is already sold out; fucking near the whole island's coming and there's still punters flying in from all over.'

JC was right: the two shows in Honolulu had been in an indoor stadium. This was an outdoor show. With Maui's population of about 8000, with people coming from outside, and seating capacity at 6500, that meant more than 1500 would miss out.

The lunchtime barbecue at John McVie's was very personalised: band members, immediate family and bodyguards were invited. The mid-afternoon sound check went like clockwork. Then that night there was a shuttle system, due to the shortage of limos on Maui. The band had made it safely backstage (a function room of the local tennis association), not bothering to eat from the huge buffet that had been prepared.

The band members had several tents for makeup and warming up. Meanwhile, the road crew had made a backstage compound by parking the tray of one of the semi-trailers off the side of the function room. This was squared off by stacking the empty packing cases to form an above-head-high wall with a two-metre gap for punter-pass access.

Then later ... 'I'm sorry sir, you can't come beyond this point.'

This islander was as big as any of the Maui Mafia: he was drinking alcohol from a glass, didn't display any backstage pass and I'd made him angry.

'Who the fuck are you, and who the fuck is gonna stop me from coming backstage?'

In my earlier gang days, this guy would've been dead meat. Then Paul Dainty's words came back, 'Bob you have to do this work without punching everyone'.

'I'm sorry, sir. I'm part of Fleetwood Mac's security. You don't have a pass, I can't let you come beyond this point!'

'Yeah, well fuck you!' He took a pace back, turned and walked off.

Had I taken this approach all those years ago, my life could have been much simpler.

I wanted to catch Richard and tell him what had just gone down. I mean, it didn't make sense: all that aggression dissolving so simply to a bad-arse almost twice my size, and one who would've thought I was just short of sucking up with all that security jargon.

Richard was working the door between the compound and function room. We were using a three-colour pass system: red got you into this media courtyard-style compound, yellow got you into the function room where the band were relaxing and mixing with friends, and green was access all areas for all immediate circus folk like us.

Just then, as I caught Richard's attention, my big bastardised behemoth had walked halfway down the trailer, and opted for crawling in between the sets of tandem wheels: on his way to mixing with the media, perhaps even telling Richard he wanted to have a drink with Mick and John or watch Stevie getting made up!

I started moving – while thinking he's mine! – and cut him off his errant journey right in the centre of the compound. While trying my best not to attract attention, I firmly said, 'Hey, shit for brains, you missed the point. Now, how about you and me simply walk on over to where this story began, and I'm sure we can work it all out – one way or the other.'

His plan was simple: he figured with his size, he'd simply walk me down and stomp over me. My sense of balance surprised him, as I placed my hand on his chest it stopped him in his tracks.

'Like I said, shit for ...' I tried to draw him back to our starting position, away from the compound crowd, who were already starting to show interest in the situation, before it was too late.

But Jesuz, it was already too late. Right then I knew he was a gang guy. Because of his black racist ego, his chest pulsated against the palm of my hand in contempt for what I'd just done.

'You piece of fucking white dog shit', he screamed, looking at my arm. He took a step back and yelled above the backstage mood-music. *'Hey white boy, you think you can touch me with your filthy fucking white hand?'* He turned and walked towards the semi-trailer and put his glass of Scotch on the side of the tray. Then he turned and was on his way, walking my walk, as I had him in my sights.

Deo gratius for the tolerance of my teachers of the arts, Jack, Tino and Sal; for the more than a dozen years on only the toughest doors; and almost as many years again with the lifestyle shit for brains here thought he belonged to. After the thousandth street fight it all became an automatic reflex of punitive reaction ...

As he took twenty steps away, with almost twenty steps on his way back to *do* me, I could read him: at this range he wasn't a boxer, there was no raising of the bodyweight to the balls of the feet, no left jab extension to gauge a reaction from me, while maintaining a safe defence distance ... There was no familiar adjustment sway with the upper body, that split-second warning all untrained street fighters give as they load a king hit ...

I hadn't been counting, but his range told me his next step would've been his twentieth, his infinitesimal step, and I couldn't allow that. He'd kept the same rhythm and pace since he'd started to walk my walk from the trailer. On this, his last step, in mid-motion, his bodyweight would shortly be transferred enough to co-ordinate his right foot to take the necessary amount of weight to perform the step. (He wasn't a grappler, at this range he should've started dropping his bodyweight. He was just a shit-for-brains street fighter!) I needed to move to take full advantage of his extra bodyweight, which was way above my own, and make heavy contact that split second before he placed his right foot on the ground.

I needed to breath out, relax and drive from the right leg, shifting my mass weight forward. Moving with my left side was very important, as I stepped away from his mobile right leg. As we were nearly head to head, my right hand struck his left cheek-bone. I needed to lock everything together, while releasing a blood-curdling scream to scare everyone mindless within a twenty-stance distance, and to concentrate all of my energy into and through the target.

My strike at his face had been snake-like, my forward body lunge meant my shoulder rotated rather than extended. I needed only a short-arm movement, my elbow and wrist locked into a slightly bent snake-like angle. Instead of two fangs striking his face, my bite came from two very calloused knuckles. The explosion was almost perfect; his cheekbone fractured and crumbled with the dynamic force of our bodies colliding. I say almost perfect because he had to be caught in movement, prior to placing weight on his next step. Second, I had to step wide to the left, outside of his stepping leg. Third, I had to make heavy facial contact with my right cross (or short reverse punch as it's known in freestyle martial arts).

The timing was faultless, he spun on his own axis. His right leg spun across and upwards. This, in turn, spun his shoulders from vertical to horizontal, causing his left supporting leg to follow suit in the direction of his already swinging right leg. His whole body flipped horizontal from the ground and in line with my hips, where he seemed to pause for a second or two before his heavy frame went crashing to the ground. Almost perfect: well, I'd gone for a knockout, hoping for an unconscious hulk of a man to crumble in a pitiful motionless heap on the ground. Instead, I got this idiot shit for brains staggering to his feet and declaring, 'Lucky shot, you lucky cunt! You haven't heard the last of me, fucking lucky shot.' He'd staggered disorientated, towards the gap between the trailer and the packing cases.

Fifteen to twenty minutes later I recalled Tokyo and that can of coffee as I heard Mick's drumsticks over the sound system. It was that ever-familiar one, two, three, four and Fleetwood Mac exploding into 'Say You Love Me'.

I took two steps past the packing cases to be in Richard's line of sight. Most of the media and celebrities had moved off to see the show. Richard and I nodded our heads as if this were the first time we'd ever heard Fleetwood Mac. There was something about the volume, the band; their songs got my adrenaline flowing ...

'Hey cunt, so you think I'm shit for brains? Well, I think you're a fucking lucky shooter, lucky shot. That's what that was – and now I'm fucking back!'

What had taken him so long? He was close, but not too close. But again, he hadn't taken advantage of my back not being covered. I looked at Richard in the distance; Richard Dashut had just lifted Lindsey's guitar several decibels. By stroking my hair, I was communicating the fact that I was about to enter a hair-, no, a Hell-raising situation.

I turned and took two steps to align myself with the backstage boundary. However, not just shit for brains, but six others, three on my left and three on my right, had made a neat semi-circle around me. (Behemoth was a sorry sight, the closed-over slit where his eye used to be, was seeping clotted blood; the cheekbone fracture was a good one (really bad for him), compressed and had dropped. Mangled blood vessels had caused internal bleeding, creating an unhealthy swelling from the side of his mouth up to the hairline of his forehead. Damaged nerve-endings twitched spasmodically within the swelling. Every few seconds the minor muscles within the area of damage formed an ugly involuntary convulsive contraction.)

Totally ignorant of his massive injuries, my Behemoth was back, fuelled with the confidence of his extra gang members, who were armed with a variety of iron bars and bottles. As he faced me, waving a broken bottle with his right hand, he'd again become my prime target.

Stay cool and make them as angry as possible, I thought. Be firm, keep the volume turned way down.

'I got you all figured out shit brain. I know what your problem is: when you were born your mumma was black. But you're fucking father was an illiterate white man.'

It worked; my primary target became so angry he spluttered all sorts of obscenities.

Deo juvante! Richard arrived, taking his place on my left as we'd trained this scenario hundreds of times in *dojo*s around the world. Richard, being a left-hander, and I, a right-hander, had we decided to go, and go with power, now would've been the time ...

Just then a member of the Maui Mafia intervened. I was pleased to see this man's broad shoulders in the centre of this *magick* circle, as he faced my Behemoth. He spoke an island tongue, maybe Samoan. To this day I don't know who he was, I don't know what he said, and I don't know who he said it to, but they all dropped their weapons and dissolved into the night. Our *magician* in his white shirt and tie turned and gave Richard and me a mock salute and a real smile.

Fleetwood Mac finished their set an hour later and knew nothing of our backstage adventure.

We arrived in Los Angeles the first week in December. Richard Norton stayed a couple of days before flying back to Australia to join Beverly and family for Christmas. I'd planned to stay about a month in California, to spend time with Fleetwood Mac to get to know them better. Richard Dashut had said he'd be pissed off if I stayed anywhere except his place.

In Hawaii, Mick's wife Jenny had asked me, once we'd got to LA, to teach her some Hatha Yoga and meditation. On early mornings I'd head off down to Malibu in my hired Porsche 928. On that first day I'd pulled up outside Mick and Jenny's Topanga Canyon hideaway. Huge iron electronically operated gates, with a lattice design of horizontal and vertical steel crossbars blocked the entrance.

'Good morning, who is this?' asked the out-of-sight exterior intercom.

The answer Bob Jones resounded in my head, like 'Shazam' from a Marvel-family comic book.

The oversized gates swallowed me up and closed securely behind me.

I drove uphill several hundred meters; the bitumen driveway had beautiful, almost tropical greenery on either side. It was a particularly cold morning as California prepared for the onslaught of a cold winter Christmas. On the crest of one of the numerous mountains of Topanga Canyon, I reached the clearing that housed Mick's and Jenny's palace of a home. The early morning mist slowly lifted, exposing a thick blanket of steam floating above the full-size heated pool. It looked like an angel-shaped bed, right at the gateway to heaven, a powerful new day of life that would make anyone want to meditate.

Mick wasn't around during my early training with Jenny. He'd either gone early or hadn't come home, due to his commitment to Bob Welch's latest album, which was almost finished and ready for release. Or he'd be catching up with Judy Wong, who was part of Fleetwood Mac's management, or he'd be over at Stevie's, fostering the latest love affair, which had started up between them during the Rumours tour.

On this affair, Mick had said, 'It started up in New Zealand. Late one night, after the concert, a Samoan limo driver took Stevie and me for a long cruise along mountains and ridges at dawn. At one point we got out and walked a bit in silence, waiting for the sun to rise. There was a mist that turned to a gentle rain, soaking us to our skin.

'We were driven back to our hotel room in a ferocious downpour, clinging to each other in the back of the car. I said, "I think I'd like to stay here tonight."'

I really enjoyed my training sessions with Jenny; there was a good energy around the house. Mick's daughters thought I was an Australian Bruce Lee (even though he'd died a few years earlier). Lucy thought it was all a big game, but Amy was at an age where I could show here simple techniques such as a left jab and right round-house kick. Instantly, she could alternate from orthodox to southpaw (she could do the techniques equally as well from either the left- or right-hand side), with everything flowing, complete with a seven-year-old's adrenaline-activated schreeech!

After training, Mick's mum and dad, Mike and Biddy, who'd stayed over with Jenny and the kids while Mick was on tour, would have breakfast going. Even they were always in good spirits, considering Mick had told me somewhere on tour that his mum had called to give him the news that his dad had been diagnosed with cancer, and that the prognosis was not good. Biddy had said Mike was declining conventional chemotherapy treatment, preferring to use other, more holistic ways to fight the disease. What particularly had me remembering this devastating news for Mick was his mum had rung him on my birthday, 25 August.

Within twelve months (August 1978) Fleetwood Mac would be locked away in Studio D at The Village Recorder in LA, which they'd custom built for recording much of their new album *Tusk*. (*Rumours* would still be holding its own on the charts everywhere: in some places it was still in top slot.)

The Mac had decided to take a break from recording and do what they loved best: playing to sell-out crowds at every arena, coliseum and bowl. They were being supported by Little River Band and Bob Welch (whose *French Kiss* was now a nationwide hit).

Then came the phone call. Mick's parents had gone home to England (so had Jenny and the kids on another of those trial separations). Mick's sister, Sally, had called and advised Mick that if he wanted to see his father while he was still alive, he'd better come quick. Mick was straight on to a Lear jet to Washington D.C., and across the North Atlantic at twice the speed of sound on the very next Concorde to London. Sally had picked him up at Heathrow Airport and he did make it, just in time.

Prior to this Fleetwood Mac tour I'd become really serious with my quest for esoteric knowledge. For almost two years, as often as I could, I'd gone to Melbourne's Gita School of Hatha Yoga and Meditation. This was what interested Jenny the most;

I think she liked Hatha Yoga because it was very relaxing, as well as being great for body-shaping.

Back in the mid-1960s Jenny and her sister Patti Boyd had been two of the most sought-after models of the time, doing spreads in everything up to and including *Vogue*.

They were two extremely beautiful young ladies. One would marry Mick Fleetwood (try several trial separations), divorce him, marry him again (try, more trial separations) and finally divorce him in just over a year, in 1979. Meanwhile, Pattie would share this penchant for rock wedlock by marrying and divorcing George Harrison/Eric Clapton/George Harrison/Eric Clapton in as many times.

After training one morning, during one of those breakfast meals, Jenny and I were exchanging trivia about our experiences with what had been fashionable for at least a decade (and would be for more than a decade to come): Indian guruism and its associated cults.

Three years earlier (in 1974) I'd been bodyguard to A. C. Prabhupada, the modern founder and guru of the Hare Krishna sect. For the three previous years, I'd had his disciples attend my annual seven-day summer training camps and teach my Black Belts and me something of their meditations. Jenny mentioned that Prabhupada had died recently, during the Fleetwood Mac tour, and that ISKON, his organisation, had been thrown into turmoil with several very nasty power struggles.

In the late 1960s Jenny had experienced a spiritual awakening, no longer looking at things in terms of Heaven and Hell. She was starting to view things in terms of Karma and rebirth, and, in 1968, had spent a couple of months at the Maharish's

Ashram in the foothills of the Himalayas with sister Patti and George Harrison, John and Cynthia Lennon, and a whole rock 'n' roll celebrity gang of budding disciples.

On the days I didn't visit Jenny I'd go and see Lindsey Buckingham and Richard Dashut, and assure Richard his house was in good hands. He and Lindsey were working on new material for Lindsey's forthcoming solo album. JC was often there. At other times I'd call into Christine's and have lunch with her and her happy housekeeper Lee, and her secretary who's name was Chris.

Most times I'd catch up with Mick, either at Seedy Management with Judy Wong and company, or down Hollywood Boulevard where they were putting the finishing touches to *French Kiss* and Bob's single 'Ebony Eyes', which in six months would be a hit. The atmosphere in this huge SIR Recording Studio was a blowout! Bob Welch was easy going, and it was with a positive energy that Mick Fleetwood managed him.

On one day when I'd called in, Mick had brought along a hotted up wheelchair. To everyone's disgust, or at times sickly amusement, he'd wheel himself around in either film director fashion or as if he were trying out for the Para-Olympics. This SIR Studio had a huge stage with the band set-up similar to a venue.

By mid-afternoon on this particular wheelchair day, everyone was blown away when Peter Green called in out of the blue. Since leaving Fleetwood Mac, Peter had constantly fought his battle with the Black Dragon, donating most of his songwriting royalty payments (a small fortune) to various charities. He'd worked as a railroad laborer, a grave-digger, hospital orderly and spent time in prison (due to producing a shotgun to convince his manager that his royalties should go to the needy). He was now attempting to play guitar again, and this pleased everyone, especially Mick.

Christmas was cold, and I'd gone to a party at Christine's Beverley Hill's cottage, which was fully furnished with antiques. Everyone was there and Christine had a roaring log fire in a huge open fireplace. As if it were a magnet, I'd headed straight for it for a bit of serious arse-warming.

After about ten minutes Curry Grant, the Mac's lighting director, came over and said, 'Hey Barb, how's the ass man? I mean is it warm yet – or should I fetch another log?'

Over at the bar quite a few of the guys pissed themselves laughing, it was some good old LA humour at my expense.

Though it was some roaring fire, it turned out that Christine's house had ducted heating and her roaring log fire was a false gas fire (this was 1977 and the false gas fire craze wouldn't hit Australia for at least another three years).

The hardest thing for me during this Christmas break was the question of what the Hell do you get for people like this, who appear to have everything money can buy? I'd searched for Christine for days, and the best I could come up with was a large-framed poster with an interesting shot of a pyramid of a dozen penguins. But maybe that would've been better as a gift for John McVie? Mick was worse; I'd searched everywhere. I wanted to give him something, that in some way would reflect my appreciation of his and the band's friendship. Then I thought of the sword set I'd bought in Japan and lugged halfway around the world, not to mention the Customs traumas a bodyguard on tour with a bloody samurai sword at his side has to go through. Mick knew I was a collector, and I'd hoped for this reason, that the gift would serve its purpose, or at the very least, be something he'd like. Luckily, it'd worked. Mic was flabbergasted, he didn't even know what to say, but that didn't matter: we both knew it'd be a present he'd cherish.

After a break of a few days up in the mountains and the fresh air and the snow, suddenly it was New Year's Eve and 1977 was about to turn into 1978.

Judy Wong had done me a huge favor. I'd asked and she'd made good, having got me Joe Cocker's address and found out he was having a huge New Year's eve party. Also, she'd told no-one, that way I could go see him early in the night as a total surprise, and then sometime in the a.m., I could go across to the Fleetwood Mac celebration party, which was for the Mac and friends to enjoy and share all the triumphs of the band during the previous year.

The Cocker connection was, as it turned out, the surprise of the decade. The electricity between Joe and me as the clock struck away the seconds beyond twelve o'clock would be almost impossible to capture in words ...

It was about 3:45 a.m. By the time I'd driven across to Stevie's villa-style house cut into the side of one of the steepest hills in Beverly, valet parking had some Mexican guy who looked really stoned whisk the Porsche out from under me, leaving me with a valet hand-card that apparently would retrieve my car with the sunrise, as reliable as a boomerang.

Inside, the number of people I knew were outnumbered three to one by people I didn't know. For a brief moment, I'd wished I'd stayed at Joe's. There was a cinema-sized screen playing a film of the Rumours world tour for those who hadn't been there. A high-tech (and loud) sound system had most people dancing. This screen was the main source of light for the entire action area. Strategically well-placed candles allowed you to see even the darkest corners. Man, if ever I'd have done drugs, on this night I would've been in a state of plethora; everyone else was.

Everywhere, and within everyone's reach, there were huge gnome mugs for the males, and dainty fairy glasses for the females, all full of smoking relaxants. There were joints as thick as fingers and twice as long. In case you became too relaxed, you could always attack a mirror with a straw. Beautifully etched, flowing Celtic artwork, with the deepest grooves, held abundant amounts of white power.

Several cute young ladies, who looked really stoned, carried trays of food. They were being run off their feet: it seemed everyone in the place had the munchies.

Within a couple of hours I'd caught up with everyone, danced with a few ladies who still had some command of the English language. I wasn't sure if it was because of all those drugs or the sunrise. Either way, it was home time.

I handed my boomerang valet hand-card to a really stoned-looking African-American. By the time I'd walked from Stevie's front door, down some very steep stairs to the front gate, there was my car. I gave the driver the customary twenty bucks; ten for the valet parking company and the other ten for the driver pool designed to keep all the staff so stoned!

I spent the following week trying to reconnect with as many of my martial arts associates as I could, although it was a difficult time due to Christmas and new year. Kickboxing in Australia was almost eighteen months old, and it wouldn't be long before I'd need to bring some industry names to fight in Australia. This had to be done to bring the sport up to another level.

I'd called into O'Hara Publications, the publishing company for *Black Belt*, *Karate Illustrated*, *Inside Kung-Fu* and a list of other popular American martial arts magazines. We did a photo shoot and a profile interview to update my last lot of coverage when I'd toured and competed in 1972. Back then, as a new second-degree Black Belt with twenty-eight clubs under my banner, I'd been tagged the 'Colonel Sanders of Karate'. This time around, as a maturing third-degree and now with fifty-five clubs across four Australian states, I was christened 'The McDonald's of the Martial Arts'. Corny? Yes, but great exposure back home: 'if it's as big as Texas, then it's good' they say, and Australia is as big as the whole of North America, but with only 7 per cent of the population.

Unfortunately, Howard Hanson, the founder of the World Kickboxing Association, was out of reach. He and Benny Urquidez were in Tokyo for one of Benny's Japanese title fights (they'd arrived there just as I'd left; I'd missed them twice). I'd also caught up with a few of the old crew (someone had said that Mike Stone had busted up with Priscilla and that he was back in Hawaii), especially Chuck Norris and Joe Lewis, two names I really wanted to have visit downunder. Though Benny Urquidez was away, his counterpart, Howard Jackson, was my favourite African-American fighter. At the time he was taking a seminar just out of San Francisco. So I took that winding coastal highway from LA to the birthplace of the Haight-Ashbury era, and made it in time to see a good friend and do his seminar.

However, when I'd asked him about visiting Australia he'd replied, 'Hey Barb, take a look at this knee under these wraps. I battle through my seminars and I'd love to come to Australia for ya, but hey, if I wind up getting a reconstruction, I'm outta kickboxing for a long time.'

The following night I got back to LA. In return for her having looked after me, including the Joe Cocker deal, I'd arranged a treat night for Judy Wong, on the town. We went to dinner, a club and back to her place for a late-night, early morning cuppa. She'd spent much of the night mentioning that the band seemed exceptionally happy with their Australian security on the tour. There was a certain attachment to the Bob and Richard bodyguard duo, and I was told that I should stay on and start a security company and martial arts training for security personnel.

'Do you have any idea, how much work there'd be here in getting musos etcetera into fitness and a bit of defence training, and perhaps a few less drugs?'

'I don't have a Green Card.'

'That can be organised as long as *you* sign a pre-nuptual to protect my assets. Bingo, you're married to a Chinese-American citizen, you live here and share ... you got your Green Card. Then you're here in California, doing what I'm talking about ...'

Jesuz, no wonder Mick Fleetwood had Judy

Wong running business at Seedy Management (which also looked after Mick, John McVie and Peter Green). I'd figured this was a concept I really had to give some attention to!

I had to return to Australia; I wished I could've stayed one more weekend, that way I would've caught Peter Green's wedding to Jane Samuel at Mick's Topanga Canyon Palace. Unfortunately, not long after this celebration of matrimony, Peter let Mick down badly by blowing a million dollar deal that Mick had battled to secure for him: simply by refusing to sign. Peter Green was feeling the lash of the tail of the Black Dragon once again, his new marriage fell apart, as did Peter one more time. Ten years later, when asked had he ever regretted leaving Fleetwood Mac, he'd replied, 'Yeah, I've regretted it, but then I also regret joining them as well.'

When asked about his guitar-playing, Peter had responded, 'I had one a while ago, but it broke.' These days Peter Greenbaun is totally unrecognisable as the Green God, Peter Green, who was once compared to Eric Clapton (in the early 1960s he was likened to the God of Rock for his blues guitar-playing). Street kids now call him the wolf-man. He is known for his unkempt clothes, matted hair and four-inch wizards' scissors-type fingernails. Mick Fleetwood had done all he could for him back in 1978.

Four weeks after my return to Australia (February) John and Christine would divorce. By the end of the year John would marry his secretary, Julie Ann Rubons.

By April 1978, Mick was spending more and more time with Stevie, and soon after Mick's parents returned to England, Jenny and the kids closed camp and went back, too.

After Mick's dad died in August, Mick could not cope. For some time he'd been abusing alcohol, cocaine, personal relationships and his own health. For some unknown reason, even to himself, he'd begged Jenny to come back with the kids to LA.

Now he had Stevie over there and Jenny over here. Celebrities always do things in threes, so enter Sara Recor. I'd met her at Stevie's New Year's Eve party. Sara was a beautiful model working for the Elite and Johnny Casablanca Agencies. She was also the wife of a good friend of Mick's, Jim Recor, who'd worked for Loggins and Messina and had managed the Stanford Townshend Band. Sara was best friends with Stevie and could also really sing. They'd get together at Stevie's for all-night singing of old country songs, under the banner of the Twang Sisters.

For Mick by the end of November it was goodbye Stevie, Jenny and Jim and a whole new beginning – with Sara.

By Christmas of that year Christine had been dealt another card from the bottom of the deck: she'd gone off on a two- to three-year roller-coaster ride with one of the wild men of rock 'n' roll who only a decade earlier had wanted to make a songwriting mogul out of Charles Manson. Like Mick, a drummer, and again like Mick, a little kid inside trying to get out, inside was a little Beach Boy, Dennis Wilson. The Black Dragon Society would call time-out for Mr Wilson, like Brian Jones of The Rolling Stones and so many of this industry. At what most would consider a young age, at 39, on 28 December 1983,

Dennis Wilson drowned, as a result of his lifestyle, in Marina Del Rey.

In 1979 Richard Norton and I tossed it over and figured he'd been at the Immigration Department long enough and it was time for a change. So off he went to make a go of it in the US.

Judy Wong had been right on the money. Richard soon became physical advisor to the who's who of LA with celebrities such as John Belushi, Peter Asher (James Taylor's and Linda Ronstadt's manager) and many others. Almost immediately, on doing security work for Linda, David Bowie and Fleetwood Mac, Richard would have a couple of bites at film offers, which was the real agenda.

By September, Fleetwood Mac had finished *Tusk*, the new double-album, and wanted Richard to go full-time on their world tour starting like, immediately!

Richard and I'd debated by phone who'd be a good representative for the Corporation, and a good substitute for us. He suggested this young guy we'd been training in the Melbourne suburb of Glenroy: Dennis Dunstan.

'You're right, Richard. Plus, he's a drummer in a garage band. That way, he at least speaks the same language. All right, he's as good as there!'

'Dennis, it's your time for a change.' I gave him the ground rules about no drugs, no this, no that, no, no.

And he was off!

With Rumours as a benchmark for large-scale, expensive touring, *Tusk* soon elevated itself to the money over-spending department. In its heyday *Rumours* was the highest selling album of the time; it supported expensive habits. On completion after twelve months of touring, *Tusk*, with a lot more going out, and much less coming in, saw the inevitable happening.

Mick, who was not one of Fleetwood Mac's songwriters, was not in the same league as Chris, Stevie and Lindsey when it came to royalties. So, on bad business advice, he started dabbling in real estate while on tour. On 16 March 1980, while in Australia, he paid three million dollars for a huge stud farm near Sydney. It was a historic landmark colonial homestead called Wensley Dale, with a mansion house on 620 acres at a place called Colo Vale. Huge loans had Mick needing to find $40 000 a month to survive. It would be a piece of cake, as long as everything held.

This Tusk tour all but fried everybody, body, brain and soul. Stevie's voice wasn't getting any better due to the pace of the tour. Christine had Dennis Wilson to contend with and John McVie had Dennis to drink with, and everybody else had Dennis to do drugs with. Sara slotted into Jenny's lifestyle, that of a rock 'n' roll widow. Sara, stuck at home, soon developed an affair like Jenny/Bob Weston (who was sacked by Mick because of this). Another saga: this time between Sara and a certain dashing technician. The result was the same: the technician found himself out of a job and he had to find a new *trip*. Mick countered Sara's affair by falling deeply in love with a telephone caller. The affair lasted eight months, with daily phone calls to 'Whitney', who eventually private detectives found to be an obese Fleetwood Mac fan employed by the New Orleans Post Office and who drove a VW. That's probably enough of the soap opera, but there was more!

Less than a month after the tour, new management entered the fold. John, Chris and Mick were still at this point with Mickey Shapiro. Lindsey had found a separate legal firm. Stevie Nicks had signed with the Eagles Legal Team. Irving Azoff had a ruthless reputation when it came to protecting any of his clients. He was now representing Stevie with regard to her looming solo career.

A *please explain* business meeting had been called for everyone. 'You should've made more money! Why isn't there more money after a year on the road?' Irving Azoff demanded, as if every last penny was his own. This fitted with his ruthless reputation.

Irving wasn't there to mince words or pull any legal punches, he was there to clean up the mess. 'Hey Mick, its over. From this point forward, we ain't paying no management commission, no office overhead, legal fees, accounting fees, nothing. We're out for now, goodbye.'

As a result of this meeting John 'Colonel' Courage, or JC, became the patsy, or fall guy. On being fired, JC went off to Hawaii to live without the pressures of the road and Fleetwood Mac.

From that point on everything was to have been reviewed by committee: managers, lawyers and business managers.

Mick, of course, had huge problems coming to grips with this, though his heart was always in the right place. Therefore, in his mind he thought he was right on the money. However, there was more: Whitney was the new undeniable love of his live – even above Sara. He was so full of drugs he didn't know who his *wives* were getting off with.

The rude awakening would come within four years when his personal life management would have him declared bankrupt. Somehow he'd managed to salvage Sara and off they'd gone to Africa to attempt some unfinished business. The rest of the Mac went their different ways on various solo adventures. Christine had had enough of Dennis Wilson's childish falsehoods and infidelities, his drinking and drug use escalated. As 1980 closed off the decade, Christine closed off the love affair.

While all this was happening, Mark Chapman, who was really responsible for the nail in the coffin of this decade, shot John Lennon.

With a little help from his friends, Mick Fleetwood and Richard Dashut finished off that African business and called the album *The Visitor*. Without as much as a break, it was off to join the rest of the Mac at a rented sixteenth-century chateau in Herouville, about ninety-five kilometres from Paris, to begin work on the new album. *Mirage* was the result and it was released in mid-1982. The first hit single off this album was 'Hold Me', a Christine McVie song reflecting her bittersweet relationship with the sycophantic Wilson.

Mirage climbed to the number one position. Due to the Fleetwood Mac band members having outside musical business interests, the promotional tour had to be cut-short. At the same time, Australia's Men At Work, who'd opened the shows for the Mac in the beginning of the tour, saw their album take over the top spot, knocking *Mirage* off the US charts, after only five weeks.

Big "D", what's happ'nin'? This is Australia calling, hope I haven't caught you in the middle of the night or anything silly?'

Dennis Dunstan, or Big D, as was his knockabout fight name before he'd left for the US, had now been there for three years working full-time minding the Mac. Never once did he suggest it was time to come home: he was at home.

'Chief! Hey God damn, it's good to hear your voice. Hey, I can't believe this: the Chief! All right!'

'How's Richard? What's he up to right now?'

'Man I don't know, we've just been touring our arses off with the new album, *Mirage*. But I do know he's only doing a bit of security now, in between movie gigs. It's all starting to happen for him over here. I mean, real crazy.'

The reason for calling was my putting together a self-defence book: *Hands Off*. I was thinking of going over and Americanising it by using FBI research and Californian rape crisis statistics. Plus, during the Rumours tour, both Christine and Stevie had said they'd liked to help out.

'Man, are you kidding? Christine and the gang would love to see you. And, hey, I get to train with the Chief! How 'bout you come for about a year?'

Though Dennis had been brought up in the tough northside suburbs of Glenroy, he wasn't a street kid, although he had a quick tongue, real quick fists and no fear of the street.

Dennis had just married flight attendant, Marilyn. They were living with Christine, as Dennis was her live-in minder.

'Big D, in about a week it'll be my birthday. Figure I'll treat myself to a trip and have my birthday twice. Good reason for a party drink, I reckon.'

Excuse me sir, would you like any papers or perhaps one of these magazines?' The voice of the flight attendant broke my concentration on the flight from Melbourne via Sydney to Los Angeles.

Well there I was, on my birthday, writing what I'd hoped would become a bestseller self-defence book for women, which was as much a book about being confident, having self-esteem, setting goals, positive thought and a physical training program ...

While killing some spare time, by finding out what was happening below on Mother Earth, I read that *Thriller* (what's this? Michael Jackson's brand new album), had knocked off Fleetwood Mac's *Rumours*, after only five years, as the biggest selling record of all time.

Then in Melbourne, according to a headline in *The Sun*, prominent solicitor Graeme Alford had been sentenced to seven years for armed bank robbery. (I'd come across his name again in years to come.) First it was the politicians, then the cops and now it's the lawyers ... What hope have we got?

And then? I couldn't believe this! John Belushi's death! Richard Norton had been working with him for months: doesn't the Black Dragon ever take a day off?

Drugs, alcohol, death: all in the one breath! Doesn't it ever stop?

Some things just keep on, keeping on.

During the first month, I'd spent most of my time sleeping, training and writing, with my research books set up all over Christine's dining room. Christine always stayed up until the early hours of the morning, as there were late-night guests (that's the nature of the industry), plus she was spending a lot of time writing, and being musically creative with future songs. Late morning's were generally when she'd request Lee, the housekeeper of the house, to prepare brunch. Chris, the secretary, would be busy preparing bills, answering the phone and setting appointments, and doing anything else that would keep a personal secretary busy.

We always stay up until Christine retired. Dennis and I'd use the earlier hours of the following morning to train. Dennis had been away so long, he'd appreciate being brought up to speed with all our latest state-of-the art techniques.

Dennis was a damned good runner and he'd been pushing it. On this particular day, my knee'd popped, arse over head. Now I was training around the bodgie knee, but I couldn't even play *brick* tennis. (Dennis and I'd play doubles every morning using a couple of rackets and a tennis ball on a long elastic band tied to a brick, that way we could hit the ball back to ourselves). Of course, Dennis had worked out a points system, for the old and young bull to compete!

Every morning I'd go swimming, convalescing the knee. While thinking about the advertorials on late-night television, where busy people got fit running on a machine, or pedalled like mad on a stationery bike, I had this image of swimming, non-stop, the second leg of a triathlon. A simple harness, securing the elastic band to either the waist or shoulders could be used to cater for either aerobic or anaerobic training. This gave birth to the swim-a-sizer concept.

Christine was very impressed and suggested we make tracks straight to her lawyer, Mickey Shapiro. 'He'll know what to do.'

Shapiro suggested he'd start the basic legals and we should get some quotes for the production of the shoulder harness, including the basic surfies' elastic cord, straps, Velcro, buckles and packaging.

During this period Dennis and I'd visited the Federal Bureau of Investigations (FBI). Two Aussies, (one with a limp!) wanted to research violence against women.

Sure, you could see them thinking, let's keep an eye on these two characters. And they certainly did! You could feel the cameras as Big Brother followed us every inch of the way. True to our word, we found more than we needed, and the cameras recorded every God damn thing.

One day we were over at Stevie's, and she'd asked how it was coming along. She was keen to understand the concept of how I intended to make it a train-at-home-alone manual.

'What can I do to help?'

'How about a photo shoot of you and me for the cover?'

Swear to God, I honestly meant this to be a throw-away line.

'It all sounds fabulous! I'd love to!'

'Great Stevie, I'll ring your publicist to do a photo shoot here by the pool.'

Stevie's publicist was astounded. 'Tell me, Bob, first, what's the concept? And, second, how the fuck did you pull this off? Stevie's flatly refused to have any photos ever. I've been in negotiation for months with one of the world's top monthly magazines ... last offer in was $250 000 and she flatly refused.

How the fuck did you pull this off?'

'Macho charisma,' Dennis joked.

'He makes me walk on fire, jump off cliffs and swim across the deepest rivers. To him, what's a coupla fucking photos: he's the Chief!'

Stevie's publicist had one of those special LA laughs: the one they use when they don't think the situation at hand is all that funny.

On this day of the shoot I was standing in my martial arts training uniform, wearing my Black Belt. Then Stevie appeared, her hair done to resemble the mane of a lion. She was psyched up for some serious photographing. Stevie wore her familiar thick-soled, thick-heeled, knee-high brown suede kid leather boots. High roll-over socks appeared over the top of these elegant Swedish boots and hung tentatively around her knees. The seductiveness of her partially exposed cleavage was the next thing any red-blooded male would have his attention drawn to ... Stevie also had on the most unusual dress, with a snow white multi-layered, multi-lengthed hem-line. The white chiffon had multi-colored flowers. With the sun behind us during the shoot, Stevie would kick, sometimes over my head, so her dress would spread like a giant Japanese fan or butterfly wing.

In these kicking-style photographs the sun also made her dress partially see-through: just enough to be artistically interesting.

'My book *Hands Off!* is centered around nine mnemonic movements, I need a shot of each one,' I'd told the publicist.

'That sounds easy. We'll do six to ten of each pose, that'll give you a good selection.' She then checked the light and selected several different lenses for the camera set-up.

This lady was a professional: in two hours I had a hundred of the most magnificent photos ever offered to the martial arts, and just one would make the cover.

I remembered what her publicist said. That a magazine had recently offered Stevie a quarter of a million dollars, and that she'd knocked it back. 'Thanks a million, Stevie!' What else could I say?

The day after the photo shoot was Labour Day at the Perfect/McVie household. Labour Day in most of the US is held on the first Monday of September. At Christine's it was the first Monday of every month. On this day over forty people would be in and out of the house over a four-hour period. Everything you could think of would have a different company servicing its need, whether it was car-cleaners, lawn-cutters, spouting-checkers, pool servicemen, rosebush-trimmers or a piano-tuner. There were other cleaners present for carpets, tiles, furniture and picture frames. Also, an interior decorator company would send three people in jazzy uniforms to water and change many of the indoor plants and there would be a van in the driveway, washing and clipping Christine's two Pekinese dogs.

While Marilyn, Dennis's wife, was away, working on a Miami flight for a few days, Dennis, Christine and I were by the pool, keeping out of everyone's way. I'd been trying out my homemade swim-a-sizer, much to Christine's amusement.

'Hey Bob, you did that photo shoot with Stevie yesterday, what can I do to help you with your book, besides reading a few pages every now and then, seeing as they're spread all over my dining room?'

Now Christine really *was* the reason I wrote that book. That was the second reason I'd come to America:

I wanted to write and complete it specifically as an omen – in Christine's company.

'Remember on tour, when you tried to teach me to play Backgammon? That was when we tried to talk about my concept of helping women to learn to protect themselves. You said I should get serious, and write a book on the subject. If I could maybe have a picture of you, and I could quote you, that would be an incredible asset in the book and add to my personal credibility.'

Christine said she had just the photo and would be glad to be of any help.

Just then Chris, Christine's secretary, brought in the mail. There was a stack of envelopes, but the third one drew a shriek from Christine.

'Tonight we go out and celebrate, dinner's on me! Well, Dennis and I get a five-star dinner; Bob gets to ride in his favourite LA super-stretch limousine,' she said humourously.

Then she gave the reason for the shriek to Dennis. His eyes rolled and he showed me his left hand, with five fingers exposed, and right, with his thumb exposed, signifying upwards of six figures. The royalty payment, for quarter-year airplay, was in the multiple hundreds of thousands just for Christine's share of how many times Fleetwood Mac's records had been played on radio stations worldwide.

Like any lifestyle, with the good news often comes the bad news. It was somewhere around this time that Stevie lost one of her best friends, Robin Anderson, who was a good friend of the band. Robin was a voice therapist and often accompanied Fleetwood Mac on the road, where she was needed to work on preserving Stevie's voice. Robin had been diagnosed with terminal leukemia two years earlier, at around the time of the Tusk tour. Although she'd spent a lot of time in and out of hospital, against the advice of her doctors, Robin desperately wanted to leave her legacy with the birth of a son; this possibly even shortened her life, but it was something she had to do. Her son had been born a week earlier, right before Robin had passed away (Stevie was the Godmother).

The best part about that four months at Christine's Lloydcrest Drive home, prior to Christmas 1982, was the nights and early mornings spent around the piano in her sound room, where she recorded the beginnings of several potentially new songs. There's something about hearing a popular hit off an album, and knowing you were there for the entire gestation process.

Plus, on these long evenings, the three of us, and a regular number of habitual houseguests, would sometimes spend intriguing hours in esoteric conversation.

Like the night Christine told us of her mother, Beatrice Perfect. 'A remarkable, very psychic lady, she was both a medium and a faith healer, and it was these strange interests and talents that often caused me anguish. She belonged to a group at one of those psychic research societies. They'd often, just up and be off on ghost-hunting expeditions.'

Apparently, Christine's mother, in an example of her faith-healing skills, once placed her finger over a wart Christine had under her nose when she was eight, prior to her going to bed. When Christine awoke the next morning it was gone!

It was now more than a decade since Christine's mother had passed away, but something in the atmosphere, probably the recent death of Robin Anderson, prompted another recollection.

'I remember a devastating time when a friend of my father's had been diagnosed with leukemia and told that she had virtually no time left at all to live. My mother requested something of the sick woman's attire, something close to her. The family of the woman sent a white kid glove to my mother, and said it was one of a pair that had been a very special present, from someone close, a few years ago.

'My mother wore it to bed several times. Within a month, she received a phone call from a relative of the woman, who said the doctors couldn't understand it as she was completely healed, not a damn thing wrong with her.'

On matters related to security, Christine respected my opinion. One late night on a very rare occasion that she and I were alone, Christine out of the blue brought up the matter of John Courage being fired, due to what the lawyers had at the time deemed 'questionable management leading to large sums of money gone missing'.

'Bob, isn't it incredible, how fast time flies. Do you know it's been two whole years since our lawyers sacked JC? It was all so confusing and conflicting at the time, I did not know what to think at all.'

Did Christine think I knew something that could shed some light on the subject?

'You're right Christine, time does fly, especially when you're having fun. At the time I'd thought, bloody lawyers!, but something had to be done; however, sacking JC, surely they could've done better than that? The lawyers weren't outside *Les Cabaret* in Japan that night JC put our lives on the line at one stage, coz someone was charging way to much for something the Mac were paying for. I don't know about the Tusk tour, but on the Rumours tour I lost count of the times JC bitched about the money he thought was being wasted.'

Of all the tours I'd done, and all the tour managers I'd worked with, JC was among the most competent and reliable.

Christine listened, but didn't acknowledge. She was either giving what I'd said serious thought, or I was perhaps out of bounds. But at least I'd got to say what I wanted to in JC's defence.

There was a simple solution: the tour manager had to be in control of the checking to be held responsible for losses!

Luckily there was a happy ending to this story: a little over a year later, Christine would ring JC in Hawaii and employ him to look after one of her tours. Any connection? I don't know, but I'd like to think so

Hands Off was finally finished prior to Christmas. I was to fly back to Australia on 22 December. A week before my departure Christine had said, 'Hey guys, today is festive season shopping day, and there's no getting out of it. I'll need you two muscle men to give me a hand. I have to get presents for everyone, and I want to do it all in the one expedition.'

About thirty minutes later my favourite superstretch pulled up. Dennis and I boarded our shopping sledge as I thought eat your heart out St Nick!

'Excuse me, Christine McVie, your other cars will meet us on Rodeo Drive in about ten minutes,' the driver politely informed.

With our three limos we went from store to store; Christine selecting what she wanted, with gift-wrapping and cards added. The limos were filled and there were almost enough goodies to open a rival store.

Next was the most exclusive jewelry store on the strip, so exclusive the front door was locked.

'I have a 1:30 appointment,' Christine spoke into the intercom.

'Good afternoon Ms McVie' answered the intercom with a very gynarchial female voice. 'About the two gentlemen, are they both security? We only have a Mr Dunstan listed here.'

'Yes, I'm sorry, they are both security.'

'Click!' The security bolts were released.

'You're welcome, please enter.'

A couple of hours later we'd unloaded everything and placed it around the beautifully decorated Christmas tree.

'Look at this, I had everything budgeted for around fifty, and I've wound up spending over sixty thousand. It's that jewelry store, they get me every time!'

Boom, boom, boom … Boom, boom, boom. Dennis had fired off an almost perfect round the next morning at our weekly target practice session at the Beverly Hills Pistol Shooting Club.

'You know, Chief, everyone should be able to at least once in a lifetime, be able to do their Christmas shopping like that – even if just once.'

We both laughed as I strapped on my Magnum, fired off a round and scored equal to Dennis.

Thank God, coz he had that old bull, young bull competition thing still happening.

'Dennis, what can I possibly buy Christine this year? I'm going home for Christmas, but I'd like to get Christine something nice. I mean, I've been living at her house for months.'

Then it hit me, Dennis was about to start working with Mick Fleetwood and Christine would be home a lot of the time on her own. I then knew what I could get her, something that was not only nice, but also practical and protective. I'd get her a Smith & Wesson revolver.

It took a couple of days for the gun club's paper work, then I took it and got it gift-wrapped like a regular present.

'That's *nice* Bob,' was Christine's only response as she unwrapped the gift-wrapping paper to what I thought was the perfect gift.

The word *nice* showed no connection between Bob, the gun and Christine McVie or Christmas. Plus, I was sure she was only being nice in agreeing to join us for an appointed private lesson with one of the instructors at the pistol club in the morning.

Annie Oakley, America's most famous female sharp-shooter, would've been proud. Christine nervously stood the way she was told and held the gun the way she was shown. She put on a set of ear muffs and a pair of safety glasses and fired again, again and again, round after round at those retractable electronic targets. Now there was a connection between Bob and her own well-being! With most of the holes appearing in the head and heart of the man-shaped target, it looked like Christine might have been settling a few old scores.

On that flight home I felt remorseful, wrestling with a decision I was thinking of making by the end of January. I'd been in a steady, the most steady relationship, since my divorce almost a decade earlier. My very beautiful lady Anne Hayward and I had now been a regular item for three years and everything had become quite serious. Another reason for my venture to the US was to give Anne and myself breathing space before we ventured into our own *united states*. It was her twenty-first birthday at the end of January; my decision seemed appropriate: as it turned out, neither of us were ready for the big commitment.

Within a month of my return, the Fleetwood Mac soap opera had given the new year a kick-start: to everyone's surprise and disbelief, on 29 January 1983, Stevie Nicks had announced this day as the marriage date between her and her recently deceased best friend's widower, Kim Anderson.

Kim Anderson was a member of The Hiding Place Church, whose born-again Christian liturgy emphasised a spiritual awareness of the charismatic and supernatural. The minister on the day, Philip Wagner, was open and forthright in his trepidation of this couple taking their vows, as he was not sure, 'Where Stevie was at with God.' In retrospect, this minister was right on the money, the marriage was short-lived. Separation papers were filed within months, the formal divorce coming through in April 1984. To this day, Stevie won't talk about it.

Stevie had at this time dedicated *The Wild Heart* album and the single 'The Night Bird' to her best friend, Robin Anderson.

These were years where the members of the

Mac had *gone their own way*. Back in 1981 Mick had bought yet another real estate property: a $2.4 million mansion in Ramirez Canyon, with Barbara Striesand and Don Henley as neighbors. Mick and Sara moved in and this became home. He named this new clubhouse, The Blue Whale, with the Mac social circle also calling the place The Ice Palace and Hotel Hell. This was where, over the next couple of years, his next musical project, the *Zoo*, would begin.

In this period Mick had about as much luck with his new endeavor, The Zoo, as he would with a few other projects (*The Visitor*). Plus, a one-night stand with a fan somewhere out in the mid-west resulted in some religious nutcase stalking him for over three years.

Everything that could possibly go wrong did, with Mick declaring bankruptcy in late 1984. He'd lost everything, including Sara, and had moved into a backroom in Richard Dashut's house, nearby in the canyon. For the next twelve months Mick would battle his inner-self, and for most of 1985 he'd have to come to terms with trying to regroup and re-order his life, now as a bankrupt. Gone were the properties and his collection of magnificent cars, which had been sold off at fire-sale prices. He'd but one consolation: relief that his father hadn't lived to see this day.

As the third year had rolled by since Dennis Wilson had joined that rock 'n' roll orchestra in heaven, Christine closed yet another page in her life's book of history and began anew, by marrying Portuguese musician Eduardo Quintela De Mendonca on 18 October 1986 in London. Alas, this union would turn out to be far from perfect.

Then things looked up, as if by some miracle of fate: first, Mick's will to survive; and second,

Christine, who'd been contracted to record Elvis's 'I Can't Help Falling In Love' for the movie soundtrack *A Fine Mess*. This miracle of fate had been due to Christine enjoying a huge hit with 'Get A Hold On Me' and now the movie deal, plus another option: her calling JC from his Hawaiian exile to make an album in Switzerland, and eventually to manage her career. This led to the Mac re-uniting with *Tango In The Night*.

Christine and JC had brought Richard Dashut in to produce and Lindsey, because of his fascination with Elvis, and then Mick and John (who was still afflicted by his ongoing problem with alcohol).

Last to join the fold for Tango was Stevie, who was busy on the road promoting her third successful album, *Rock A Little*, with her own hot band.

As 1986 unfolded, John's twenty-five-year battle with alcohol finally caught up with him. He'd suffered an alcoholic seizure while on St. Thomas, his sailing hideaway in the Caribbean, which scared the life out of him and Julie, his wife. With the aid of a therapist, John finally got himself off the grog and on with a new life worth living.

Stevie was in Australia, and I hadn't seen her in such a long time. Some of her press was not that becoming: there were reports that she'd twice fallen off stage. Aussie industry gossipmongers had her drinking heavily and doing excessive amounts of cocaine. I'd called into the hotel where she'd been staying after one of her shows. As usual, I'd been out with a bunch of bodyguards that lived at my house. We were sitting around in the bar, I'd just finished telling my guys how one of the last times, or in fact the last time I'd seen her, it'd been a total blow-out.

One night during that four months I'd stayed at Christine's, late in 1982, all of us – Dennis, Chrissy and I – had gone to the Roxy, a nightclub where Stevie was promoting the release of her latest single. After the set, backstage at the Roxy in front of a bunch of management and media people, most of her recording magnates, and the whole band, Stevie had come straight over to yours truly (please, don't think I'm suggesting any sexual overtones or anything of the like) and raised her arms above her head, bending her forearms, thus cloaking her head and upper body with the long-draped sleeves of her dress.

This alone had everyone's undivided attention. Stevie then lowered herself to the floor, so small that she was barely recognisable! Here she stayed for about ten seconds, which seemed like ten minutes. I'd stood there looking at everyone, and everyone was staring at me, probably thinking, who in the...? Then, she slowly raised her arms, her overhead stretch seemed to have lifted her body from the floor, back to a standing position. This was every bit as elegant as what she'd done for years when presenting the Welsh witch, Rhiannon. Slowly, she lowered her arms with a Gothic romanticism and announced me as her Gnostic *Pillar Of Strength*, her martial arts guru.

Swear to God, this had come as a bigger surprise to me, more than any of the hundred plus industry people in the room that night.

Four years later, back in Australia in 1986, in this hotel lounge, again with around a hundred plus industry people, I'd just finished telling this story to my bodyguards, when Waddy Wachtel, Stevie's lead guitarist, and the rest of her band had come in and said 'G'day Bob, owyadoin?' in their send-up Aussie accents. They'd moved into the bar area to check out the girls, who'd come to check them out.

My guys all knew, there was no reason on

earth I'd ever lie to them, but still I could feel them digesting my tale. Just then I saw Stevie at the reception desk. I could read the porter's lips, as he told Stevie that Bob Jones was waiting in the lounge area to say hello, as I'd requested. As she'd walked on down, oblivious to her crowd of well-wishers, she'd finally caught my eye. Before I even had a chance to react, the tears came streaming down her face. Without any of the theatrics of the Roxy in LA, Stevie collapsed on the floor between my legs. With her head buried in her forearms, which were spread over my knees, she cried and cried. I let her cry herself out and sometime later, as she sobbed and regrouped herself, I asked myself what was wrong and what could I possibly, if anything, do to help?

Staring into my eyes like a lost soul, Stevie kept apologising, telling me I would not be proud of what she'd been doing to herself recently, but, how she really was planning, and seriously working on sorting herself and her life out.

Four years later, early in the new year of 1990, Rod Stroud, my Western Australian BJC state manager, introduced me to a really beautiful Perth girl after a kickboxing event he had me in town for.

'Hey Chief, this lady's for you!' This was Rod's way of introduction.

A week later I'd invited Stacey-Lee Delahaunty to visit me in Melbourne.

A month later, on her twenty-second birthday, we became engaged and life had never been better.

During 1990 and 1991 Christine McVie, Stevie Nicks and Rick Vito (he and Billy Burnette had replaced Lindsay Buckingham when he'd quit the band prior to a world tour) would all leave Fleetwood Mac, although they'd all worked together on tracks for the twenty-fifth anniversary set *The Chain*. Mick, this time as much as necessity and desire, turned to the other members of his Zoo.

By 1992, at Dennis Dunstan's suggestion, the Zoo had taken on Australian icon Billy Thorpe for his powerful lead vocals. To balance this, and perhaps give the Zoo a little of the Fleetwood Mac sex appeal, they'd enlisted Bekka Bramlett, the daughter of white rock/soul duo Delaney and Bonnie. This put Bekka out front with Thorpie for their *Shakin' the Cage* album, named after the recent tour of the Mac, then consisting of the Zoo front line-up.

Meanwhile, in Australia Jeff Fenech, Australian two-time world boxing champion, had been signed for a rematch with Azumah Nelson at Melbourne's Princes Park. Jeff Fenech had given the Bob Jones Corporation the contract to the world merchandising rites to this fight and for the following two years. For this reason I'd taken three of my Black Belts, all with a mixture of manufacturing, marketing and sales backgrounds, to the US to set up Fenech's merchandising around the world. In LA, Mike Tyson had recently been charged for raping beauty pageant contestant Ms Desiree Washington (eventually convicted with a six-year prison sentence). Boxing was not flavor of the month, and we were there, an Australian marketing team selling boxing.

We'd hooked up with Dennis Dunstan and he'd taken us to see Mick Fleetwood, Billy Thorpe, Bekka and the gang recording the finishing touches to *Shakin the Cage*.

Billy Burnette and Rick Vito, just in passing

conversation, mentioned that earlier in the day, their studio had been visited by representatives of the Triads. As I had a quick look around the studio for bullet holes, they laughed and said 'no', that it wasn't the Chinese Mafia, it was a leading band management company in the US. (I still had another look around, to make sure.)

The planned single release of 'Shakin the Cage' was one of the best training singles for me and my bodyguards to train to that I'd heard, and I'd told Thorpie that I had to have a copy.

'That's good!' Billy had this great smile. 'I really like that Jeff Fenech World Tour jacket you're wearing. I just have to have it!'

So we swapped.

One night I took my marketing team for a bit of a get together at Christine's. It was great to spend quality time with her, and my Black Belt, Michael Bikiki, whose background was design and manufacturing, had been a classical concert pianist since his youth in Yugoslavia. He'd also written many songs. A highlight at Christine's party was Michael playing Christine's grand piano and singing many of his original songs.

A couple of months after this trip to the US, the Zoo were in town. Mick Fleetwood, Thorpie, Bekka and the whole tour group all visited my house for an Aussie barbeque.

In 1993 the US would have a new, and its youngest ever President, Bill Clinton. He took office in January, requesting a Fleetwood Mac grand performance at his inauguration party at the Whitehouse. This had brought together for the first time in years that original Rumours lineup. The President also requested his favourite band to play his favourite song, 'Don't Stop'.

Very early in 1999 I'd received a phone call from the secretary of the Mariah Carey World Tour. She'd asked if I could come into the Melbourne Hyatt Hotel, as the tour accountant Mr Taylor wanted to have a talk to me.

I couldn't believe it! Mr Taylor was Dwayne Taylor, the bodyguard from Fleetwood Mac's Rumours tour (and at *Les Cabaret* on our party night out). Before Mariah, he'd done a world tour with Barbara Striesand. Wow, had he been through the mill with the Black Dragon, and he'd told me it'd been much worse for our town crier Greg Thomason who'd got done big time on a Mac Tour with a large dose of heroin!

'You know Bob,' he'd said. 'Someone should write a book on the Fleetwood Mac band members and associates, and their bodyguards and their immediate crew and hangers-on that have fucked up ... fucked up big time over the years. That'd be a real good book and some.'

Of course he didn't say who.

Right at the end of 2000 I was on a martial arts training camp on Queensland's Sunshine Coast. Richard Norton and his wife Judy Green were supposed to be with me, but he was stuck in Afghanistan or somewhere, held over on a late shoot, finishing off yet another one of his movies.

Then Steve Panebiango, one of my fourth-degree Black Belts, was having a cool drink with me during a break.

'I was in the bank on Friday and I'm organising finance for this guy out from America. He was looking for an investment here, and he'd heard Noosa was the place, and he'd found a bargain. So while I'm shuffling paper work and getting his details like employment etcetera, suddenly he gives me Fleetwood Mac's name and I know that's the Chief's favourite band. Then I notice inside his casual collar, he's wearing a BJC square cross around his neck. When I ask, he says,

"Sure, I've trained in martial arts since I was a kid with the Bob Jones Corporation."

'Then I told him you were here this weekend on the coast, on this camp – and that's him standing behind you!'

They'd set me up beautifully. I hadn't seen him in years, and there he was like the prodigal son come home. Dennis Big 'D' Dunstan. You know, we would've spent the rest of that weekend in some sort of old bull, young bull competition.

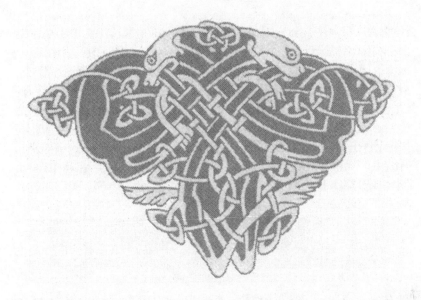

When Linda Ronstadt first took to the stage as a solo performer in the early 1970s, she'd score an easy two-digit rating on any male-oriented scale that evaluated the natural innocence of her girl/woman sexual naivity, when judged on a one-to-ten points system.

Even with the help of expert makeup artists, the best they could do was make her appear somewhere between twenty and twenty-two. This was during her Australian tour in our summer of 1979. By then she was already thirty-two years of age!

Linda wore no makeup and dressed in mini-skirts, cotton frocks, bobbysocks, with strap-over patent-leather adolescent-style shoes. For much of the time I thought I was the minder of a sixteen-year-old!

Born in Tucson, Arizona, Linda picked up the basics of music when she learned Mexican folk songs, while still at home, from her guitar-playing father. After she finished her freshman year at The University of Arizona, she moved over to the West Coast, settling in LA where, together with friends Kenny Edwards and Bob Kimmel, she formed the Stone Poneys, anacoustic trio known more for their spirit than their style. Nevertheless, the Stone Poneys were signed by Capitol. Now, even though this venture produced three erratic albums, their second contained the Mike Nesmith-penned 'Different Drum', and it was as this single was released that both the Poneys and Linda catapulted to fame.

The pre-hype had started earlier than usual for this particular tour, possibly because there was only one female singer up front, as compared to the usual acts that come touring; for example, Fleetwood Mac. Bands with multiple singers meant a whole barrage of marketable identities.

In the past, I'd told the bodyguards, 'no press about us and martial arts until after the tour'. That was because Paul Dainty had drilled me on occasions for capitalising on media interest on us minders. However, this time around Paul's publicist Margaret St. George had released to the media that Linda was a physical fitness addict. Seeing that the weather in the US at this time of year was extremely cold, this had restricted Linda's training regime. At the time Melbourne was experiencing a brilliant summer, so Bob Jones and Richard Norton were engaged to not only be Linda's protectors, but to prepare a rigorous self-defence program and to put Linda and her entourage through strict workouts every day, until they were all fighting fit.

The Melbourne Cricket Ground (MCG) was to have it's second-ever rock concert, the first being only the previous year with David Bowie. The sound check on the day of the concert was at 3.30 p.m. Richard was with Linda, which meant she was in safe hands. I'd had a deal going with Russ Kunkel (one of the best session drummers in the business) that we'd do a martial arts workout in the mornings and he'd give me my exchange drum lesson in the afternoons. At 2.30 p.m. we'd gone to the MCG ahead of everyone and, as I'd learned when touring with Bad Company and exchanging drumming/fighting fit lessons with Simon Kirke, that drummers were the easiest guys to teach martial arts to, that the hand–foot timing thing makes them very co-ordinated, but not so in reverse; well, not this martial artist anyway.

During the session I was deep in alpha concentration. All my focus was on that bloody snare drum, trying to get that basic beat that Russ was pressuring me on. Once I was head down, arse up, that astute world tour boss Eric Barrett yelled, 'Okay drummers, let's get serious. It's now 3.30 in the p.m. and Linda will be here shortly. C'mon Jonesy, don't make me get tough!'

As I'd knocked off, and looked up for the first time in an hour, there was a spontaneous burst of applause and raucous laughter. The 120 BJC Melbourne Black Belts that had gathered in front of the stage were bemused to see that their martial arts mentor had two left feet when it came to playing drums – even with the best teachers in the business.

In a Melbourne newspaper article published on 24 February 1979 they ran an unusually large photo of Linda. It was one of those typical naive sexually appealing shots, caught by photographer Bruce Postle.

This is the report by Bill Birnbauer with the headline:

Miss Ronstadt Sings To the Tune of $60m

Linda Ronstadt arrived in Melbourne yesterday looking vulnerable despite her two hulking bodyguards.

But the sex/song goddess and million-dollar poor rich girl did not need anybody's help at her first Australian Press conference.

Miss Ronstadt, whose voice and naive sex appeal have sold more than 17 million albums, is here for tonight's MCG concert.

Unlike her Sydney visit where she refused to answer press questions, Miss Ronstadt yesterday kicked up her thin summer dress, showed ample leg and faced a barrage of kid-glove questions.

Question No. 1: Did she play last night?

'Oooh, yes, we certainly did,' she said, giggling suggestively.

She juggled questions, teased television interviewers and flirted with camera lenses.

Male groupies? 'That's what girls do, I mean what would a male groupie do?'

The highlight of her career? 'Well today when we were trying to go down the elevator we had to lay on the ground because we couldn't stand ... we were so tired.'

Only one person asked the 32-year-old girl/woman about her much-publicised relationship with California Governor Jerry Brown.

Her 'rather not comment' answer echoed a

similar reply from an overworked public relations woman.

Miss Ronstadt, whose last five albums have grossed $60 million, admitted that there are times when singing is not easy.

I sometimes pick up a song and think I'd like to do it, but just fall flat on my face,' she said.

And the bodyguards? 'The promoters assigned two very large people who stand around all the time, which gives me a certain sense of security, I guess.'

During her three-week Australian concert tour, Miss Ronstadt's love of the wildlife and animals has led her to sanctuaries and zoos in every city. At Melbourne Zoo after the press conference yesterday she was presented with two young kangaroos by radio station 3XY to take back to America with her.

Miss Ronstadt looked truly surprised and kept asking unbelievingly whether she could take the kangaroos with her.

A crowd gathered as she cuddled the kangaroos and other native animals.

Now, I don't know what happened to 3XY's well-intentioned gift of the two kangaroos, but I do know how different the whole Australasian media, followed by the world press, would've been if they'd had an inkling as to what was actually going on behind the scenes ...
That night in my hometown, Linda took to the stage dressed to kill: she looked like the answer to every young man's sexual fantasy. She was dressed in an outfit that would make New York's fashionable

hookers eat their hearts out: a leopard skin low-cut shoulder-less Lycra top that sat low on her hips, and around her waist she wore a five-centimetre black leather belt. This was the perfect accessory to her black leather hot pants, which had double-sided hip-splits right up to her waist. From the splits at her thighs to her toes she wore the ultimate turn-on for 1979: thick, black mesh stockings that she would've imported direct from the Paris Blue Belles Dance Troupe.

Melbourne's Cricket Ground, the normally staid MCG, had never had it so sexy. More that 28 000 fans were treated to the fantasy as Linda pranced her way through just on two hours of her mainstream hits from as far back as the Stone Poneys.

That night I took the guys out. This included my drum coach Russ Kunkell, the boss of this tour, our inestimable tour manager, and a very personal friend, Eric Barrett, lead guitarist Waddy Wachtel, and one of the best keyboards players to come out of a session studio, Mr Don Grolnik (who sadly passed away in the early 1990s), and some of the crew. We really hit the town. Meanwhile, Linda wanted to stay in, Richard offering to hang about in case she needed anything, which was great: it gave me the chance to party with the guys.

Melbourne was really happening so our limos did my circuit from St. Kilda's restaurants in the red light district by the beachfront at dinner time. We moved on to the Crystal Ballroom and Chapel Street for Chasers, to the city early for Billboard. Then we headed out to Brunswick's Bombay Rock (Gangster City at the time) where you could see three, maybe four bands any night. Next it was back to town for the elaborate King Street scene, where there were more night clubs grouped together over only a few blocks than anywhere else in the world. That way my overseas guests would've seen a variety of bands from Midnight Oil, INXS and Australian Crawl to one of the hardest workers of the day, Joe Camilleri, who at the time fronted Jo Jo Zep and The Falcons.

A couple of nights earlier we'd done a similar trek through downtown Sydney. Russ Kunkell had asked me who was a good band to see there, and I'd checked with my man about town Norm-e and off we'd gone to the Stagedoor Tavern, near Central Railway Station. Though the Americans loved this place, it was soon off to the Civic Hotel near Chinatown, then it was the choice (depending on who was playing where) of a dozen inner-city gigs, or out west to the Brighton Hotel. In the south we had the Manly Vale, or we'd head north to the Royal Antler. After all that it was into King's Cross to see my gangster associates at the Manzel Room on Springfield Avenue. The Manzel opened when all those others closed, and never faltered pre-sunrise.

The Manzel, a glamorous sleaze pit, coexisted in an underworld atmosphere of sex and drugs, which bought in drug-dealers and rockin' groupies. Backgammon tables were booked out all night, it was just the place that all overseas performers fell in love with every time I took them there. Russ was real pleased, he'd seen a band that Norm-e said we just had to check out: its name was Flowers. Sydney columnist Tom Zelinka had tagged the group recently with the line: 'Flowers Bloom on Local Scene'. Out front was guitarist/singer Iva Davies (his real name was Ivor; a printer's mistake put it out as Iva, and the singer figured it suited him better). A year later

Flowers changed its name, but on this night it was thumbs-up from all of Linda Ronstadt's backing band. The other bands we saw, before we'd finished up at Benny's, as the sun came up–down at Potts Point, included Mi-Sex, Cold Chisel, The Angels and Mental As Anything.

As we touched down in Japan I looked out of the first-class porthole window, half expecting to see a big banner with 'Welcome to Tokyo' backed up by:

RINDA RONDSTADT

but no, that gag would not be repeated.

Almost the whole day after our arrival was spent at the all-Japan Zoological Gardens in Tokyo. For Linda this was one of these days of absolutely no makeup, a double bow and her hair in pigtails. Once again she didn't look a day over sweet sixteen. Linda would walk between us, her arms hooked at the elbows to each of ours, Richard's and mine. However, media people ever so politely had banded together at the major exit area, with TV cameras, radio microphones and the tell-tale pen and pad. On moving her grip from our elbows downwards, and taking the both of us by the hands, Linda said quietly,

'Come on you two gladiators, get me to, and through that mob as quickly as possible! We can't give them too much, the promoter has organised the national press conference tonight at our hotel. Come on, last one in pays for dinner tonight!'

As we all ran together, holding hands, I breathed in the euphoria, thinking that if anyone should try harming this beautiful specimen of human eminence, they'd find themselves in a lot of harm: Richard and I were prepared to go all the way, as protectors of Linda Ronstadt.

Linda gave the media crew at the zoo enough to keep them happy. Then the three of us had a light, early dinner. She didn't want much to eat due to the prodigious Tokyo press conference that night.

The boys in the band had backed Linda up at this press conference, although she didn't really need it. Linda was more than capable of going head to head with the press.

The Japanese media are normally very well researched and knew that Linda was touring with session musicians. They wanted to know about each of their background. There were a couple of annoyances. One American journo wanted to know all about Jerry Brown, Governor of California, and the recent safari she'd supposedly had, venturing into the wilderness with him.

The European paparazzi were intent on pursuing some aspersion about Linda's being quoted as saying that she wouldn't have minded sleeping with a priest!

It was true, like anybody else, Linda had a bit of the devil in her, but this press conference was about her musical tour of Japan, and the introduction of the support band she'd brought to play the music ...

'While I do what I do, sing the songs ...'

The conversation swung to her recent hit albums, *Hasten Down the Wind* and *Simple Dreams*, followed by the hit singles of the time, released off the 1978 album, *Living in The USA*.

In watching her work the media it wasn't hard to see why Linda would shortly after this tour be in demand to appear on both the stage and screen in Gilbert's and Sullivan's *Pirates of Penzance*. This would soon be followed by a trilogy of albums on which she sang standards backed by Nelson Riddle and an orchestra. In 1987, Linda collaborated with Dolly Parton and Emmy Lou Harris on *Trio,* which included a revival of Phil Spector's classic, 'To Know Him is To Love Him'.

In 1987 *Canciones De Mi Padre*, probably influenced by her guitar-playing father, was an album of Mexican folksongs, and *Cry Like a Rainstorm, Howl Like The Wind* (1989) included duets with Aaron Neville of the Neville Brothers, one of which, 'Don't Know Much', was a major hit in 1990.

The day after the press conference Linda, Richard and I had a limo take us from the hotel to the Ginza. Linda was keen to have a look around and to do some Japanese shopping.

Tokyo – once again it was a good tourist day, and with its thirty million people the traffic was unbelievable. We were at the Ginza, one of Tokyo's busiest, if not the busiest shopping area. The Ginza is a multiple-angle intersection, and it has this bloody traffic going in all directions! The Ginza also comprises of tall, high-rise business buildings, and shopping complexes, multiple cinema centres and thousands of moving, talking billboards advertising in incredible Japanese character displays that mean little in sales value to the Western eye, except for, over there, look at that – we can buy a Coke or go to McDonald's!

Synchronised traffic lights and Tokyo uniformed police somehow kept this traffic moving – not fast, but flowing – as our limo had pulled into the curb. Richard and I'd jumped out followed by Linda...

Bang! Crash! Smash! Three cars collided, and you could tell it was only the beginning.

Richard and I are about the same height and of very similar athletic condition. Both of us had long hair, but that wasn't the problem, it was the fact that Richard's was blond and mine (back then) was bright Irish red. Add to that sneakers, blue jeans and our Linda Ronstadt world tour jackets, and our *little* Linda. Now I've described her already and she was as cute as ever on this Japanese spring day.

Screech! Crash! Honk! Honk! Boom! Two more cars collided. The cops came from everywhere. We'd only just worked out that we'd been responsible for the mayhem. The sight of us was too much for them to take in (at any time during the day or night, in this area of the Ginza there'd be at least 25 000 people in and out of the cars travelling to as many destinations. Everyone would be the same height, at least head and shoulders below Richard and me, they'd *all* wear dark-colored suits or dresses, they'd all have black hair and they all wore glasses). Cars were now skidding to avoid one and other, and the traffic had begun to jam up; pedestrians stopped to check out the crashes and stood there staring at us.

One uniformed cop spoke our language; well ... 'Oh prease, gentermen, you must take Rinda and get back in car – or go to store. But prease, you must reave the Ginza now!'

We smiled and bolted with *Rinda* to the revolving doors and revolved ourselves into this incredibly large department store.

There were no more cars piling up outside, but 'Oh how embarrassing,' Linda said.

'It's sort of funny in a way,' Richard replied.

Wherever we went everything came to a standstill. On entry this large store had been incredibly noisy: tills rang up, supervisors yelled commands at staff and thousands of customers prattled in their native tongue. Then suddenly, silence.

'Oh no, I've had enough of this already; I can't take anymore. Let's go back outside, get into the limo as quick as we can. Shut the bloody doors and let's get ourselves back to the hotel!' Linda ordered.

We'd gathered around reception on the night of the first concert to decide the order of events for our assault on Tokyo's nightlife. About nine months earlier a new club called the S-Ken Studio had opened in Roppongi. It catered to the Tokyo Rockers Movement bands, and it was by far the most sought-after club in this city.

We had quite a group: about a dozen or more band members and crew. As usual, emotions were mixed, some of the crew had worked very hard during the gig. They were hungry and going to eat. Some were dying to find out the answer to that age-old question, and see what Japanese women were about: were they really horizontal, or vertical like every one else? This group were off to the bathhouse 'B' district to find out for themselves, so we all decided to meet up at S-Ken Studio at 2:30 a.m.

Russ, Waddy, Eric Barrett and I opted for the city centre and a club known as Dukes Bar to see Lizard playing. Dukes was an old favorite of mine from earlier tours; it was definitely mob-connected and run by Mitsuhiro Yamamoto. He was one of those Japanese businessmen you knew would be unhealthy to mix it with on his own turf. Everyone called him the Duke, and Dukes Bar had its own currency. Through a couple of well-positioned teller's windows in the club, you could exchange any country' money, including Japanese Yen (for a small broker's exchange fee). In return you'd be given the Dukes Bar very own quasi-currency, which looked and felt exactly like US dollars. The only difference was that this money carried a mug shot of the Duke himself, and if you read the small print, it stated that it was good for the Dukes bar trade only. This was the only currency traded at the Duke Bar, and at the end of the night you went to the teller and for a small exchange fee she'd transfer back this credit, to your original currency.

The Duke was pleased to see me with the guys. He knew this normally meant that the main act might be close behind. The usual, drink cards and only the special hostess, worked our tables. Eric Barrett and the Duke got into a rave as to whether a chain of Duke joints would work in California and what a great idea it was to stop pilfering among the staff. The Duke acknowledged theft was no longer a problem, but that with every day of trading, due to the Duke's trade being mostly tourists, he could always count on an 18 to 25 per cent loss of his counterfeit currency as a result of souveniring. Patrons would get drunk enough to forget, not care, or they'd just want to hold on to this funny money to show the folks back home.

'Every week I have to order 75 per cent turnover on booze, and I have to print off 25 per cent new money. With the cost of restocking the alcohol and the printing cost of the fake money the profits are both comparable.' The Duke had an educated American accent. 'In fact, I think I make slightly more on my quasi-currency.'

By around 3 a.m. all of our gang had arrived. Most were up 'n' dancin' here at the S-Ken Studio. Everyone now knew we were in town. Waddy Wachtel had become the life of the party and the crew was becoming more outrageous. The power of the good ol' tour jacket had started to show its significance. As bathhouse 'B' girls had finished off their professional duties, they'd started to arrive in their customary mini-skirts and with some bugger's tour jacket on. Some diligent sound guy in control of volume lifted the band up a couple of decibels to keep in time with our party machine. Almost the whole Ronstadt entourage had now arrived, those missing included Linda, the boss herself, and my best buddy, that other Aussie bodyguard, Richard Norton.

Before the sun had come up the Duke had wanted to show some of the gang the town. He'd arranged for cars so off we went on the grand tour of Tokyo's dark side: a couple of the usual gay bars complete with trannies, just like any major city. A club-bar brothel had some of us playing the pool and a couple playing the fool. Then it was downtown for a taste of illegal casinos for those who wanted to take a punt. Pretty soon that familiar old sunrise had started to show us the light. This had been the aftermath of the first concert, there'd be four more concert nights over the following two weeks with more of the same.

There'd be time for some sleep on this first concert night – now that was the best idea we'd had for a coupla hours!

Linda's remaining concerts in Japan got better and better, which helped her records sell more. The usual press conference lunches, sound checks and after-gig parties only grew wilder due to the success of the tour.

However, as bodyguard to Linda Ronstadt, I'd seen very little of my client. In a Melbourne newspaper article (24 February 1979), Bill Birnbauer had asked Linda if she played the previous night?

'Oooh, yes we certainly did.'

Birnbauer had picked up on the inference, by reporting that Linda had giggled suggestively. But of course he couldn't pick up on who was who in the zoo!

Then when he'd asked her what had been the highlight of her career, he must have wondered when Linda replied, 'Well today when we were trying to go down the elevator we had to lay on the ground because we couldn't stand. We were so tired.'

This had been another of those early nights Linda had stayed in for, with my buddy Richard being on hand in case Linda had wanted anything. There are no prizes for working it out ...

After the tour Richard had gone home direct as he had to get back to work at the Immigration Department (at this stage he'd not yet left). I'd gone home via Hong Kong and Taiwan on some martial arts importing business.

About ten days after I'd returned to Australia, Richard and I were having lunch and he confided, 'Bob, I've got this real problem that maybe you can help me with. You've already been there and done that, so, I'd like your ... in fact I value your opinion. On the one hand, I'm very much in love. Maybe it's time I got married, planned a family, settled down with my job at the Immigration Department, and stopall this gallivanting round the world with you and all these rock stars.

'My other problem: my thing with Linda Ronstadt is, ah, pretty serious. She wants me to drop everything here, pack up and shift over to America.'

What could I say? There was only the one piece of advice I could give my best friend ...

It was really hard for Richard the first couple of years in the US, fitting in his bodyguard work with the physical fitness training and nutrition programs he'd put together for his rich and famous clients. Then life got really difficult as he started to get his breaks in the movie industry. It wasn't long before the get-fit programs and his security work suffered.

Now for more than twenty years Richard has had to travel the world making movies!

Shit of a job, but one of us had to do it.

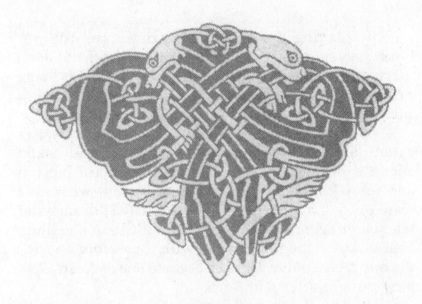

Glenn Ruehland as a young adolescent had gone to a martial arts demonstration featuring the most famous martial artist in Australia (I wrote the copy) one Saturday at Albert Park. Some time later as a teenager, Glenn started training with this Bob Jones. A few years later, as a young Black Belt (young as in first-degree), Glenn had become so keen as a disciple of my lifestyle that I'd offered him the opportunity of live-in *course de comitatus* to learn bodyguarding. This for Glenn, at this stage in his life, was on a par with a big lottery win. It meant an apprenticeship of five years, living the role twenty-four hours every day as a full-time bodyguard to the Chief.

    This meant full-time martial arts training in all its aspects: physical, psychological and spiritual. It would mean regular weight training and dietary supplements; it would mean periodic abstinence of all vices for predetermined extended periods of time.

By playing the live-in bodyguard twenty-four hours, seven days a week, it meant that when Glenn was contracted out professionally, the client was being protected by the real thing. Hence, things were running along quite nicely for Glenn Ruehland.

At the time I'd tried to launch a television series called 'The Bodyguards' (back in 1975) and asked Glenn if he wouldn't mind helping Richard Norton and me with some fight scenes and stunt work. We were putting a pilot together to show to sponsors and television agencies. This also being Glenn's calling, he'd enjoyed the stunt work with a passion, and for the next twenty-five years he became one of Australia's most sought-after stuntmen.

During those early years Glenn had got his experience working around the traps, then I'd started working him on the tours around the pits, backstage and so on, until he'd gotten used to how we secured massive concerts featuring The Rolling Stones, ABBA and David Bowie. Then he was ready for his first tour as a bodyguard for Olivia Newton John. He went on to be a personal bodyguard for the Electric Light Orchestra (ELO), and his next big challenge was Demis Roussos. However, his most unusual assignment was Evil Knievel.

Glenn remembers fondly his time with Demis Roussos and Roussos's ability to speak some eight languages fluently. Glenn would look on in awe as he and his client would eat at a variety of restaurants and Demis would order off the menu and conduct lengthy conversations with the staff and management in their particular language.

Glenn had moments of paranoia when protecting Evil Knievel in public. This was due to a walking stick Evil carried with him, which was an item of luxury.

The handle was a model of Evil Knievel doing a mono on his favourite motor bike. It was covered in clusters of diamonds and rumoured to be insured for $US750 000. Added to this, on average, was another half a million dollars in gold chains and diamond-studded medallions that hung around the man's neck. On more than one occasion, Evil Knievel (especially in the heat of summer) would lift all this jewellery over his head, fold it into his hand and tell our young Glenn to put it all into the pocket of his jeans, until they got back to the hotel!

When Glenn attained his fourth-degree Black Belt he ventured off into the world of *stuntman extraordinaire*. After several years on the Paul Hogan and every local television series that had anything to do with special-effect stunts, Glenn moved into the movie industry and his life was to change forever. He paved the way and set high standards for many new young stuntmen to follow in his path.

In 2001 he was contracted as stunt co-ordinator for the highest budget film in Australia to this date: $100 000 000 for the actor/animated movie *Scooby Doo*.

World-profile kickboxer-turned WCW wrestler Sam Greco featured in an epic battle with the star of *Buffy the Vampire Slayer*, 45-kilogram Sara Michelle Geller, also lead actor for Scooby Doo.

David Pendleberry was known to other martial artists as Dave Berry, and to me he was known as 'Bungles', a term of endearment referring to the fact that he wasn't much good at anything other than fighting – but he did that well.

From the time I started teaching professionally, Bungles was my very first student. He fitted into the story very early in the piece, helping me to renovate my first premises at 48 Elizabeth Street, Melbourne, which would be the first of eventually more than a thousand martial arts schools. David had got the name Bungles because we learned from the experience that he and I would never open a business in the area of renovations.

David had worked doors at the clubs with me and we'd gone off to the festivals together. He was there on that first concert tour of The Rolling Stones in 1973. After The Stones tour Bungles got married (to Christine) and started a family, which limited his gallivanting around the world with me.

Peter Iken was the Australian head of Warners (WEA), which was starting to bring out on tour young overnight sensations of the pop scene. Peter Iken, or 'Iris', as he was known to us, had asked state manager Steve Hands to co-ordinate security for these young teen-idols. Steve Hands was a good friend of the BJC and in 1975 it was organised that Dave Berry, alias Bungles, would tour as personal bodyguard for the Australian visit of America's Shaun Cassidy.

In Melbourne, Shaun had made a public appearance promotion at Brash's Record Bar in Collins Street. There was enough publicity and fanfare to create a riot. Thousands of teenagers, mostly very young girls (Shaun was a young teenager at the time), had crowded the store and street out front. They'd screamed and clamored to see their young idol, all wanting a souvenir piece of his clothing or hair if they could get it. For these girls, worked up to a fever pitch, even having Shaun's skin under their fingernails was the ultimate connection!

Bungles had rung me for support and I'd gone to Brash's with four of our best Black Belts. The limos were parked in a lane way at the rear of the store; the lanes were narrow and the limos could only get within fifty metres of the record store's exit doors. When it came time to leave the building, we formed a circle around Shaun to shield him all the way to the limos. When we opened the store's exit doors there were hundreds of his fans jammed into these narrow lane ways as we locked arms to confine our circle of protection. The aggression of this wild, out-of-control mob of teenage girls was almost as threatening an obstacle as any gang I'd encountered.

Shaun had been crouched in the middle of this magic circle, and as we'd neared the rear of the limo, Bungles had reached out to take control of him so that we could flank him into the safety of the car.

However, 'Chief, where the fuck is Shaun?' There was instant panic, with all of us focused outward into the crowd. None of us had noticed at what point our client had disappeared. Then again, in this scenario, how the hell could our client just disappear?

Shaun's disappearance was the best thing that could've happened: it brought the screaming crowd to a standstill. The girls were as bemused as us. Where is Shaun? they asked.

Just then the limo driver caught Dave Berry's attention, by pointing over the front seat to the floor of the car. As it turned out, at the peak of the excitement, our mischievous Shaun Cassidy had gone to the ground. On his hands and knees he'd crawled all the way through the legs of these girls to the blind side of the car, opening the door, sliding in and simply laying on the floor. As hundreds of his fans stood around bewildered, we'd all driven off in the limo, with one consolation: as we'd scrambled into the back seat, we'd pretended he wasn't there, and kept him pinned on the floor until we'd arrived back at The Southern Cross Hotel.

But meanwhile, 'Hey guys, your feet are crushing the life out of me!'

'That's funny, I thought I heard Shaun's voice,' Bungles remarked. 'But it couldn't be, he disappeared ages ago!'

These days (more than twenty-five years later) Shaun Cassidy has produced many fine television series including *Roar*, a medieval adventure exploring Celtic culture.

Some time later (in 1978) Steve Hands organised Bungles to work in the capacity of personal protection for the Australian tour of overnight sensation Leif Garrett. Leif was only sixteen when he toured here. In every state he drew crowds of between 10 000 to 30 000 screaming teenage girls. His fans were so young Steve Hands organised a well-known twenty-six-year-old Sydney model to keep Leif company, and safe from so many underage teenage girls.

Leif also had a passion for women in any style of uniform. His sexual conquest of a young Victorian Police woman, complete with her constable uniform, at the Hilton Hotel Melbourne, was an event that he'd remember for many a year!

Another memory of OZ, that may have haunted our young Leif Garrett for sometime, was the fact that Steve Hands used to grow, for personal use only, some home-heated plants primarily known as *Mentone Poison*, also referred to endearingly as Creeping

Norman. This plant would seem to be a very mild form of mind-expansion drug before *boom*, it would strike like a Mike Tyson swinging left hook.

Dave Berry recalled, 'One night, after a hectic day of public appearances in Queensland, we were back at the Brisbane Park Royal. We were with a bunch of Leif's recording studio people, PR guys and some local DJs. They were all commenting on the mildness of this Melbourne Mentone Poison when suddenly Creeping Norman did his thing: *boom*, everybody was asleep.

'One by one I had to drag all these fuckers out into the corridor and prop them up with their legs crossed. They looked so peaceful, like a group of meditators. Leif was away with the leprechauns. I put him to bed and he slept the night away until midday the next day.'

Almost ten years later (in 1985), while I was on a martial arts training camp in New Zealand, and being sworn in by a Catholic priest as the godfather of newly born Ishoa-Rose Sidey-Renato, Dave Berry was on the road with Twisted Sister for their Australian tour. While in Sydney, Bungles had the assistance of Noel Rush (fifth-degree Black Belt). Shortly after Twisted Sister, Noel Rush would start a more-than-fifteen-year relationship as personal bodyguard to Billy Joel.

This was also the year that Jimmy Barnes' half-brother John 'Swanee' Swan released his *Bushido* album and used my personal Celtic Cross as part of the album art work.

Spandau Ballet had used Australia as a springboard to their 1985 world tour, and I'd given them two of my best: Mark 'the Bear' Warren and Joe Vidovic. The Bear had been a live-in *comitatus* for the full five years and both he and Joe were fourth-degree Black Belts.

Spandau Ballet were so impressed they took the guys on the world tour, thus off to Europe and America as protectors. The Bear and Joe had the whole band and crew training in our martial arts from the very beginning. This was particularly so for lead singer Tony Hadley and saxophonist Steve Norman who took the first grading to Blue Belt in my system.

However, an unfortunate accident occurred one night at a sell-out performance (of more than 65 000 punters) in Orange County, where Steve Norman went into his floor slide during his saxophone solo and tore knee ligaments. A stint on crutches meant that some gigs had to be cancelled, but rumour had it that Steve was equally distressed at missing out on his martial arts training.

The other key members of the Spandau Ballet line-up were brothers Gary (guitar) and Martin (bass) Kemp, with the fifth member on drums being John Deeble. Gary's and Martin's theatrical training undoubtedly gave the group an advantage with their stage performances, and later with their video productions.

Chart success had eluded them for a while. Then in 1982 *Communication* reached number twelve in the UK, and the title track from the album 'True' gave them their first UK number one; a suitable riposte to the critics who dismissed them as more hype than talent.

Shortly after their UK success, they established a world market for themselves with the *Parade* album. But Spandau Ballet had more than their fair share of contractual disputes, which affected their true worth and growth.

Gary and Martin Kemp later received rave reviews for key roles in their portrayals as the Kray Twins, those notorious British gangsters. Later, Gary went on to support Whitney Houston and Kevin Costner in *The Bodyguard*. Martin also did a stint in a well-known British soapy.

Joe Vidovic went on to look after Mick Jagger's better half at the time, Jerry Hall. This was during the Australasian release of her summer-wear fashions, released nationally through the David Jones network.

Then ten years after Glenn Ruehland had looked after Olivia Newton John, it was Joe's turn to protect this popular Australian singer. Olivia had been brought home from the US to sing in the opening ceremony of the Victorian Football League Australian Rules Grand Final.

Along with Jerry and Olivia, the BJC toured with Kim Wilde, Cyndi Lauper on her True Colors World Tour 1986–87, and many other artists of the time.

In between protecting the fabulous females of rock 'n' roll during the mid- to late 1980s, one of my Sydney Black Belts, 'Big Kev' Kevin Gerraghty, toured with Bruce Springsteen.

According to Kevin, Springsteen was the most energetic rock performer he'd toured with. 'He sings and plays flat-out for anything up to four hours, constantly maintaining an extraordinary feverish tension and communication with his audience.'

Bruce Springsteen has the knack of writing songs that capture readily identifiable characters in identifiable situations, and these experiences are shared experiences. This is different to Bob Dylan, who in the early part of his career wrote about social issues; instead, Springsteen concerns himself more with their effect on individuals.

Springsteen's 1985 mammoth tour played to full houses in arenas around the world. The Born In the USA album, with not a bad track on it, brought him large record sales as a result of songs such as 'Dancing In The Dark' and 'I'm On Fire', and to cap it all, Bruce had a short-term love affair, which would lead to a short-term marriage to twenty-four-year-old model Julianne Phillips, who'd entered and exited from his life within a space of three years.

Joe Vidovic had paired up with Peter Costello (third-degree Black Belt) for the Paul Dainty Corporation tour of Julian Lennon with his album *Vallotte*, which included the hit single 'Too Late for Goodbyes' and his follow-up single 'Say You're Wrong'. During this tour Julian had shown extreme interest in the martial arts, thanks to his two Black Belt bodyguards. This had led to lengthy conversations between the three of them; Joe and Peter would talk extensively about the discipline and its attributes. A good yarn about their Chief Instructor ensued, and eventually Julian requested a communication with the Chief.

When they finally rang, Julian and I talked non-stop for over two hours about everything from the history and philosophy of the martial arts and its original source with music. Julian showed a deep interest in my spiritual search through the martial arts, as compared to the world's big three gurus that had captured the West's interest in the past decade, including his dad and his ex-Beatle buddies.

Julian learned of my connection to each of the three gurus, how I'd been bodyguard to the founder of the KRSNA consciousness movement, A. C. Prabhupada during his world tour of 1974, and how the both of us were connected to the elite of rock performers. Prabhupada had been invited to stay as a guest on John Lennon's estate, at Tittenhurst, in 1969. He would die peacefully on 14 November 1977 during the period when I was on tour in Japan with Fleetwood Mac.

The second guru who'd gained notoriety in this era of spiritual experimentation was the sexual scallywag Bhagwan Shree Rajneesh. He had a feminine powerbroker from Hell, Ma Anand Sheela. Multiple fraudulent activities saw her sentenced to twenty years of imprisonment and the Bhagwan was eventually ordered by the courts to leave the US.

Five years after my conversation with Julian (in 1990), Bhagwan would die at the age 59. He maintained that he'd been poisoned while in US custody (others suggested he was poisoned, but by someone from within the cult, while others have implied the guru died from an AIDS-related illness).

Julian and I'd also spoken about guru number three, due to our connections with Mick Fleetwood's wife Jenny, her sister Pattie, George Harrison and The Beatles, Mia Farrow, The Rolling Stones and The Beach Boys, and the many others who'd given the then little-known guru with long straggly hair, Maharishi Mahesh Yogi, so much notoriety in the 1960s.

Prabhupada had shared with both John Lennon and me the belief that Bhagwan and Maharishi were a couple of gurus with questionable sexual beliefs. However, after Prabhupada passed away, his own organisation would spiral out of control as a result of greed and paranoia.

When Julian's father had accused the Maharishi of womanising and publicly announced his disassociation, the guru had declared, 'I know I have failed. My mission is over.'

Instead of retiring, as he initially declared he would, Maharishi successfully reinvented his organisation. Now an octogenarian with a long flowing white beard, Maharishi leads a reclusive life in The Netherlands, where he controls his now, multi-billion-dollar empire.

Our two-hour rave must have confused the young Julian Lennon. That night he indulged in a cocktail of drugs and alcohol with Australia's own icon of self-destruction, INXS' Michael Hutchence. Together they'd done the town in Kings Cross and Julian had brought a young maiden of the fold back to the Sebel Town House Club Bar for drinks and then it was up to his suite for whatever would eventuate.

Her distress arose when Julian called in his bodyguards to evict her, demanding that she not go off into the night wearing one of his best silk shirts. Joe and Peter, having heard my story of Mrs Richards from The Stones' tour, promptly stripped her of the shirt, and threw her naked arse out into the corridor followed by her clothes. After this tour, Julian humorously signed the tour poster: 'To Bob Jones – Thanks Vallotte'.

Joe Vidovic for years represented my organisation as a protector of the entertainment industry, covering many top-name tours. He recently told me that one of his favourites was the 1987 Glass

Spider World Tour as David Bowies' personal bodyguard.

58 College Street, Hamilton, Queensland, was a live-in training facility, as was my Melbourne residence. One of its earliest successful trainees was Tony Quinn. Tony was one of those fanatical martial artists who built his positive thought levels to a point where he felt he could do anything he put his mind to. His successes in personal well-being, business and social acumen all were balanced through the attainment of each of his Black Belt degrees.

At first degree Tony started in the security industry. As was expected by our corporation he started working doors.

At second degree he began managing the bars where he'd begun on the door and he graduated to working security at the festivals.

At third degree he started his own seafood restaurant business and employed a manager and several young Black Belt security guys to work his doors. And I graduated him to touring as bodyguard with various visiting overseas bands.

By fourth-degree Black Belt, as well as all of the above, Tony was operating a chain of BJC Self-defence Academies. He'd become Australia's first National kickboxing champion: ranked number five in the WKA (World Kickboxing Association) world ratings.

At Brisbane's Festival Hall, I'd matched him to fight a top seed from New York, Kraiger Dupré. Tony made short work of this African-American athlete, by knocking him into dreamtime in the third round. This boosted his ranking to number three and I took him to fight in Hong Kong.

By the time Tony Quinn had received his fifth-degree (halfway on a scale of ten degrees) I'd reward him with the contract of protecting one of the biggest bands of the era, the Eurythmics. Dave Stewart and Annie Lennox, both Celtic Scots, had met in a north London restaurant in 1977 and subsequently formed a group, the poppy, post-punk Tourists. Failing to score a hit with their own songs, Dave and Annie finally resorted to a desperate retreat, covering Dusty Springfield's 'I Only Wanna Be With You'. This at least had them in the charts.

However, the Tourists didn't long survive this small measure of success. When Stewart and Lennox resurfaced, it was as the Eurythmics, with a flexible line-up based around the two of them for a very different sound and image.

Lennox's savagely cool voice dominated their space, uncluttered synthesizer pop, while her continual disguises – costumes, wigs, the occasional male drag outfit – caused her to be cast by the press as a female counterpart to the gender-bending Boy George.

In 1982 the title track of their second LP *Sweet Dreams (Are Made of This)* became their first hit as the Eurythmics followed swiftly with 'Love is a Stranger'. US success followed and a third hit single 'Who's That Girl' featured cameo appearances by a host of stars from Bananarama and Marilyn to Kiki Dee.

This tour was the last time I ever saw Tony Quinn; he continued on overseas as the Eurythmics' bodyguard. From here, Tony worked his way into management level when Dave Scott and the band sent him to New York and put him through a scriptwriting course for their future plans in films. Now, he lives between France and England, and manages several of Europe's name bands.

Although I haven't seen him in twenty years, I always speak of Tony Quinn with my usual pride.

Paul Jeffrey lived at my house for two and a half years; however, halfway through his apprenticeship he returned home to New Zealand. In the early 1980s he laid the foundation of today's network of our martial arts clubs across both the North Island and the South Island of New Zealand.

He also instigated TAG-War Games (Tactical Adventure Games) franchises for our higher ranked Black Belts. Besides our martial arts clubs, the Black Belts could expand this natural extension of our business: a strategic league of teams spread across both the North Island and the South Island, drawing not only from our BJC but also involving the corporate sector.

TAG is played along the lines of a football match, with two teams scoring goals, strategically defeating their opponent, with the aid of automatic firearms that shoot a blood-dye pellet that bursts on contact. The more opponents you *kill*, the easier it is to score goals.

Paul's claim to bodyguard fame was his stint on the 1984 world tour of Boy George and Culture Club.

When George O'Dowd, an exceptionally flamboyant character from the so-called New Romantics set of London night-clubbers, decided to form his own group, observers were cynical. Far from being a mere mannequin, however, Boy George, proved to possess an outstanding musical talent, as well as the gift of being able to charm everyone from pre-pubescent pop fans to their grannies.

After a couple of flop singles, George and his Culture Club – Jon Moss, Roy Hay and Mikey Craig – shot to number one in 1982 with the lilting, reggae-ish 'Do You Really Want To Hurt Me'.

The UK press threw its hands up in horror at George's long plaits, makeup and knee-length tunics (worn over trousers), which they never failed to describe as dresses. However, when they discovered he was jolly, articulate, sensible and determinedly asexual, approval followed. He soon became a British media obsession, almost on a par with the late Princess of Wales.

Both the group's first LP, *Kissing To Be Clever* and 1983's follow-up *Colour By Numbers* received world acclaim and showed Culture Club as a multi-talented band. They'd blended everything from reggae and soul to MOR and country music to achieve this smooth brand of 1980s pop.

At the height of all this action my organisation had rewarded Paul Jeffrey with his probationary sixth-degree Black Belt; this was designed to coincide with his apparent personal success. Paul would perform his martial arts training with a passion; he'd established Bob Jones martial arts clubs all over both islands. Already we'd become the largest self-defence organisation in New Zealand.

Paul was also instrumental in establishing my latest venture of this period: Convenience Advertising. This was a concept another of my Black Belts had devised. Hence, we sold advertising space on the back of convenience (or dunny) doors at airports, restaurants and our pubs and clubs (today

Convenience Advertising is found in six countries).

After only six months TAG war games were turning over more than $40 000 a month. On top of this, Paul had found the time to expand our Bob Jones-associated security company into the pubs and clubs; this was important, as it created employment for a lot of our students as they came through to their Black Belt (first-degree gradings).

Paul's sixth-degree Black Belt philosophy of the grading structure within our organisation was, 'man's own abilities to put his ideas into practice.'

Now, for ideas known only to himself, Paul went off and did something that totally alienated him from all my teachings and philosophy. In retrospect, I've always said to my Black Belts, 'If you don't want to do the time, don't do the crime.'

The *crime* got Paul four years. While in prison, Paul directed all his energy to library pursuits and arduously studied the healing effects of pharmaceutical products on physical injuries.

Two years later, and out on good behaviour, Paul met his Ms Right, settled down and put his research into practice and, between the two of them, they developed a line of products. Today he operates, with his other half, a multi-million dollar business and is involved in the healing of people.

Andrew Wolveridge, one of my fourth-degree Black Belts, was exceptionally astute when working the concerts. His communication skills made him another one I could always trust to leave in charge of the backstage area, including the pits. He'd worked on all tours during the late 1980s and now runs his own Security Company. He works extensively in the entertainment industry and recently secured the World Masters of Business Seminar Circuits. These featured famous international speakers, including Russia's Mikhail Gorbachev and US military diplomat, Norman Schwarzkopf. Andrew's company also secured the Australian 2000 tour of Nelson Mandella.

Recently, Andrew and I were having lunch together and he suggested that I take a look at a book he'd just finished reading.

It was the biography of Graeme Alford, the story of a guy down on his luck and his personal battle to get himself back on track.

Graeme Alford, I'd heard of that name. Way back in 1982 I'd read an article about him during a flight to the US. He was that solicitor who'd developed a drinking and gambling problem, siphoned out his trust account, then tried to square up by robbing a bank.

As it turned out Graeme Alford did his time for the crime, got his act together and wound up promoting the seminar circuit known as The Masters. It proved that if you *Never Give Up*, as his book was titled, and you can conceive and believe, you will achieve.

During Gorbachev's and Schwarzkopf's lecture tour of Australia, Graeme Alford had given them copies of his biography.

After he got out of prison, Graeme Alford married a client's wife (this client had died while he was doing his time). His wife-to-be would visit him in gaol for legal advice, as she'd done with her husband. A deep affection had developed and they'd married. Her daughter Lee had been dating Andrew. Here again a deep affection had developed and they also married. During this time both men entered into a business partnership in the area of entertainment management. Their first act, rock 'n' roll band Drive 55, recorded their first album in the same studio where Michael Jackson recorded *Thriller*: the Ocean Way Recording Studio on Sunset Boulevard, California. Mid-september 2001 Andrew's company secured the Bill Clinton tour of Australia.

John Forsyth has worked for me and now with me since 1983. In those early days John worked the doors in Melbourne on the infamous King Street strip. He was training in my martial arts organisation when I realised that he had something special. Paul Jeffrey had just left the house for New Zealand, leaving a position vacant, so I felt the timing was right to ask John to live-in as a full-time training bodyguard, twenty-four hours a day, seven days a week. John quickly worked his way through the ranks and began organising numerous martial arts events. He helped co-ordinate national tours with Frank Sinatra, Sammy Davis Jnr and Liza Minnellie, Luciano Pavarotti, Billy Joel, Fleetwood Mac, Olivia Newton John, Stevie Wonder, INXS, Jimmy Barnes, Kylie Minogue, Jerry Lee Lewis, Chuck Berry and Michael Jackson, just to name a few.

John Forsyth also showed promise beyond my martial arts and rock tour security industries. His bodyguard tactical driving and pistol-shooting skills were honed, and he'd started close-quarter armed personal protection several years earlier with fellow live-in bodyguard, Craig Larsen.

In 1990 Dave Hedgcock and I'd started a nationwide security company, Combined Security Industries (CSI). John went to Sydney to manage and control the New South Wales division of CSI.

In 1993 a longtime friend, Pat Condon, contacted me and asked if I could handle putting the television series of the Gladiators together for him and Kevin Jacobsen Promotions. The series was contracted to go to air on Channel Seven and it needed regular gladiators and new contestants for each episode. John and I put the Australian series contestants together and then we helped form a Malaysian team. With that John toured Asia and England as security liaison head trainer and assistant tour co-ordinator of the Gladiators international spectacular.

From my experiences of working in security and years of working in close personal protection, John Forsyth, Craig Larsen and others decided to take what they'd learned from living-in and working on all of my corporation's projects and supply to the Vocational Education Training Accreditation Board (VETAB) for Government approval, training courses in security, private inquiry, first aid, close personal protection and defence tactics.

Beyond 2001 John Forsyth now operates Australia's only full-time Close Personal Protection School. Having travelled extensively to examine this type of training, I can honestly say this course is on a par with any of its kind anywhere in the world.

Craig Larsen first caught my attention during a

national seminars tour of my martial arts organisation in mid-1987. Originally from New Zealand, he was living and training in the Coffs Harbour area of northern New South Wales. During training he had that certain attitude: a type of arrogance that came from feeling good about himself and a self-confidence that came from his physical prowess.

As a live-in bodyguard this attitude grew to the point that he became quite unpopular with even his counterpart live-ins. As my personal student and aide, this suited me at the time because due to business pressure I really did need a buffer. Since my other four bodyguards were all *nice guys*, I had a buffer that actually enjoyed being unpopular!

Along with John Forsyth, Craig really worked on his close personal protection skills. My security company got him his pistol licence, and he and John worked great together with that age-old good-cop, bad-cop routine.

By the time Craig had attained fifth-degree Black Belt, he'd served a quick apprenticeship on the Melbourne pub and club scene, working the doors as part of the usual training ground process. Almost immediately, his management skills stood out as he moved into the many diversified areas of my corporation, making himself even more unpopular – while getting the job done.

When it came to romance, after Craig managed to find the time, he found himself in a serious relationship with television presenter from 'Who Dares Wins', Tania Zaetta. Craig had her training at my home gym and Tania became a very competent Thai boxer. He also did personal martial arts training with Michael Hutchence (up to his tragic death) and Garry Beers, the lead singer and bass guitarist of

INXS, respectively. Ex-Miss Australia and television personality, Michelle Downes, and AFL Collingwood football star, Richard Osborne, became regular Thai boxing enthusiasts, all training at my gym. He'd met all these personalities thanks to the security work my company had given him.

Next up, Craig formed a partnership with fellow live-in, '$crooge' Madigan (a thirty-year plus veteran associate of my corporation), and together as FiteNite Productions between 1990 and 1995 they promoted more than forty Toughman and Thai-boxing spectaculars all over Australia, including Darwin. Their final super show was the production of 'The Crowning' in 1995, a $300 000 production at the Melbourne Sports & Entertainment Centre.

During this period Craig found the time to organise, co-ordinate and tour manage six annual training tours for one of my companies, The World Kickboxing Association (WKA). These kick/Thai-boxing tours to Thailand had WKA fighters from all over Australia and New Zealand touring with Craig and me for intensive training with Master Sennin Yodtong, my personal Thai-boxing Master, at his training camp set in the jungle near Pattaya in southern Thailand.

In 1988, the year I brought him down from Coffs Harbour to live at *The House*, Craig worked on concerts with Jimmy Barnes, his first time with INXS, John Mellencamp, The Pogues, The Vietnam Veterans at the Music Bowl and a street kids concert on Princes Wharf. That year culminated with the spectacular Tall Ships celebrations, which drew a record crowd of 1.4 million people. During the next eight years Craig would secure more than forty major tours and international concerts.

INXS took him on as security co-ordinator (in 1993–94) and personal bodyguard and trainer to Michael Hutchence for their Dirty Honeymoon world tour. His final tour while with me (in 1996) was with magician David Copperfield for his Beyond Imagination tour. By now, Craig had moved from Melbourne back to Coffs Harbour, where promoter Michael Barnett tracked him down.

Craig has since worked out of Coffs Harbour, New South Wales, as a tour manager/security co-ordinator. He has worked with the Warner Bros. On Ice tour; Kenny Rodgers and Reba McEntire in concert; George Benson Still Standing tour; once more with David Copperfield and his Journey of a Lifetime tour; from the Ultimate Rock Symphony featuring Roger Daltrey (The Who), Alice Cooper, Gary Brooker (Procul Harum), Peter Frampton, Paul Rodgers, Nikki Lamborn, Jimmy Barnes and Billy Thorpe; to Suzi Quattro and her Devil Gate Drive 2000 tour; Al Jarreau Live In Concert tour; and then a stint with the Superstars of Wrestling Downunder tour featuring Denis Rodman.

Craig toured in April 2001 with the Paul Rodgers Bad Company outfit. These days Paul is off the drugs and grog, and is working out regularly. He looks and is singing as good as he ever has.

Noel Rush, a fifth-degree Black Belt, after fifteen years of touring with Billy Joel as close personal protector, has a million stories of his own. In 1998 Billy Joel and band and their Bob Jones bodyguard toured on a dual promotion with Elton John.

I'd gone to the concert on invitation of Noel and Billy Joel with my now ex-fiancé, Stacey-Lee Delahaunty (we'd gone our separate ways in November 1999 after a nine-year relationship), and several bodyguards from my house (Kevin Smith, Gary Stewart and Adrian Gurney).

Backstage, one of our premier promoters, Michael Chugg, was taking the piss out of me, 'Hey Bobby Jones, have you heard how Billy Thorpe has given you up in his new book, *Most People I Know – Think That I'm Crazy*? In that chapter about the Wallacia Outdoor Concert he's really done you up!'

(Chuggy had a copy of Thorpie's new book. He gave it to me, I read it and what you're now reading is mostly a result of this encounter.)

After the concert, we all went back to the hotel and both touring bands staged a party till dawn. It was a funny party: all the gay guys were on one side of the bar with the Elton John crew and my guys and me were with the macho team of the Billy Joel crew. All the ladies congregated in the centre.

Bekka Bramlett was part of the backing vocals, it was good to catch her. The last time we'd seen each other was in LA in the early 1990s when she was singing lead with Thorpie in Mick Fleetwood's Zoo.

Another female at the party that I classify as a good mate was Tina Arena. I was working the club scene when she was just starting off with her singing career. Tina and Bekka, my lady Stacey-Lee and a few of the girls had teamed up and were in a right party mode. Tina was in Australia on a break from her busy Paris schedule, where the inclusion of her duet with Marc Anthony, 'I Want To Spend My Lifetime Loving You', on *The Mask of Zorro* soundtrack, was giving her wide recognition. The following year would land her the lead role as the gypsy Esmeralda in a British production of *Notre Dame de Paris*.

Tina would return to Australia to sing at the opening ceremony of Sydney's 2000 Olympic Games, this would coincide with the release of her new album, *Souvenirs*.

Michael Gudinski, Frank Stivala, 'Molly' Meldrum and many of Melbourne's elite entertainers were at this after-party event.

Noel Rush had for fifteen years been the exclusive bodyguard of Billy Joel. Billy was now seriously thinking of cutting back on his touring schedule. Thanks to Noel's professional attitude towards his work, he already had several offers in the pipeline.

Wow, talk about getting the creative juices flowing! I really enjoyed reflecting on how well all my guys have done (especially the ones that served their time at *The House*, honing their skills and protecting me), through the success of the various career paths each of them has followed.

Bodyguard work and reminiscing go hand in hand. There's nothing like getting a few of the guys together, having a few drinks and just letting them go for it to simply *Let The Good Times Roll!*

During breakfast one morning, when the guys were living inhouse, we were all together and it came to be that while they were still bouncing the local club scene and learning their future trade as bodyguards (of course, this was after their early morning training session), they'd discuss their sexual exploits.

'Have you guys noticed,' ventured John Forsyth after a particularly late-night encounter, 'girls that live on the north side of Melbourne are easier to score than those on the south-east side?'

'Nah, western suburbs, they're the nutters! Don't even wait till ya get them home, they're at ya while you're trying to drive the fucking car,' replied the 'Bomber', a local bouncer buddy of Johnny Forsyth who often visited the clan, especially at breakfast time, when he could smell the bacon and eggs.

'Well, I agree with John,' added Joe Vidovic. 'But I reckon the ladies on the south-east are worth the effort, especially the middle class. They're better educated – they tend to get down and dirty.'

These observations brought to mind a night in the early 1980s (actually 1983) at the Roxy, a popular club in LA. I was in the US, having just finished my book *Hands Off*. Dennis 'Big D' Dunstan (from Australia) and Wayne 'the Wedge' Cody (from New Zealand), and a whole bunch of local US bodyguards, were having a free night. We'd all arranged to go to the Roxy to see Robin Williams doing a stand-up comedy routine.

Come to think of it, even Robin Williams freaked me out that night. He'd started his set off by walking backwards through the stage curtains, and into a small spotlight that covered his head to feet. He was dressed in extremely baggy trousers and a very sloppy T-shirt, and, as he turned to a full-frontal view of the audience, he had, protruding from his fly and hanging down halfway between his knee and ankle, one of those lookalike almost-real male sex organs. (I'm sure he would've got this from that same Japanese department store that Mick Fleetwood, Richard Norton and I had done our Christmas shopping a couple of years earlier.)

Robin Williams did half his sketch with that penis banging from side to side against one leg and then the other. Eventually he pulled it out of his fly and, like a wet towel trick, he flicked it over the heads and bodies of both male and female audience members; that is, the ones that weren't already rolling on the floor in hysterical laughter.

For a taste of this brand of humour, you might want to rent out that Chopper movie. There's a really funny scene where Eric Bana (the lead actor playing Chopper) pulls off this Robin Williams stunt, during a conversation with a couple of cops in a bar. Then again, maybe that thing hanging out of Eric Bana's fly was the real thing?

Back to Robin Williams ... After he'd finished his sketch and left everyone ill from laughing so much, us bodyguards took over a section of the bar (it was a night were none of us were working). There were about a dozen of us, plus another dozen lighting, sound and crew guys. The opening conversations were about, yep, you guessed right, sexual exploits.

'Have you guys noticed,' began David, who'd worked on the Rod Stewart television special at the LA Forum the previous December, and who'd just got back from the London tour with Stewart, 'girls in London are easier to score than girls in either France or Germany?'

'Nah, Asian girls, they're the nutters! Don't even wait till ya get them back to the hotel; they're at ya while you're still in the fucking limo!' replied a bodyguard who even looked like the Bomber.

'Hey Chief, some things never change, eh?' observed Dennis 'Big D' Dunstan. 'It's not all that long ago, we were at *The House* back home, comparing a chick from Frankston to one from Broadmeadows.'

A couple of rounds of drinks and these tour tell-tales were warming up and beginning to compete with Robin Williams' routine.

The Bomber look-alike, who'd done world tours in the 1960s and 1970s with Led Zeppelin, Pink Floyd and The Doors, recalled a night after an outdoor concert at a speedway arena. One of the above mentioned bands had decided to stage a rock 'n' roll Grand Prix from the venue for the eight kilometres back to the hotel. A couple of hours had passed since the concert had finished, the 60 000 odd fans had long gone. The band had been partying in their caravans and at the backstage tent, complete with ample amounts of grog and excessive amounts of the Black Dragon's substance. Plus, there were an over-abundance of slutty backstage groupies practising to be sexual contortionists.

'Now it was time to get serious: the race was on and we'd lined up at the starting barriers five late-model (almost new) hire cars, complete with a chequered flag raised by one of the roadies. Each car was loaded up with booze, drugs, groupies and driven by a member of the band.

'As the chequered flag dropped, the planned circuit was three times around the ground track. Then out on to the streets and the first one back to the hotel was a rotten egg.

'Off they went, tyres skidding, smoke all-about, and drunken drivers – out of control more than in – crashing in to one another and the barriers. After three laps they'd broadsided out of the stadium and into the night of their urban racetrack. One of these hire cars seized up almost immediately after leaving the venue. Another couldn't respond to its driver's demands and wiped out against some parked cars, and another couldn't handle the high-speed flogging as it raced down the freeway and burst into flames. Number four hire car got lost and wound up back at the wrong hotel, one rotten egg made the circuit intact and arrived home safe but unwell.

'The reason, besides the obvious, for this rock 'n' roll Grand Prix being so catastrophic was the one rule they had all abided by: it was illegal to change out of first gear!'

Following up with a story that was a close second to the Grand Prix tale, our Bomber look-alike narrated another episode that concerned the same band: another famous race, but this time in the late 1970s, which was staged at one of a large chain of hotels across North America (it's probably better not to mention the chain). For the times, these hotels were extremely large complexes, built with high ceilings and very wide passageways that always ran the complete length of the hotel.

As always, these travelling circuses booked out entire floors due to the amount of entourage and support crew. On this particular night in question, the band had used the hotel's goods lift to smuggle up several Harleys to *their* fifteenth floor. For several hours they'd raced up and down the *straights* and cornered around the complex network of hallways.

Luckily, I hadn't thought about telling my Fleetwood Mac story about that flight from Japan to Hawaii. Mick Fleetwood had creatively stuck his first-class food utensils and cutlery all over the wall of the plane during his business rave with the band's manager, John 'JC' Courage.

Lucky? I say lucky because the next story to surface was from Wayne 'the Wedge' Cody as he started telling an old yarn out of New Zealand. It had been rumoured that during a Who tour just prior to September 1978, when Keith Moon had been struck down by a Black Dragon drug overdose, after a great gig and a post-gig night of revelry, Keith had called up the chippies from the crew. For the rest of that night he had them fix everything from the bed, dresser, settee, tables and chairs, reading lamp ... *everything* had been stuck or bolted to the ceiling.

Rumour also had it that somehow even the bed was neatly made, complete with phone book and Bible attached to the sideboards.

When the maids had gone in to clean his room the following morning, Keith had simply said that he'd missed the northern hemisphere since he'd been downunder.

The management of that Auckland hotel used that suite as a promotional gimmick for at least the next six months. It was a sort of:

Who were Here!

Someone bought up the fact that it had been only one month since Keith Moon had gained after-life membership of the Black Dragon Society and that the lead singer of the Sex Pistols had been charged with the murder of his American girlfriend, Nancy Spungen. While Sid Vicious was out of prison waiting to be tried, the Black Dragon would strike again through a heroin overdose. Sid Vicious would die on 2 February 1979 (within five months of Keith Moon).

This got a lot of cliches going about the things in common between these two bands: the one that stuck in my mind (although I'm not sure why) was the story about this or that chick, being in or out of the gang. The bodyguard that told this yarn called it the Show Us Your Tits story.

With a name like Sex Pistols being a reference to the male reproductive organ, the band had become famous for bringing rock 'n' roll anarchy to the UK. It shook the rock establishment to its very foundations and created a *new wave* of aggressive, exciting and sexual music to a younger generation who'd been too long without rebels to rouse them. Plus, out the front of the band you had guys with green teeth and names like Johnny Rotten and Sid Vicious. This set the scene for the kind of young ladies calling back to the hotel after the gig who just wanted to fuck anybody in or even remotely connected to the band.

'Show us your tits!' the roadie would say as he'd flash his instamatic camera. Then he'd walk the corridors to either the Vicious or Rotten abodes, knock three times and slide the photo under the door. Either the photo came back out from under the door, or the door opened and it was, 'Tell the bitch to come on in.'

Whenever the photos were slid back out from under the door, they were taken back to the elevators. The photo would generally be given to the young lady responsible for the pose.

'Show us your arse, love!' would then be the immediate question to the buxom lady next in line ...

'Nah, you'll have to do better than that!'

'Nah, you'll have to show me something else!'

'What else you got? If I'm gonna walk all the way down that corridor, there's no point in you getting a knock-back, now is there?'

Seemed logical enough ...

'What else you got?'

By that time all the rooms were full of more girls and photos than anyone could handle. Man, you wouldn't believe me, even if I told you what these roadies could get those girls to do at the elevator/ corridor photo shoots!

This game of Show Us Your Tits! saw the stories degenerate for a while. After a few more drinks, and a lot more smut, eventually one of the guys gave us one to think about. I'm not sure what band this little ditty belonged to, but between all of us and those who all of us knew, we'd covered every one in the zoo ...

It appears this Hole In One story took place during a world tour of either The Rolling Stones, The Doors or Status Quo. Either way, again it's one of those times the actual group needn't be identified.

As the story went, it was the usual fabulous outdoor gig, with more than 60 000 fans. There was the great backstage after-gig party, and back at the hotel those present had gotten into one of those typical *what's next on the agenda* frame of mind ...

The promoter had hired a couple of prostitutes, who also performed as strippers and who were all-round massive drug-taking connoisseurs. Someone had turned their music up and they'd alternated dancing and almost stripping down from teenagers' outfits and the usual nurse, secretary and even a nun's costume. Their timing showed them to be professional, just as the band and a dozen or so of the crew were getting into this stripping-almost-naked routine; that is, the strippers had got everything off except for scanty panties. Next up, both girls appeared together for the first time, and after stripping, this time totally naked, they'd joined together and gone into a raunchy lesbian act, which came complete with Mick Fleetwood/ Robin Williams strap-on rubber dongers!

That's when the bodyguard telling the story admitted, 'Man, every guy in that room was aroused and envious!'

Now the time had come when these girls wanted to play Hole In One. They lay on their backs, with legs wide open and high in the air. Both of them had stretched their vaginas wide open. Now the rules for playing Hole In One is that the guys play in pairs about two metres from the girls. The guys take it in turns to flick peanuts at them. If either one scores a hole in one, the other guy has to go and get that peanut out of the vagina using nothing but his tongue.

Now its real late, all the guys are pretty much on their way with the alcohol. The Hole In One story caused a deeper degeneration in the yarns: this one and that one were outdoing each other with lots of stories like the US Sandwich. Here the girls wind up being the meat in the sandwich, in between two pieces of guy, one on either side. Then there was the European Sandwich, which was almost the same thing, except the pieces of guy become three, four or more. When it was time for the story of the age-old Asian Sandwich that was when I thought enough was enough ...

I tried to bring it back by offering a yarn about an Australian promoter who one time threw a very valuable grandfather clock (it had hung on the lounge room wall) off the balcony of the third floor of an exclusive Perth hotel, and it had landed in the swimming pool.

Then David the New Yorker saw where I was coming from and began, 'How about the time Keith Richards threw a bottle of Mateus Rosè through a television screen, just because he was pissed off with some interview.'

This caught everyone's imagination so David continued. 'Yeah man, I did the *Some Girls* gig with The Rolling Stones a couple of years back, and they were all really pissed off about some interview that had gone down. I was working the elevator security and ya could hear the band raving and ranting: "Fuck them, who do they think they are? Fuck this, we don't need this in our lives! Fuck that!"

'It was at that point we heard the explosion as the TV screen burst and the bottle of wine had wedged itself where that interviewer's face had been.

'Just then the elevator doors opened and off stepped the night duty manager, complete with tuxedo and the hotel's network corporate tie.

'"Good luck, buddie," I said, as ya could see he was responding to some sort of noise complaint or whatever.

'Now, the conversation that followed for the next twenty minutes was totally unbelievable – if I hadn't been there and heard it myself! After almost banging the door down, Keith finally opened it. He and this night duty manager eventually got into a game of psychological warfare.

'The manager's official duty in this hotel network is to follow up on any noise pollution, infringements of the rights of house guests, check general wear and tear or damage that may have occurred between the changing of guests ...

'Whereas the unofficial duties of The Rolling Stones lead guitarist and his stereo-blaster is to make as much noise as is humanly possible ... Plus upset Mick Jagger and the rest of The Rolling Stones whenever he felt the need. And if he felt the need to cause damage to any of these fucking hotels, then that's exactly what Keith would do!

'Now then, with the fact that neither of these men agreed with the other's basic philosophies of life, or about the basic principles of running a successful business, the following debate began ...

'"Ah, excuse me, sir, but how did the television get damaged in this way?"

'"Wha'? The TV? Oh yeah, I smashed the fucka!"

'"Well, firstly sir, I am to advise you, this damage will have to be added to your account, and secondly, for the filing of my report, why did you cause this damage to the television?"

'"Who are you again? Oh yeah, the fucken' manager. Well, that's your job i'n it? Just stick it on the bill, like every other fucken' hotel in the world. Matter of fact, work it all out, then double it for the bill, that's also wot every other fucken' hotel in the world does."

'"Wot was that second part of tha' first question? Oh yeah, why did I do it? Did you hear wot that cunt said? Pissed me right off, so I 'it 'im right in the face with me fucken' Mateus!"

'Now, both men went into an intellectual debate as to why the principles and ethics of the other was completely wrong. Plus, both men gave an account in point form of the advantages as to why each of them responded to issues in their own way."'

David had the uncanny ability to sound like an American hotel manager and more so, to mimic Keith Richards. He really did have the accent and mannerisms down. This New Yorker was nearly as funny as my old Southern Cross mate, Pat Housley.

After licking the salt, and a quick suck of the lemon, David downed his tequila-slammer and followed this with a whisky-chaser, as only bodyguards can do on a night when they're not working.

David went on ... 'Now this is the part that was unbelievable. Keith had made reference to how all managers always doubled the tab for his post-gig playful escapades. The other points of his debate were job pressures: how travelling constantly around the world and forever suffering the effects of claustrophobia during airline travel, Customs clearances, limousines and fucken' hotel rooms ...

"Stress release woz doing wot makes ya feel good, let some steam off, get it all out in tha' open and tha most important thing of all, ta fuck everybody!"

'Somewhere between "'itting the fucka in the face with the Mateus and fuck everybody!" this manager was becoming sympathetic to the cause.

'Keith seized the opportunity. He'd turned the

manager's suit coat inside-out, coz he'd figured that the purple satin lining with the sleeves rolled up to the elbows was a good transitional starting point. It also gave the whole thing a bit of an Elton John flare. The network corporate tie converted to a head band, so this manager almost doubled for Jimi Hendrix! A quick line of coke and a joint in one hand, and a straight Scotch in the other – and instant transformation! This manager had become an honorary member of The Rolling Stones.

'In no time at all Keith had convinced the manager to help him throw the broken TV set out through the plate glass window into the swimming pool. Then they both launched on a journey of mayhem and destruction, from one room to another, freaking everybody out. All the while, Keith kept reminding the manager, "Don't forget, mothar fuckar, keep an eye on the tab, then double it. What ya reckon we're on?

'"Approximately ten, twelve and a half, fifteen! Now you got to double it, thirty thousand fuckern dollars! God damn, now everybody's fuckern happy!"'

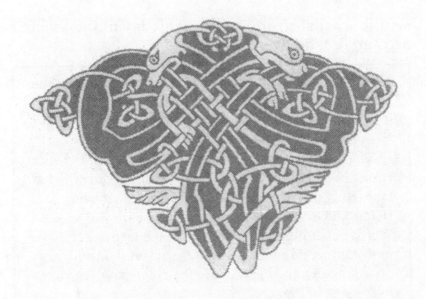

Last, but not least, I'd like to flash back to mid-1977. Joe Cocker had already played Darwin and attracted 12 000 fans to the outdoor venue. He'd been flown on to Great Keppel Island, where the Australian media had been invited to visit for a national press conference. This would culminate with a concert on Keppel, which had a population of 160, including tourists, Joe and his entourage, resort staff and the intermittently arriving media. Of course, it was expected that the concert crowd would swell: the promoter had chartered boats from Rockhampton during the weekend.

The media must have thought this to be a great location, everyone was arriving: Ian 'Molly' Meldrum and his ABC Television film crew, national current affair programs of the day and most major newspapers and radio networks.

The Australian had a feature section in its Sunday edition, The Weekend Australian Magazine, and had sent journalist Colin Talbot. This is an abbreviated account of what went to print:

> ... Joe Cocker leans across to insert another cassette into his music machine. His cassette player is huge, like a suitcase covered with switches and dials because Joe likes his music L-O-U-D.
>
> The rock star fossicks in a large satchel packed with cassettes and selects ... well, guess what? A Joe Cocker tape. He's singing along with the music, that hoarse cry rising above the tape. A series of grunts and groans. Words put through the Joe Cocker language mixer down in that throat. Mumble, mumble, and slur. The only ones crying louder and harsher are the crows up in the trees to the side of the pool.
>
> Joe tugging at tufts of his hair, in the style of Phyllis Diller, was drinking more beer and slurring his speech. He's talking to a bearded reporter, whom he's been told to 'watch out for'.
>
> The marauding press.
>
> 'You're from the local smut paper I hear,' snaps Cocker as he leans across to face the reporter.
>
> 'No, that's not true. We're national,' replies the reporter with a smile.
>
> 'National Smut,' muses Cocker. It's late afternoon, and Joe has been poolside for a couple of hours here on Great Keppel Island.
>
> Bob Jones stands to the side, watching the exchange. Arms folded.
>
> 'I don't know why people pick on Joe,' he says to me. 'He's a quiet, lovely guy. In fact he's the nicest guy I've worked with.'
>
> Bob Jones casts his gaze around the pool, checking out, sizing up the talent. His steady blue eyes come to rest upon two gentlemen in deck chairs and sipping at beer cans down the far end. They both wear the sort of

T-shirts that show plenty of arm, and these arms are showing muscle, and a lot – a real lot – of tattoos.

The two tattooed guys are looking at Jones but without looking too hard – some casual glances rather than full-on study. And who could blame them ... what they see is a six-foot messenger of doom, with shoulder-length red hair and a stare that says he could be quite mean if he wished. A Viking Warrior.

I tell Bob that the fellows from the meat works in Rockhampton, just a few miles across the sea there, are said to be invading the island for the Cocker concert. Maybe some fireworks there I say.

'If there's trouble, it's my job to guard Joe. And I'd die trying to protect him, if I had to.' And by golly, I think this Viking means it.

I've been on Great Keppel Island for a couple of days now. It's being promoted as the new playground for the young, a teen scene ... that's why Joe Cocker and band have been brought here to play.

But it's a slow process ridding the island of the old, as it were, and replacing them with the new. For instance, when I arrive by air (and you can only fly to the island via TAA Light Aircraft, and the resort on the island is run by an offshoot of the TAA Board), I am shunted immediately to the dining room. Here I am faced with at least 60 people, all septuagenarians. Most unusual for a youth resort. Quite bizarre in fact, Joe Cocker is going to play here?

Is this a joke? I do not have an answer, and after eating the lunch – which is remarkably free of fish, considering this place is an island surrounded as usual, by water – I return to the booking office. There the ladies are discussing the arrival of the tour.

'Mr Crocker is due in tomorrow.'

'It's Cocker, not Crocker.'

'Oh, it doesn't make a bit of difference to me.'

> And back outside in the dining room the conversation isn't all that much different.
>
> 'What do you think about Cocker coming to play on the island?'
>
> 'Oh Barry ... Is Barry coming here?' an elderly lady gasps. Thus I enter my first day. I hire a boat and take it around part of the island, looking at nature's gift to the young tourist. Beaches with rusty, empty cans lying around. Beautiful white sands stretching three miles, with no-one in sight.
>
> At night the full moon rising over the bays, turning the placid water to the color of milk. Possums that will eat from your hand on the path back to the resort. In a certain light, this place is idyllic. Quite, quite beautiful...

The day after the two gentlemen with the tattoos and Colin Talbot and company were down by the pool, the afternoon's entertainment for more than a hundred of our *younger* tourists was the ABC's 'Countdown' interview, which must have been a shitload of editing for Ian 'Molly' Meldrum and his crew: they'd set up at a barbeque table on the lawn area between the pool and beach.

Joe, pianist Nicky Hopkins and saxophonist Bobby Keyes (both session players from my Rolling Stones and many other tours) were quite drunk. With the mid-afternoon sun they were in right good form. Between these three madmen there was no end the humour: Monty Python skits and plenty of Paul Rodgers'-style, 'Wot's tha worse job yoo evar had?' and 'Wot would yoo do?'

There was more grog, many more drugs and eventually Molly was happy: he had plenty of what he was after.

On that night, as was the plan, the fans came in

their thousands. Joe and the gang played a fantastic show and TAA's Great Keppel Island would never be the same.

The appearance of Sheffield-born John Robert Cockers' first long-player in 1969 *With a Little Help From my Friends* proved that this white man could sing the blues. Joe vocalised in the vein of Ray Charles and the Four Tops, and many others.

After attending a local technical school, young Joe Cocker had his sights set on a career as a gasfitter. However, his real love guided him to his first band: playing drums with a group called Cavaliers. As the band mutated to Vance Arnold & The Avengers, Joe slipped into the role of lead singer. The repertoire included Beatles covers, as well as Cocker's blues and soul favourites.

A failed recording of a Beatles tune 'I'll Cry Instead' saw him back in the gasfitting trade in 1964. A couple of years later, Joe used the stage name Joe Cocker to head up a new group called The Grease Band. This saw him develop a long-term relationship with musical partner Chris Stainton. Within a couple of years (1968), a meeting with producer Denny Cordell resulted in a Cocker self-penned single, 'Marjorine' (based on a puppet show character). This reached the UK top fifty.

Joe gained international status a year later with 'A Little Help From My Friends'. An album of the same name and a promotional tour had critics comparing him with Janis Joplin: both wrenching out bottomless emotions from their songs' lyrics; both being white blues interpreters. Lillian Roxon in her *Rock Encyclopedia* states that Cocker becomes so physically involved with his music that he often appears grotesque to some fans. With arms flailing like a jitter-bugging epileptic and face contorted into a life mask of agony/ecstasy, the bellowing newcomer would become the cause célèbre of the 1969–70 music scene.

His first bad taste of business dealings saw him lose his first hard-earned fortune as a result of the misdealings of some musical and business associates. Disappointed, Joe split from the Grease Band and set off for LA, arriving on 11 March 1970. With no band and an agency mix-up, he had seven days to get ready for seven weeks of tour dates – all this with a warning that he could find himself blacklisted and banned from appearing in the US.

Joe had little knowledge of the local scene, so he enlisted friend Leon Russell to help out. Leon had written two tracks for Joe's album *Joe Cocker!*, 'Delta Lady' and 'Hello Little Friend', and co-produced with Denny Cordell. He organised ten of LA's finest within twenty-four hours, including my mates Bobby Keyes and Jim Price.

After lengthy rehearsals on 15, 16 and 17 March, the group recorded and produced both sides of a single 'The Letter' and 'Space Captain', which would become a huge hit. As the band and its crew, numbering thirty-six, prepared to board a plane at the start of the tour, someone suggested the tour be filmed. This meant a much bigger plane had to be found. The circus eventually flew to Detroit on 19 March, ready to open the next day. On 16 May, sixty-four days later, they had a double live album, and a feature movie of a touring circus, both titled *Mad Dogs and Englishmen*.

Although Joe was the centre-point for this whole deal, the tour wound up doing a lot more for the careers of Russell and the sidemen than it did for him. In fact, many years later Joe and I were downtown in some city somewhere, and he'd confided that he'd actually got hit with a six-figure law suit over responsibility for losses incurred in production costs of the album and the movie, despite the worldwide distribution and sales of *Mad Dogs and Englishmen*.

After getting busted in Australia in 1972, Joe came back in 1974 with the aid of manager Jim Price and the album *I Can Stand A Little Rain*.

Paul Dainty had both Richard Norton and me work the tour, to make sure the biggest danger to Joe would only be Joe himself.

Everything ran like clockwork. Although Joe was drinking heavily, his performance each night of 'You Are So Beautiful', the single off his latest album, went into the top ten everywhere. For the first time in nearly five years, success seemed assured.

The only real thing that happened out of the norm was that last night of the tour in New Zealand. After the show we'd all gone to downtown Auckland and wound up after several clubs and haunts at a Les Girls Burlesque Show. The lead singer was a cum-*comedienne*, cum–mistress of ceremonies.

Joe'd taken one look at her and said, 'Man, that's the best-looking chick I've seen since ...'

'Joe, it's a bloke,' I'd tried to warn.

'Nah, fuck that! She's just too cute.'

'Joe, she might have had the cut 'n' tuck, but it's still a bloke in anyone's language.' This was my way of reasoning back in 1974.

'Bob, will you listen to me! These Les Girls Shows are the same everywhere, it's all a con. They always stick in one or two of the real thing, just to suck you in.' Joe's reasoning convinced the lead guitarist and drummer with such ebullience that they all had second thoughts.

Well, while no-one was looking and the alcohol flowed, I'd snuck off to the backstage area and invited them all, the whole cast – the sound, lighting and production team – back to Joe's penthouse at the hotel, for an after-show party. But, I didn't mention this to Joe or the band.

All the next day, even on our way to the airport, Joe's mood was one of 'mums the word'. He simply wouldn't talk about the unexpected late-night guests (and every one of them did come) or the sexual condition of the Les Girls' libertine lead. That remains still today one of our tour secrets.

Here's another of those tour secrets: it's a fact that Joe is not half bad as a tennis player (if he hasn't had too much to drink that is). One time during some tour or other, Richard and I'd played doubles against Joe Cocker and Paul Dainty. I really shouldn't talk about who won, except that we were playing our two bosses, and sometimes discretion is the better part of valor.

Another tour secret about Joe Cocker is that sometimes even when he hasn't had a drink he can well be at his drunkest state. That first time we went to Adelaide, the visit after he'd been busted there, he'd made a point of staying stone sober: Joe really did want to impress South Australia. For this tour he'd brought a great mix of session studio people to back him as a band and he had this new album with the 'You Are So Beautiful' single; in other words, he had a lot of things about his music – and business – that he wanted to talk about.

In one of the side lounges, the media had set up a massive press conference for the local entertainment industry, and there they were with their microphones and metres of leads for the cameras. The star's seat was floodlit and they were in semi-darkness.

Joe took up his position in the hot seat. Microphones were thrust at his face, cameras started rolling and the very first questions were asked.

'Does your drinking affect your performance on stage?'

Joe took one look at me, winked, then leaned down to his carry bag. He pulled up a full bottle of Jim Beam and with a full healthy swig he replied, 'I reckon my dick would get as hard as yours, anytime!'

The whole thing went downhill from there, with not one question directed at Joe Cocker's business.

For a national current affairs show for Channel Nine in Sydney, Joe, knowing this would be important, didn't have a single drink all day. We'd reached the studio on time. In the main studio there were Cameras one, two and three, lights, overhead boom microphones and technicians everywhere. They had a type of sofa for Joe, and he was being interviewed by Sue Smith, one of the best at her trade for that era. For Sue they had a four-legged stool, which had her sitting higher and thus looking down at Joe, with her clipboard and list of questions written out for her.

I was doing my thing standing off to one side. Sue was asking Joe about trends in the US, about

Europe, about touring, who he'd brought as his backing band for the trip ... It looked like it would have been a great interview once it went to air. However, Sue was suddenly called to one side by the producer. She'd left her questions on the stool. Joe, as inquisitive as a little kid (he's like that when he's not drinking) had leaned forward and took a peek at her list.

Sue had come back; she was one of the beautiful people of television of the day. She was elegantly dressed in her twin suit ensemble: pin-striped business grey jacket and moderately short mini-skirt (it was the 1970s). She'd perched back on to her stool and given her skirt the appropriate hand tug that women did to mini-skirts back then. She'd placed her clipboard strategically over her thighs as she'd crossed her legs.

As they were all set to count us in with that familiar 5, 4, 3, 2, 1 point-the-finger, you're-on routine, Joe took one look at me, winked, leaned down to his carry bag and pulled out a full bottle of Jim Beam. With a full healthy swig he'd asked Sue Smith some terrible question he'd just made up about her and the three camera guys.

'Is it true?' Joe asked, as if he really did expect an answer for such a disgusting question.

Sue Smith did exactly what you would expect her to do under the circumstances: she'd burst into tears and run out of the studio.

'Hey Bob, I guess we won't be doing "A Current Affair" currently.'

As I'd hoisted him off his studio sofa, I'd glanced at Sue's clipboard and its questions. His actions now made some sense, even as they'd had the perfect conversation interview off-camera: the go-to-air questions were the same format, almost identical to those in Adelaide.

My fondest memories of that first tour was one afternoon in Melbourne. Richard was away. I'd asked Joe to take a couple of hours off from this tour-city hotel lifestyle and visit my home for a typical *Aussie* put-a-shrimp-on-the barbeque.

I was showing Joe around, particularly my favourite area: a large gymnasium with enough weights for a professional gym. Although I don't think the gym did that much for Joe, there was, however, at the bottom of my block a waste area that I didn't use.

'Look 'ere, Bob, at this piece of your property, after you and your guys work out on the weights, I can see it there, a kidney-shaped swimming pool surrounded by winding paths ... Over there a rockery bordering beautifully landscaped gardens ... Umbrellas and deck chairs over here, and a Cocker Cocktail full of rocks!'

After the tour I'd called a local landscape designer and had him do the drawings as Joe had described it to me. Here's the weird part, when the price of the quote came in, it was exactly the same as the wages I'd earned off that tour with Joe. A little poetic licence allowed me to tell my friends at home barbeques that Joe Cocker actually designed and paid for this entertainment area of my block, which used to be a wasteland!

As I'd transferred from the commercial TAA jet in Rockhampton to the TAA six-seater light aircraft, I'd experienced some trepidation, not from the flight or the landing on the makeshift condition of the Great Keppel Island airstrip, but I hadn't seen my friend for almost three years and I was wondering if he'd even remember me.

'Bob! Bobby Jones!' He was poolside with about fifty tourists, band members and media people. He let me know our friendship was beyond shaking hands: we hugged each other, two men with their arms around one and other, both slapping each other heartily on the back, like a couple of crusading Celts.

'Bob, how's your wife Pauline and your daughter Tracey-Lee? If you don't mind me saying, I felt a problem in Jonestown last time I was here!'

And I'd thought he wouldn't remember me! How did he do that, after all the things he did to himself, the constant travelling and the meeting of people all day, every day?

It was almost three years since we'd last met, he'd even remembered my ex-wife, and that we'd had a problem, and my daughter. Jesuz Christ, I couldn't even remember my flight number!

I'd explained that the Jonestown problem had gone past its expiry date, that Pauline and I had divorced not long after that 1974 tour.

From Joe's reaction I could tell that a friend was genuinely saddened by this news.

Anyway, later on during the tour we'd called again to my house and Joe had laughed when he'd read the copper plaque inscription on the gate (which, by the way is still there, almost thirty years later):

THIS AREA RESERVED –
'FOR THE MAD DOG AND AN AUSTRALIAN'

On hot summer nights, I often sit poolside with friends, and sometimes we drink Cocker Cocktails – full of rocks!

During the drive years earlier when Norman-e was chauffeuring us towards Gosford, on our way to do that gig in Newcastle, I'd looked to the back seat and saw the Mad Dog about to come out to play with that look in his eye that spelled out 'What Are You Doing With A Fool Like Me?'.

Well, we'd got to the gig but things were a bit crazy. I remember thinking, Joe must have dropped a tab of acid or something. He was really out there, spending a lot of time sitting on the floor, carry-bag inside out, bottle of Jim Beam half empty and his cassettes (from his carry-bag) spread everywhere. Joe was holding some of them real close, reading all the small print, as if he'd never seen them before.

This was to be the second-last show, before the finale in a couple of days' time at Sydney's Hordern Pavilion. For this reason, all the crew, everyone including Norm-e and me, had put in an amount of dollars each to surprise Joe. The crew had also wired the place and stage with fireworks. And during the last encore, that last song, we'd planned to surprise Joe and his fans with a spectacular fireworks floor-show!

All right, here it came, with little bit of this, a little bit of that: the marijuana, the Jim Beam, the cocaine and the tab had all kicked in. Joe was nowhere in sight and the Mad Dog had come out to play, and play he and his band did, probably the best set of the tour. Joe'd come off stage for the break before the first of two encores that he was supposed to do. The problem was that Joe had really believed in his mind that he'd already done the encores. The more I'd told

him to go back on stage, the more he'd said the show was done.
The more I'd told him that the audience chanting was for him, that the audience wanted more, the more he'd say 'what a good show it's been'.

On the way home I'd wanted to tell Joe how fabulous the fireworks were, when really they were the only things that had stopped that lot from rioting – due to the short show. But Joe was snug as a bug, stretched out on that back seat. Little did I know the Mad Dog was resting for what was about to unfold.

Norman-e Sweeney had got us home safe and sound; he'd swung into the shallow in–out driveway of the Chateau Commodore in Macleay Street, Kings Cross, right across from Benny's, our entertainment industry people's palace. Joe was there, in the driveway, to stay. For the life of me I couldn't get him to budge out of the car, short of dragging him off his arse and on to the bitumen.

The second car pulled in behind us with Nicky Hopkins and Bobby Keyes on board.

'Hey Barb, wha's up man? What seems to be a problem?' Bobby Keyes had as much interest as me in Joe's welfare.

'Ah, Bobby, it's Joe man, can't budge him. We've been here for ten minutes already.'

'Here, let me try, we've been here before, eh!' With that Bobby leaned over Joe's comatose body and said some magical code, in muso's monologue, that tapped instantly into Joe's monomaniac mentality.
Joe immediately sat up, slithered across the seat and stood up, out of the car.

'Whazzup, whearze it all happernearng?'

I'd figured I should've asked Bobby what it was that he'd said to Joe, for next time, but it was a tour secret.

As we'd come off the elevator, Joe's penthouse door opened. I'd arranged a key for Sally (you remember Sally, the working girl with the python and the spider fixations) to my room.

As usual, Joe and I'd exchanged rooms.
He never could stand the penthouse. 'Too big,' he'd say, 'I can never find my cassettes.'

In my room with the twin beds, he'd use one for sleeping and one for his tapes and anything else he needed to find in a hurry.

This suited me fine, I liked penthouses about as much as I liked limousines.

Meanwhile, Sally was leaning against the doorway with her arms folded and one of those extremely long legs of hers crossed over the other. It was habit, I suppose, or maybe a taste of her humour.

'Hello Sally, how are you, my darling?' Joe was about as articulate as anyone in the world could be in his current condition.

It was another one of those times when I'd thought, how does he do that, in that frame of mind? He'd remembered Sally's name from an encounter almost three years earlier.

Norm-e had opened Joe's door with my key and let him in. We'd all settled in the penthouse with the door fully open, in case anybody had wanted me. Sally had the cricket on the TV with the sound turned down and what else but a Joe Cocker best of tape playing quietly in the background. She'd poured a double Scotch for Norm-e and an orange juice for yours truly. There we were, one of my best guy-friends, and definitely one of my best girlfriends, Joe

Cocker on audio and the cricket on TV. Life doesn't get any better than that!

Then boom-crash! Joe had swung around the corner, into the penthouse and face first on to the carpet. He'd stood up laughing, and walked sideways into our en-suite and swung the door over behind him. I'd looked at Norm-e and Sally, they'd looked at me – he likes the smaller room, maybe he just wants to use a bigger toilet!

Approximately ten to fifteen minutes had elapsed, Joe was shoeless and the door ajar. I'd listened at the door, in case of any problem. I'd peered through the opening of the doorway and in the mirror I could see Joe behind the door and sitting on the floor, with his legs tied together in what a serious yogi would call a full lotus position. However, Joe's elbows rested on the sides of the toilet bowl, with his head supported by his cheekbones bridged against both palms of his hands: usually the classic vomit position.

I had to strain my ears to comprehend ...

'Out! The linesman has called a very controversial decision, many feel this shot was good for the white line. Advantage Cocker!'

I'd called Norm-e and Sally over, to check if what was happening was real.

Joe Cocker was at Wimbledon and playing an elimination match against the world's number one seed, a tall black guy, a 1970s' version of a Tiger Woods-type tennis player. It was the first set, and four games apiece. That linesman's call had taken it from deuce to Cocker's advantage.

Sally poured Norm-e another Scotch and me another orange juice. We went back to the cricket on the TV and Cocker on the tape.

About an hour later Joe'd come into the main room, looked straight through us, turned and walked to two giant doors that housed a linen cupboard. He'd opened both doors, sat on the floor, crossed his leg's into a full lotus position, and without as much as a falter, only this time to the acoustics of this linen cupboard, he'd continued, 'Cocker bounces the ball three times, throws it high in the air, arches his back, powerful swing, and straight down the centre for another ace. That was Cocker's twenty-second ace so far in this match!'

Just then Bobby Keyes came in, it was now about 4 a.m. 'Hey guys, where's Joe? I been callin' next door, but there's no answer.'

'He's playing tennis!' I replied as Bobby walked over to the cupboards.

'Yeah, it's Wimbledon! That bloody black guy again! Joe never beats him. Oh well, I'll catch you guys later.' Bobby left as quickly as he'd come.

Australia was ahead in the cricket. What else is new? Sally had put on the just-released *Rumours* album by Fleetwood Mac (whom I'd meet and tour with a few months after this experience with Joe at Wimbledon) and turned the volume up.

About twenty minutes later Bobby Keyes came back. By then our numbers had swelled to include Jenny, the mother of Norm-e's child, Nicky Hopkins and the drummer, and a few extra girls. However, he didn't see any of us. Bobby had to simply go over to Joe, sit down next to him and cross his legs.

I'd given them about fifteen minutes, then I'd gone over to tune into whatever in this world could've been happening. And there they were three games down in the second set. They were now playing doubles, wait for it, with two black chicks, and this was years before the Williams sisters were even born.

A couple of days later it was the final performance day of the tour at the Hordern Pavilion's sold-out show. Joe was tied up with a financial meeting. Norm-e and I were having dinner at Chèz Guy, a French restaurant in the arcade down in Springfield Avenue, opposite the Manzel Room. Jenny, Claudie (Claudie is like a niece to me, she's Norm-e's and Jenny's daughter) and Sally were with us, along with some of my Sydney BJC Black Belt instructors.

Norm-e was doing what he and I enjoyed best, telling tour stories: 'Man, what about that Wollongong gig last week?'

This was a story that Norm-e and I had both thought was going to turn out nasty for the lot of us.

'That local Wollongong newspaper quoting the local cops down there that if "Joe Cocker thought he could come into their town with his onstage swearing and profanities in front of the youth, then they'd drag him and his band off the stage. They'd lock them all up!" Even the local radio stations are beefing it all up here in Sydney.'

On the way down that night to the Wollongong show I'd confided in Norm-e, 'No one's forced them to buy tickets and if they think they can drag Joe off stage, they'd better bring a bloody good team – they'll have to contend with me before they get to him or any of the band.'

I must admit I was thinking, not too many coppers, please! Or even better, Joe might do one show without any swearing. Maybe!

One thing about the publicity: it sure drew a crowd and a half. There was a full house with thousands outside swearing profanities coz they couldn't get tickets to see an international show that had bothered to come to their town.

'How the fuck are youze? Bring on those fucking boys in blue, let's see what they can do! Fuck 'em ...' Joe screamed into the microphone. He'd looked over to me and winked as if he'd just declared our death wish and couldn't be happier.

The crowd went nuts, totally ape-shit, acknowledging his defiance of their town's authority.

Joe had taken on icon status. If the boys in blue were anywhere in the wings, they'd have been well aware of the situation, as I was. Any action on their part would've caused a riot, and Bob Jones cum-bodyguard would've been the least of their problems.

And what an electric show it was! Joe, the guys and that crowd rocked the auditorium to its foundations.

There are more law-defying memories. During another tour in Perth, Western Australia, backstage at the entertainment centre on my second or third tour with David Bowie (to this day I don't know if they were on or off duty) there were five cops and they'd been drinking, seriously drinking. The leader and one other fronted me at the backstage door (that ran off a long corridor running parallel to the stage and the stage-loading zone).

'Step aside son, we're going to backstage to take a look around and check out this Mr David Bowie character.'

'I'm sorry sir, you don't have a backstage pass. I can't let you back here or anywhere near Mr Bowie.'

'We don't need any stupid, fucking backstage passes, we've got these ...' He flashed his police ID.

'What can I say? I'm sorry, you still don't have what it takes: you need a backstage pass.'

The officer was really pissed at me! The other

three started to mill around.

'Wait a minute, you think you can stop us, all of us from going wherever we want to go?'

It was time to stop pissing in the wind, time to pull up stumps. The game was over. Five coppers, this was real life or death stuff. Oh well, it was a good day to die, long as I was fighting for what I'd believed in.

'Well, the one thing I do know, there's only one way any of you are coming backstage and that's over my dead body. For that you'll need to draw guns. If that happens, you'll have to shoot that witness standing there.' I nodded at Richard Norton.

'After that you'll have to shoot the boss.' I'd figured it was time to include Michael Chugg, the tour manager (after all, it was him who'd said, don't let anyone in here without the proper access-all-areas backstage passes).

As I'd nodded to Chuggy, the head copper turned his head to check who I was referring to. Then he saw what I'd been facing the whole time: at least another twenty witnesses had accumulated around as word had spread about the cops and this crazy situation!

There were loading guys, venue staff, a couple of Bowie's band members. I think even Paul Dainty was buried in among that crowd somewhere.

'Lunatic, that's what you are: an absolute fucking lunatic!' With that the boss cop started laughing. Then they'd all started laughing as they'd walked off to the side door leading into the arena.

The lead copper turned, his eyes were focused to thin slits and his voice was three times colder than the backstage air-conditioning. 'You haven't heard the end of this, one day this'll come back and bite you on your arse, lunatic. What's your name? Bob Jones, isn't it? That's easy enough to remember.'

He wasn't kidding, either. Twenty years later the Western Australian coppers would bite me on the arse so hard, I'd thought it was a pit-bull! Actually, it was worse than that. It was Chief Inspector Bull, the Western Australian Commissioner. He'd lock horns with Rod Stroud (my WA chief instructor) and me. However, that's another story!

'What about Joe Cocker's incredible memory?' I was offering a bit of tour trivia to lighten up the conversation here at Chèz Guy, and giving the girls a chance to stock up on their French wines over dinner.

I'd told them how, about a week earlier, Joe had woken up after a real heavy night on the town, disorientated.

'Where the fuck am I?'

I didn't even think he was sure which country.

'Joe, east coast – between Melbourne and Sydney. Closer to Sydney in the ACT, capital of this wonderful country, Australia–'

'Oh Canberra! Yes, now I know, of course, Canberra. Lovely place, lovely city. Lots of government public servant workers that have to be off the streets at 6 p.m.! But you can have a real good time here long as you know a local to show you around, like we had last night.' He'd placed both hands over his throbbing head, a reminder of that good time.

Norm-e took over the story-telling stage at Chèz Guy. He remembered with enthusiasm, '... that last tour, again when we were in Newcastle. We'd driven up there, mid-afternoon on the day of the show. With a few hours to kill, Joe said he wouldn't mind a shot of pool, and a bit of a chat with some of the locals.'

Norm-e went on to tell how, after three or four games of pool with the locals, and three or four trips to the toilets, from his last urinal excursion, Joe hadn't returned. 'We'd checked the toilets, both male and female. We'd checked the corridors, both upstairs and downstairs. We'd checked the fire escapes ...

'I couldn't believe this! It was 5.40 p.m. and no Joe on the day of a show. The hotel manager helped us check twenty-four bedrooms, under beds, cupboards and en suites. Still no Joe! The hotel restaurant wasn't opening until 6 p.m. That way no-one noticed, and we didn't think to look under the tables in the restaurant.

'Apparently, after his fourth trip to the toilet, he'd wandered into the dining room, had taken off his shoes and socks and curled up under one of the thirty-five tables for, I guess, a quick snooze, coz those locals sure had him socking a few pots away.

'But the next thing we knew, after more than an hour of searching, this couple came into the hotel and I heard the guy tell a couple of mates, "Hey guys, you're not gonna believe this. You know Joe Cocker's playing in town tonight, we just saw him walking barefoot down the road, about three blocks from here."

'Turns out that as people started to file into the pub's restaurant after 6 p.m., Joe'd scared the lifeline out of some elderly couple who sat at his *bed*-table and woke him up. Have you ever seen Joe woken out of a drunken sleep? It's not a pretty sight.

'We found his sneakers and socks, and then we found him that few blocks away wandering aimlessly.

'"Norm-e! Bobby! Some fuckin' minders I got! I've been roaming around this city for an hour or more just looking for you two! Where the fuck 'a ya been?'

'Then came the white Rolls Royce sweeping its way on to the Chateau driveway, looking like it had arrived to take Cinderella to the concert. We'd finished dinner at the French restaurant, and we were waiting for everyone down at the Chateau Commodore's reception, admiring the white Rolls, when off the elevator comes Bobby Keyes and a glamorous blonde lady friend. She was wearing a long white satin dress and Bobby was wearing all-white long tails – a dinner suit with white shirt and bow tie and a gentlemen's white bowler hat. It wasn't hard to guess who the white Rolls was waiting for!'

Just after the band had started playing their last set for the Australian tour, the manager had approached Norm-e and me.

'Hey guys, you know where we can get a stack of apple pies with plenty of cream? Bobby Keyes looks so good starring tonight with that all-white ensemble. I think a massive pie fight on stage would make for a great encore for tonight, the last night.'

Norm-e got the pies somewhere down the bottom end of the 'Cross'. I got a few cans of shaving cream to bolster the effect. As it turned out, everyone threw these apple pies with shaving cream at everyone! Several flew into the audience and they responded by throwing pieces at one and other, and back on to the stage.

It was all very funny from my safety-zone behind the drummer. Until Bobby Keyes came from the side and caught me flush – right in the face!

How does your memory compare to Joe Cocker's? Do you remember some time ago I was telling you about the valet parking dudes and everything at Stevie Nicks' Beverly Hills New Year's Eve party, to celebrate the success of the world Rumours tour? Well, I haven't had the chance to tell you how the night actually began. I'd been staying for some time at Richard Dashut's house and earlier on that evening I'd called into Christine McVie's, over on Lloydcrest Drive. She was having a few friends over for drinks before going on to Stevie's before midnight. Judy Wong had done me a favor and got Joe Cocker's address, where he was also having the big New Year's Eve celebrations. Judy said I could make it to Joe's easily and safely with about thirty minutes of driving.

At around 9.30 p.m. Christine and Judy had drawn me a map of the destination. I'd figured to have reached Joe's some time shortly after ten o'clock. It would take a couple of hours to see in the new year with Joe, then over to Stevie's by about 1 a.m. This was to have been a good plan ...

Have you ever driven around Los Angeles on the freeways on New Year's Eve, on the wrong side of the car, and on the wrong side of the road? It was mayhem; I'd gotten lost. At first it was a bit of fun. Then, as it turned 10 to 10.30 to 11 o'clock and I was still lost ...

By 11.30 p.m. I was panicking; I mean, I wanted to see the magic moment of the old year becoming the new in the company of a good friend.

Finally, the street names and Christine's and Judy's map were beginning to gel.

Still, it was left up a couple, right down about six blocks. Nope, that was a no through road sign ... It must have been there on the other side, no problem.

Then 11.50 to 11.55, thank Christ, there it was, and I had to find a place to park. But stuff it, I parked on the nature strip.

Knock, knock! 11.57 p.m. Three minutes to midnight. A very sociable security guard dressed in black, complete with a black bow-tie, opened one of two huge oak doors.

'Good evening, sir. Do you have the correct invitation card for this evening's function?'

Oh no, here I was, two minutes to midnight, and I was having flashbacks to me and that drunken copper backstage in Perth. Hang on, I hadn't even had a drink: tell him who I am and why I'm here, that'll do the trick.

With about one and a half minutes to go, just as I was trying to think how I'd tell this total stranger the Bob Jones' story, there was a cry of, 'Bob, Bobby Jones! God damn, can that really be you?'

Joe'd seen me from the other side of the room. He'd been sitting with a group of friends in front of a big open fire (and a real one, I think). He'd walked over and told the security guard, 'Everything's fine, it's my bodyguard from Australia.'

A surge went through my body; it'd been almost six months since Great Keppel Island. We stood in the doorway hugging and slapping like a couple of crusading Celts, Joe was on the doormat facing the street and me looking at around the 150 people present from the LA recording industry and management and personal friends. There was this huge grandfather clock on the mantle piece over the fireplace. All those eyes looked and wondered who was this? Meanwhile, that big clock's second's hand had ticked its way uphill for the last time that year: 10, 9, 8, 7, 6, 5, 4, 3, 2, 1 ...

'Where did you come from?
'How long have you been in America?
'How did you get this address?
'How the fuck have you been?'

Joe kept firing questions at me as that damned old second's hand ran a bit faster downhill (or so it seemed with everyone staring at me): 26, 27, 28, 29, 30 seconds past midnight.

Somebody eventually came out of the crowd. 'Ah Joe, it's that time – it's new years!'

'Oh, would you look at that!' Joe'd faced everyone.

'Everybody, this is Bob Jones, a very good friend of mine from Australia …'

The place exploded: whistles, balloons and all the new year's gadgets, and everyone now hugged, kissed and sang the praises that came with the new year.

What was about to happen was the reason I was so late in arriving at Fleetwood Mac's party at Stevie's house on this same night.

'Bob, come here! There's something I really need to show you'. There, right on the floor near where he'd been sitting was Joe's old faithful satchel, the carry-bag for his cassettes, bottle of Jim Beam and anything else he might have needed.

Off we headed into the night for some new adventure. It was then that I'd realised how sober Joe was: he'd had hardly anything to drink.

Now the adventure was a real-life Jack-and-the-beanstalk experience. This huge old tree in the yard had a circular staircase winding it's way around the trunk.

I'd looked up to the clouds – high enough that God could well be there – well, almost, to an octagonal tree house.

'C'mon, follow me!' Joe said, his carry-bag under one arm. We climbed around and around, towards the heavens.

We'd eventually come to a trap door. Once we were inside Joe'd closed it, and we were inside a mini-sound room in an octagonal-shaped room with glass windows that gave fabulous 360-degree views.

While high up in this tree, high enough to be able to see most of LA floodlit for New Year's Eve, it was all of five minutes past twelve and the LA revellers were still going at it, too far away to hear. But what a fabulous view LA was from this height at night, especially with those magnificent fireworks still lighting up most of LA and the horizon!

'Now I want to know what you think. I want your totally honest opinion.' Joe for the next three hours would play a host of songs that he'd compiled. It was a case of which songs would go on the album, which ones would not, and what sequence would the singles follow on the album. And 'what did I think?'

This was reminiscent of the subject matter conversations I'd had with Tamiko in Japan. Sometimes it'd been a little difficult to understand what's going on..., but I'd listened intently and made suggestions. Joe asked me questions; we communicated. Plus, we both had a couple, of Cocker Cocktails – full of rocks and with just a usual dash. Well, I wasn't working, was I?

That was one of my best New Year's Eves ever!

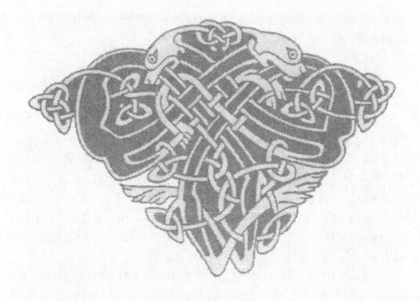

My having been born in the Year of the Dragon is undoubtedly the reason why I've developed such an empathy throughout the years for the symbolism and mythology of this birth sign.

My personal logo, which is an identification with this symbolism, appears on the cover of each book in my autobiographical trilogy. A white circle lies within the triangle, and around this circle are enclosed the three primary colours: red, yellow and blue. These colours symbolise body, mind and spirit: the three primary principles of my personality, which in turn are reflected in the three adventures within my trilogy.

The white circle also symbolises life's balance (between birth and death); the battle throughout my life's journey to be conscious of always keeping these three principles in harmony.

My personal ideals of how Bob Jones should live his life in harmony with the energy of the universe have always been seen through my connection to the mythology of the Dragon.

The Dragon is not only the oldest of all mythical beasts, it has a place in almost every mythology. In the New Testament Book of Revelation XII, 7–9, Saint Michael did ferocious battle with the Red Dragon as it had acted improperly in the Garden of Eden within Heaven's boundaries. The punishment was to be cast out of Heaven for eternity on Earth.

Centuries before this Biblical interpretation of the Red Dragon, mythology told that the fiery Dragon – the firedrake – was the protector of a massive fortune of gold and sparkling gems for 300 years. Eventually, while it was feeling the need for sleep, a thief who stumbled across this fortune decided to steal a golden cup studded with jewels.

When the Red Dragon awoke it was furious, and went in search of this thief and the stolen golden cup. In its anger it flew around the world sending flames upon the earth and leaving behind a black trail of ruin and death.

The colour yellow characterises the ethereal Dragon who lives mostly in the clouds. From this cosmic vision of the world the Yellow Dragon gains insight, intelligence and much wisdom.

During the bodyguard years of my life, I spent

much of my time flying through the clouds. My mythology thus sees me experiencing life from a different perspective.

For the Druids and Warrior Celts in Pagan times, the Dragon was all-powerful with undying universal energy. Due to such reverence it was adopted as a heraldic device.

In my journey through life, my dedication to the martial arts and to the mythology of my Celtic heritage has taught me that the Blue Dragon is associated with the element of water, with storms discharging rain, with clouds and thunder. Initially these forms appear to be the weakest and softest of substances, yet they overcome the strongest and hardest.

Without noise, without effort, they find their own level and penetrate all things subtly. Now with this ability to penetrate and with the ability to unite the three primary principles,

associated with the power of fluidity,

my life is dedicated to becoming one Dragon, the symbol of the infinite, so that one day I may be recognised by my peers as the ultimate *Pendragon*.